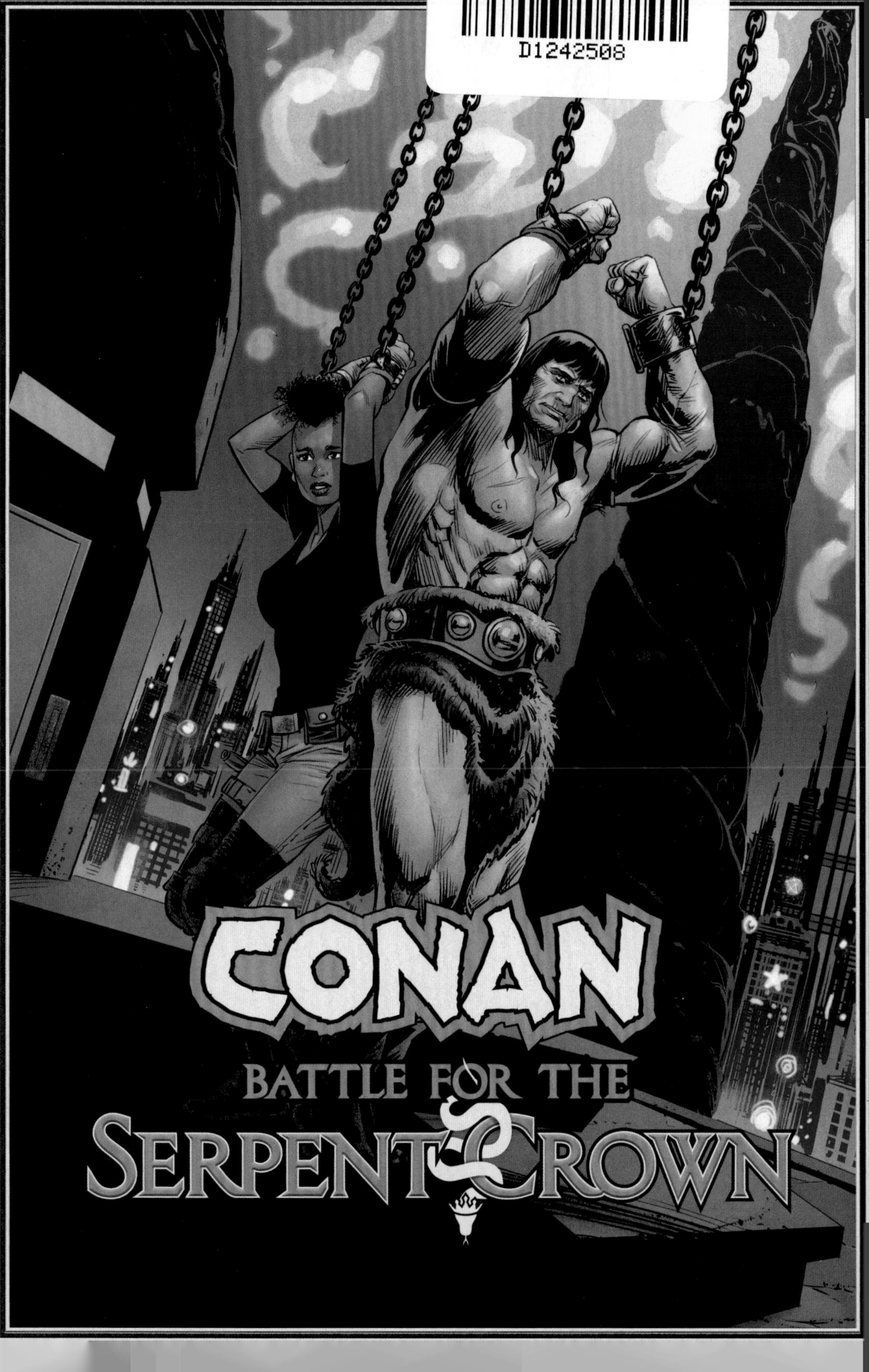
D1242508
CONAN
BATTLE FOR THE
SERPENT CROWN

CON
BATTLE
SERPENT

From the hills of his homeland in Cimmeria, Conan traveled, survived and thrived by cutting a bloody swath through the Hyborian Age. His most recent travels have found him in yet another strange new place... the modern world!

CONAN CREATED BY **ROBERT E. HOWARD**

COLLECTION EDITOR **MARK D. BEAZLEY**
ASSISTANT MANAGING EDITOR **MAIA LOY**
ASSISTANT MANAGING EDITOR **LISA MONTALBANO**
SENIOR EDITOR, SPECIAL PROJECTS **JENNIFER GRÜNWALD**
VP PRODUCTION & SPECIAL PROJECTS **JEFF YOUNGQUIST**
BOOK DESIGNER **JAY BOWEN**
SVP PRINT, SALES & MARKETING **DAVID GABRIEL**
EDITOR IN CHIEF **C.B. CEBULSKI**

FOR CONAN PROPERTIES INTERNATIONAL

PRESIDENT **FRED MALMBERG**
EXECUTIVE VICE PRESIDENT **JAY ZETTERBERG**
CHIEF OPERATING OFFICER **STEVE BOOTH**
COORDINATOR **MIKE JACOBSEN**

CONAN: BATTLE FOR THE SERPENT CROWN. Contains material originally published in magazine form as CONAN: BATTLE FOR THE SERPENT CROWN (2020) #1-5. First printing 2020. ISBN 978-1-302-92446-1. Published by MARVEL WORLDWIDE, INC., a subsidiary of MARVEL ENTERTAINMENT, LLC. OFFICE OF PUBLICATION: 1290 Avenue of the Americas, New York, NY 10104. © 2020 Conan Properties International LLC ("CPI"). CONAN, CONAN THE BARBARIAN, HYBORIA, THE SAVAGE SWORD OF CONAN and related logos, characters, names, and distinctive likenesses thereof are trademarks or registered trademarks of CPI. No similarity between any of the names, characters, persons, and/or institutions in this magazine with those of any living or dead person or institution is intended, and any such similarity which may exist is purely coincidental. Marvel and its logos are TM Marvel Characters, Inc. **Printed in Canada.** KEVIN FEIGE, Chief Creative Officer; DAN BUCKLEY, President, Marvel Entertainment; JOHN NEE, Publisher; JOE QUESADA, EVP & Creative Director; TOM BREVOORT, SVP of Publishing; DAVID BOGART, Associate Publisher & SVP of Talent Affairs; Publishing & Partnership; DAVID GABRIEL, VP of Print & Digital Publishing; JEFF YOUNGQUIST, VP of Production & Special Projects; DAN CARR, Executive Director of Publishing Technology; ALEX MORALES, Director of Publishing Operations; DAN EDINGTON, Managing Editor; RICKEY PURDIN, Director of Talent Relations; SUSAN CRESPI, Production Manager; STAN LEE, Chairman Emeritus. For information regarding advertising in Marvel Comics or on Marvel.com, please contact Vit DeBellis, Custom Solutions & Integrated Advertising Manager, at vdebellis@marvel.com. For Marvel subscription inquiries, please call 888-511-5480. **Manufactured between 10/2/2020 and 11/3/2020 by SOLISCO PRINTERS, SCOTT, QC, CANADA.**

10 9 8 7 6 5 4 3 2 1

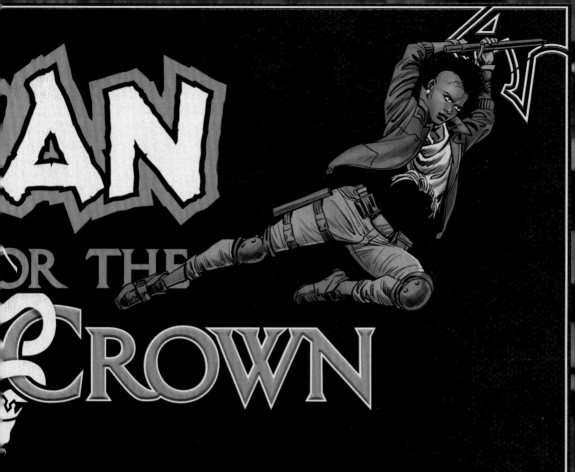

SALADIN AHMED
WRITER

LUKE ROSS
ARTIST

NOLAN WOODARD
COLOR ARTIST

VC's TRAVIS LANHAM
LETTERER

MAHMUD ASRAR
WITH **DAVE McCAIG** (#1)
& **MARCIO MENYZ** (#2-5)
COVER ART

MARK BASSO
EDITOR

**MARTIN BIRO,
SHANNON ANDREWS BALLESTEROS
& LAUREN AMARO**
ASSISTANT EDITORS

RALPH MACCHIO
CONSULTING EDITOR

SPECIAL THANKS TO **BRIAN OVERTON**

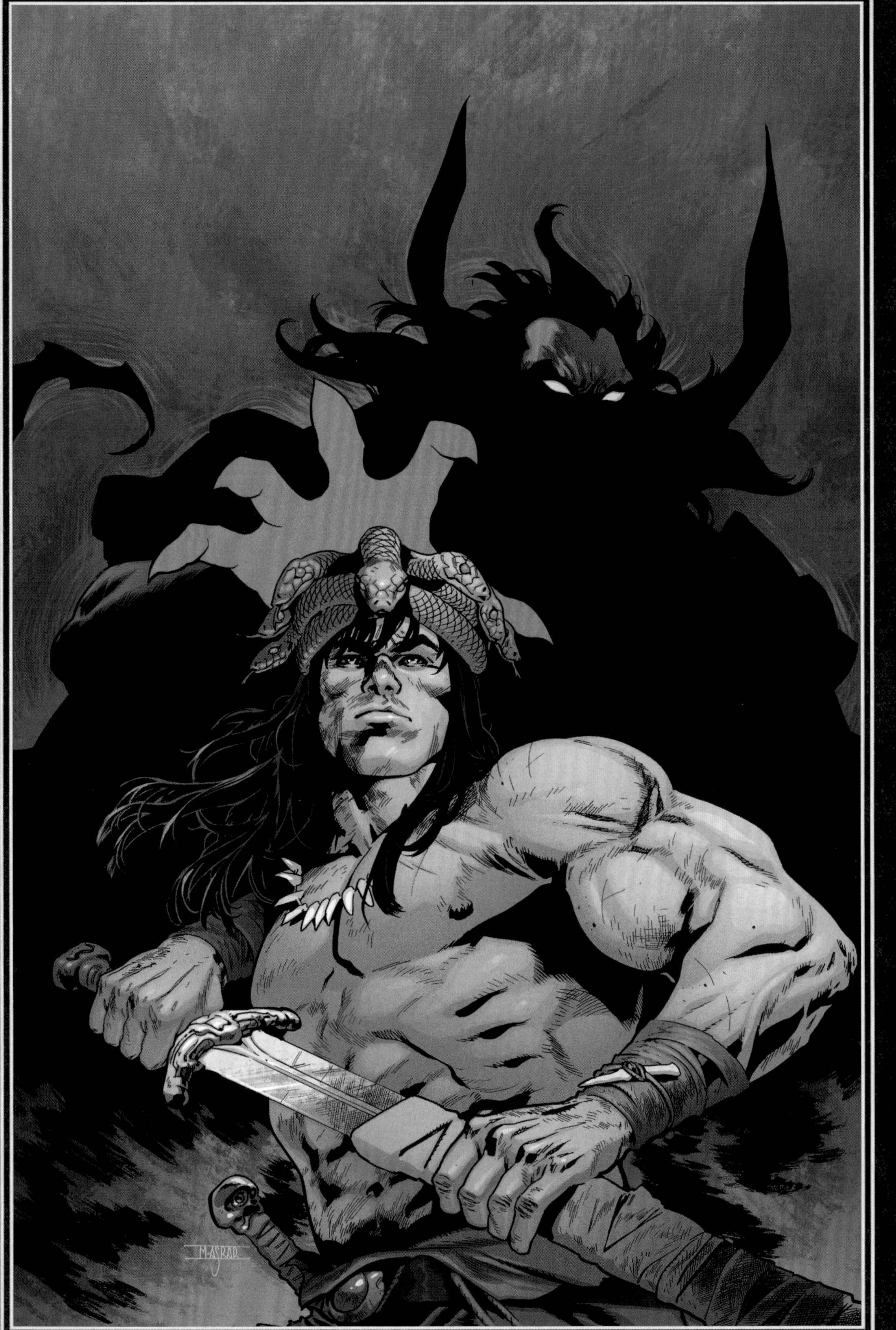

I

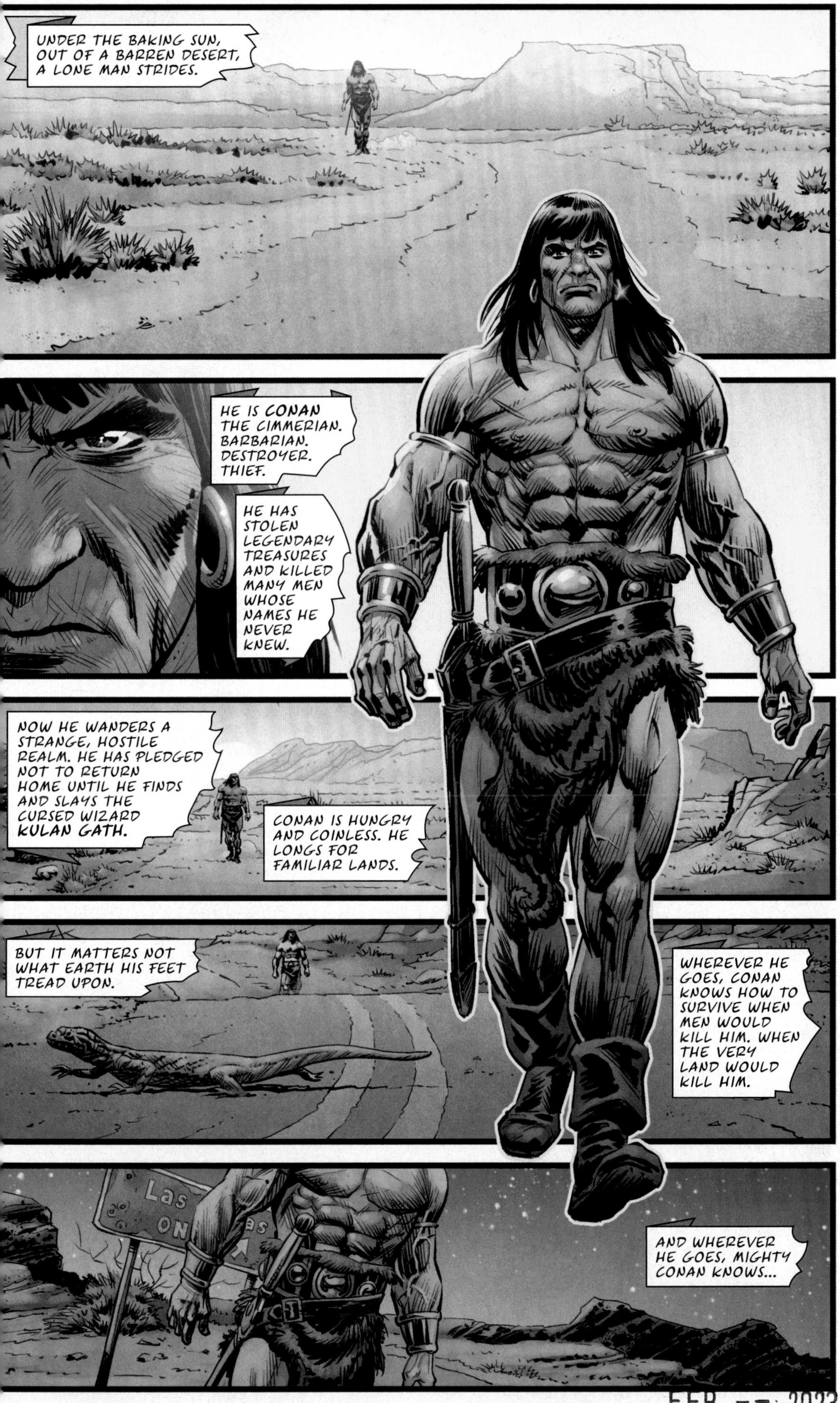
UNDER THE BAKING SUN, OUT OF A BARREN DESERT, A LONE MAN STRIDES.
HE IS CONAN THE CIMMERIAN. BARBARIAN. DESTROYER. THIEF.
HE HAS STOLEN LEGENDARY TREASURES AND KILLED MANY MEN WHOSE NAMES HE NEVER KNEW.
NOW HE WANDERS A STRANGE, HOSTILE REALM. HE HAS PLEDGED NOT TO RETURN HOME UNTIL HE FINDS AND SLAYS THE CURSED WIZARD KULAN GATH.
CONAN IS HUNGRY AND COINLESS. HE LONGS FOR FAMILIAR LANDS.
BUT IT MATTERS NOT WHAT EARTH HIS FEET TREAD UPON.
WHEREVER HE GOES, CONAN KNOWS HOW TO SURVIVE WHEN MEN WOULD KILL HIM. WHEN THE VERY LAND WOULD KILL HIM.
AND WHEREVER HE GOES, MIGHTY CONAN KNOWS...

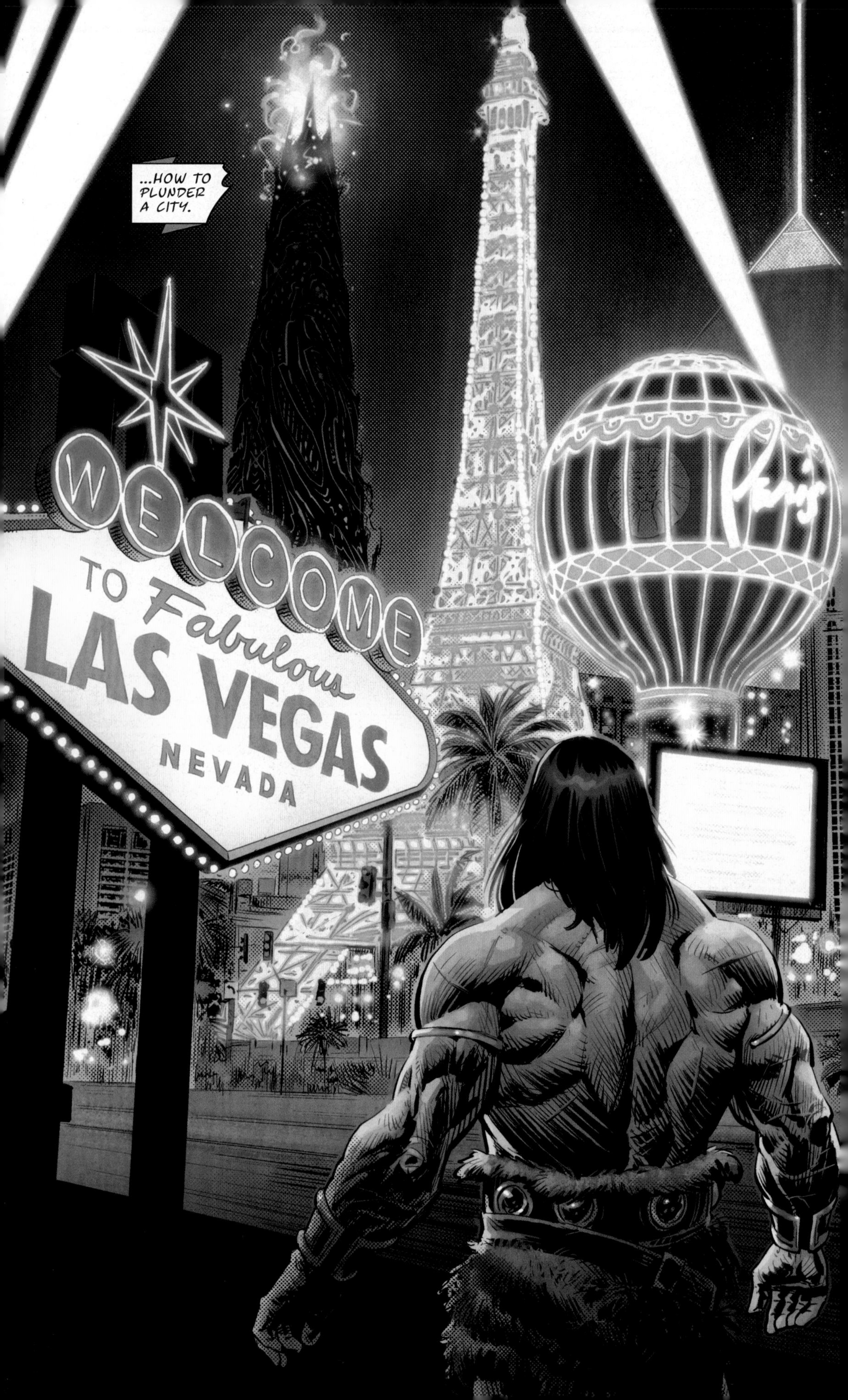

...HOW TO PLUNDER A CITY.
WELCOME
TO Fabulous
LAS VEGAS
NEVADA
Paris

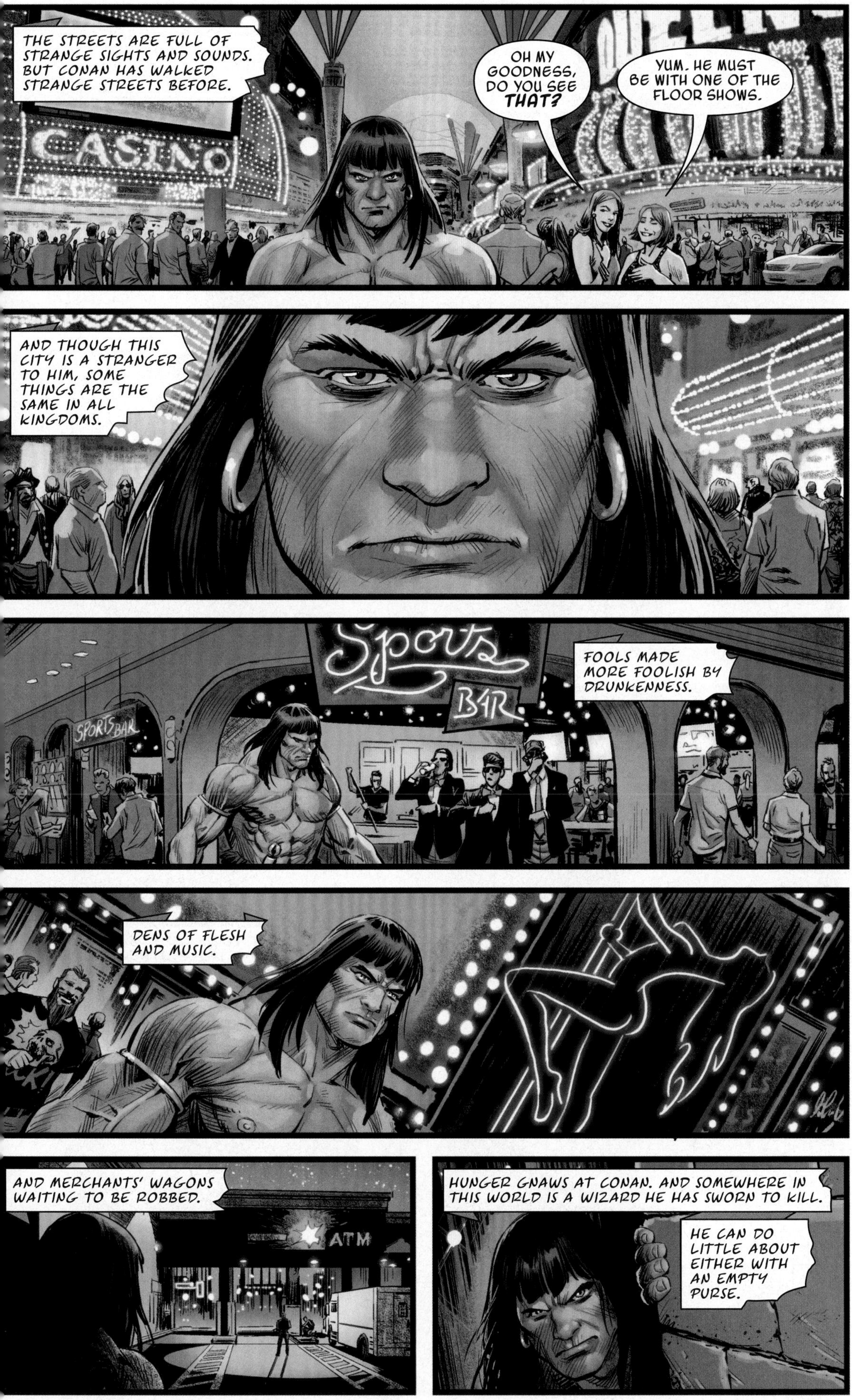
THE STREETS ARE FULL OF STRANGE SIGHTS AND SOUNDS. BUT CONAN HAS WALKED STRANGE STREETS BEFORE.
CASINO
OH MY GOODNESS, DO YOU SEE **THAT?**
YUM. HE MUST BE WITH ONE OF THE FLOOR SHOWS.
AND THOUGH THIS CITY IS A STRANGER TO HIM, SOME THINGS ARE THE SAME IN ALL KINGDOMS.
Sports BAR
SPORTS BAR
FOOLS MADE MORE FOOLISH BY DRUNKENNESS.
DENS OF FLESH AND MUSIC.
AND MERCHANTS' WAGONS WAITING TO BE ROBBED.
ATM
HUNGER GNAWS AT CONAN. AND SOMEWHERE IN THIS WORLD IS A WIZARD HE HAS SWORN TO KILL.
HE CAN DO LITTLE ABOUT EITHER WITH AN EMPTY PURSE.

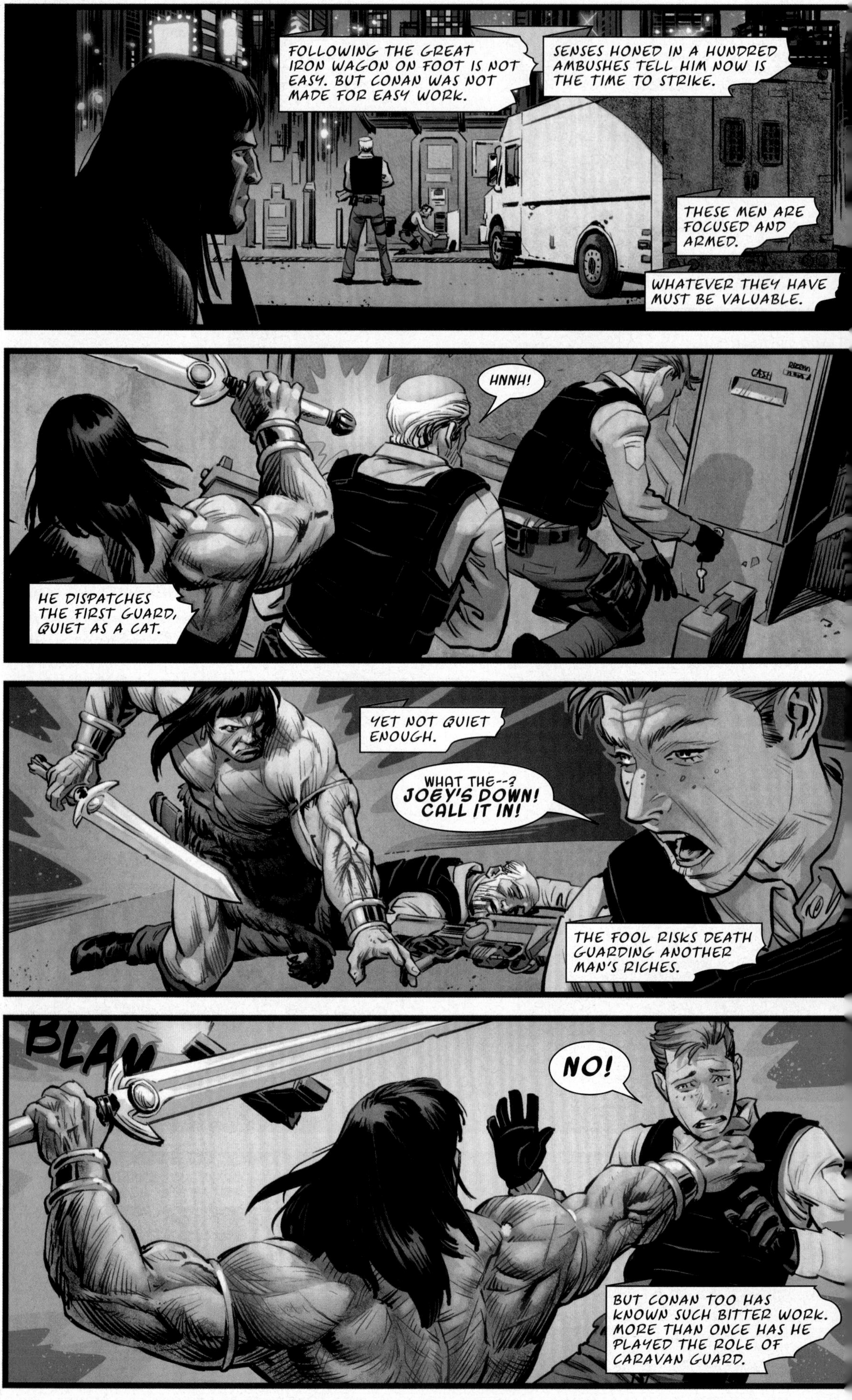
FOLLOWING THE GREAT IRON WAGON ON FOOT IS NOT EASY. BUT CONAN WAS NOT MADE FOR EASY WORK.
SENSES HONED IN A HUNDRED AMBUSHES TELL HIM NOW IS THE TIME TO STRIKE.
THESE MEN ARE FOCUSED AND ARMED.
WHATEVER THEY HAVE MUST BE VALUABLE.
HNNH!
CASH
HE DISPATCHES THE FIRST GUARD, QUIET AS A CAT.
YET NOT QUIET ENOUGH.
WHAT THE--? JOEY'S DOWN! CALL IT IN!
THE FOOL RISKS DEATH GUARDING ANOTHER MAN'S RICHES.
BLAM
NO!
BUT CONAN TOO HAS KNOWN SUCH BITTER WORK. MORE THAN ONCE HAS HE PLAYED THE ROLE OF CARAVAN GUARD.

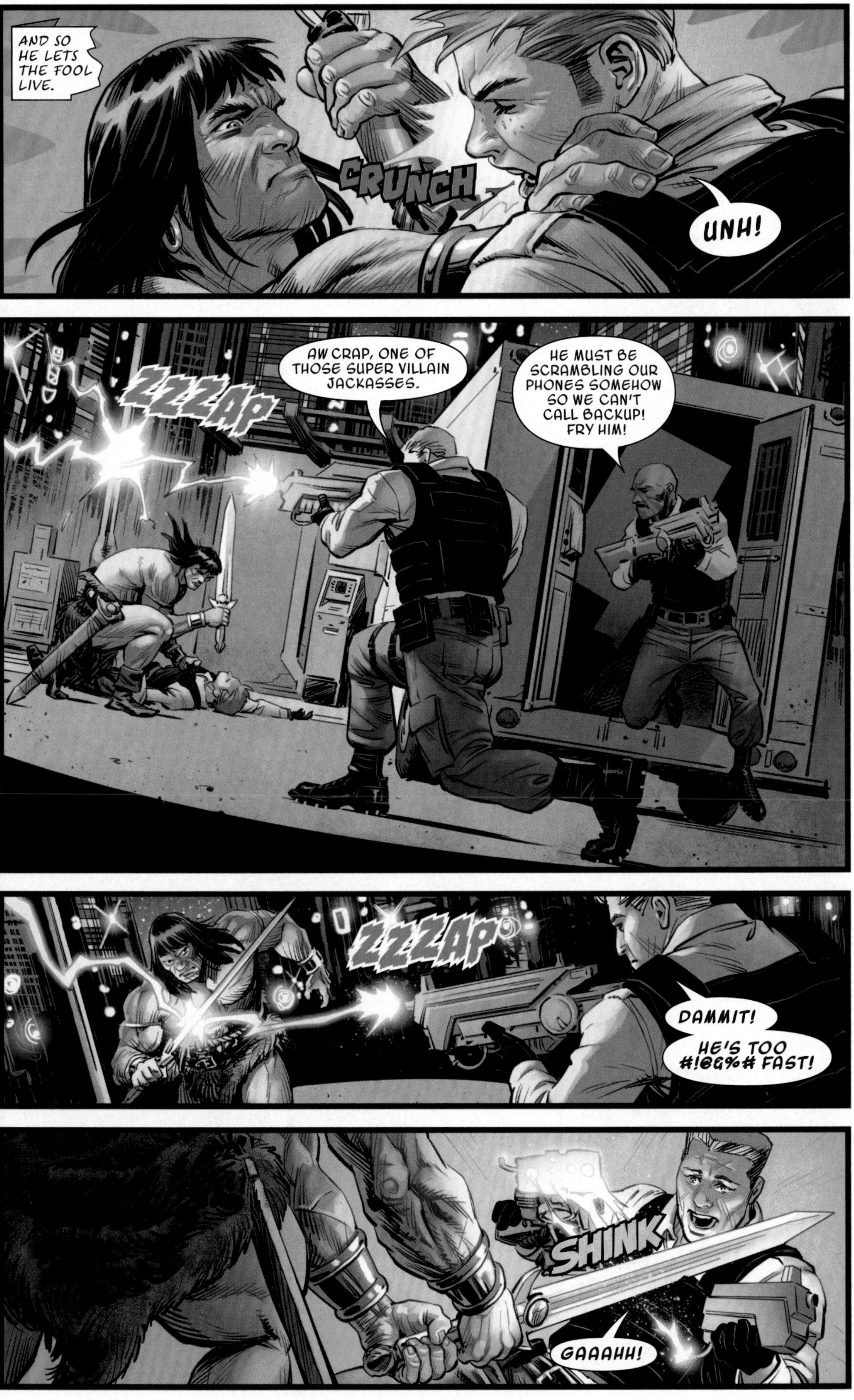
AND SO HE LETS THE FOOL LIVE.
CRUNCH
UNH!
ZZZAP
AW CRAP, ONE OF THOSE SUPER VILLAIN JACKASSES.
HE MUST BE SCRAMBLING OUR PHONES SOMEHOW SO WE CAN'T CALL BACKUP! FRY HIM!
ZZZAP
DAMMIT!
HE'S TOO #!@G%# FAST!
SHINK
GAAAHH!

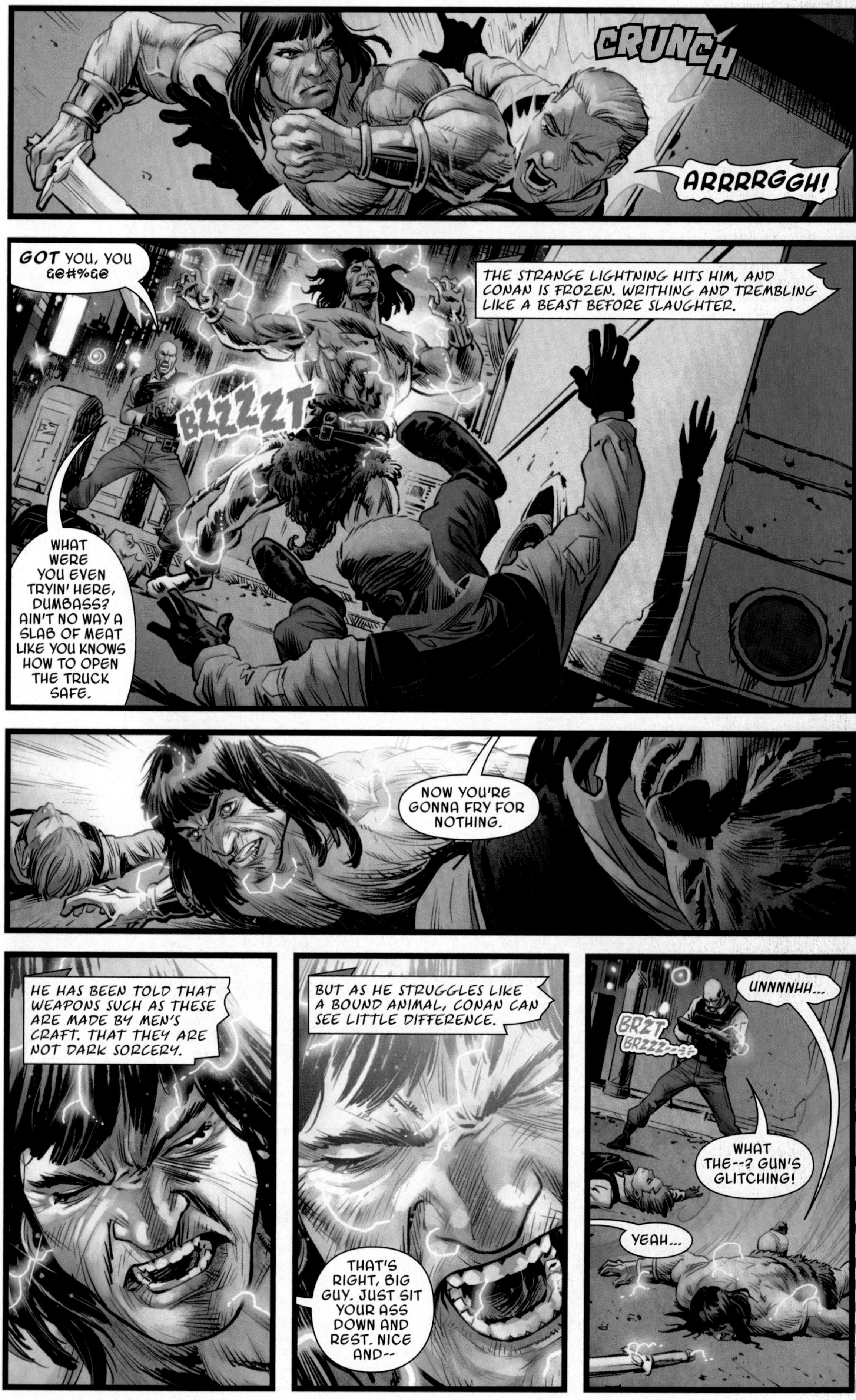
CRUNCH
ARRRRGGH!
GOT YOU, YOU &@#%&@
THE STRANGE LIGHTNING HITS HIM, AND CONAN IS FROZEN. WRITHING AND TREMBLING LIKE A BEAST BEFORE SLAUGHTER.
BZZZZT
WHAT WERE YOU EVEN TRYIN' HERE, DUMBASS? AIN'T NO WAY A SLAB OF MEAT LIKE YOU KNOWS HOW TO OPEN THE TRUCK SAFE.
NOW YOU'RE GONNA FRY FOR NOTHING.
HE HAS BEEN TOLD THAT WEAPONS SUCH AS THESE ARE MADE BY MEN'S CRAFT. THAT THEY ARE NOT DARK SORCERY.
BUT AS HE STRUGGLES LIKE A BOUND ANIMAL, CONAN CAN SEE LITTLE DIFFERENCE.
THAT'S RIGHT, BIG GUY. JUST SIT YOUR ASS DOWN AND REST. NICE AND--
UNNNNHH...
BRZT
BRZZZ
WHAT THE--? GUN'S GLITCHING!
YEAH...

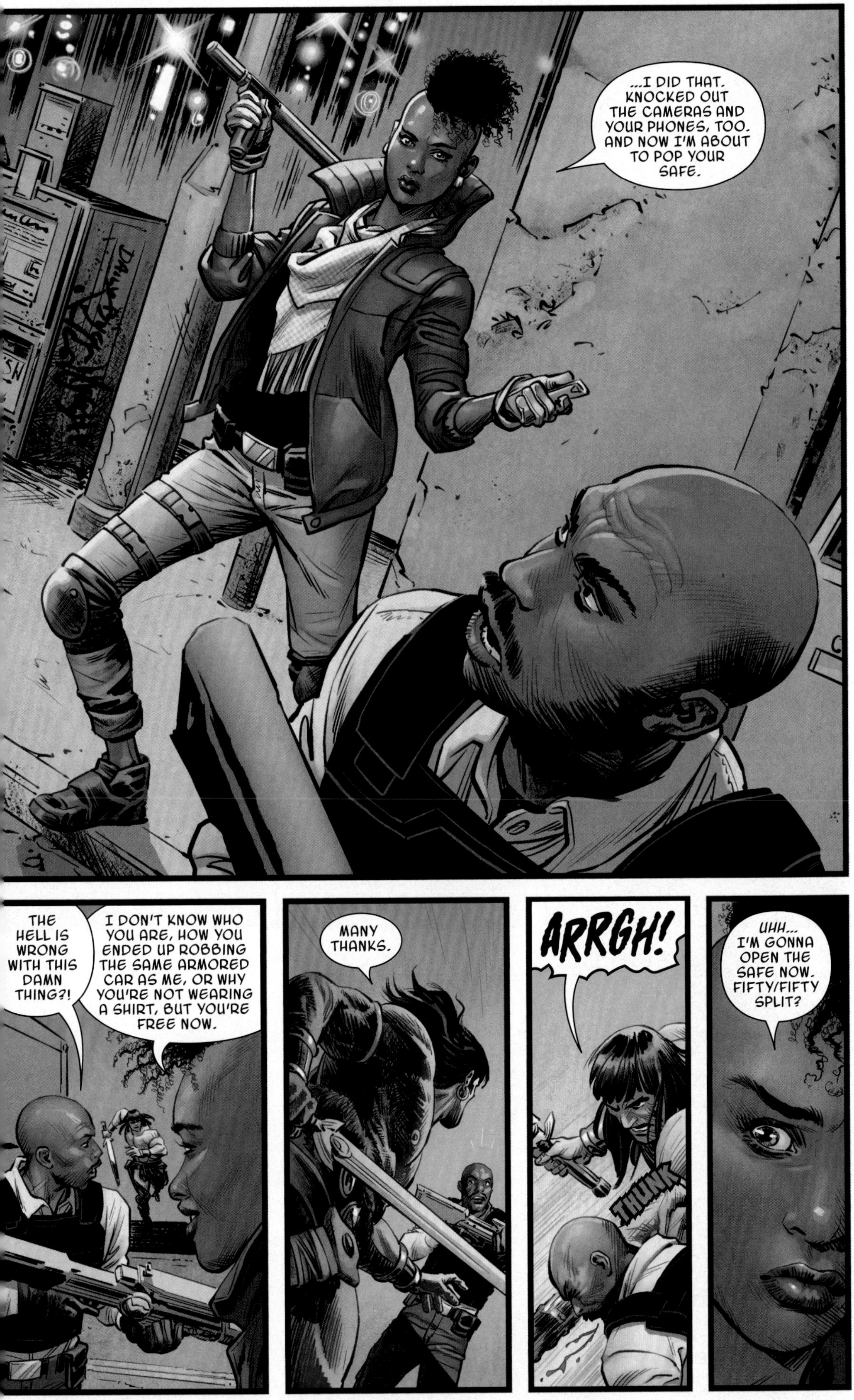

...I DID THAT. KNOCKED OUT THE CAMERAS AND YOUR PHONES, TOO. AND NOW I'M ABOUT TO POP YOUR SAFE.
THE HELL IS WRONG WITH THIS DAMN THING?!
I DON'T KNOW WHO YOU ARE, HOW YOU ENDED UP ROBBING THE SAME ARMORED CAR AS ME, OR WHY YOU'RE NOT WEARING A SHIRT, BUT YOU'RE FREE NOW.
MANY THANKS.
ARRGH!
THUNK
UHH... I'M GONNA OPEN THE SAFE NOW. FIFTY/FIFTY SPLIT?

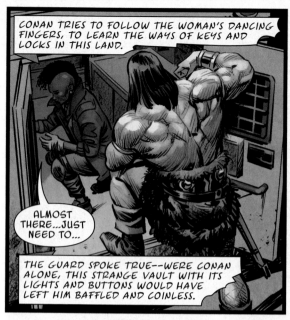

CONAN TRIES TO FOLLOW THE WOMAN'S DANCING FINGERS, TO LEARN THE WAYS OF KEYS AND LOCKS IN THIS LAND.

ALMOST THERE...JUST NEED TO...

THE GUARD SPOKE TRUE--WERE CONAN ALONE, THIS STRANGE VAULT WITH ITS LIGHTS AND BUTTONS WOULD HAVE LEFT HIM BAFFLED AND COINLESS.

HELL *YES!* PAYDAY! HALF OF THIS IS YOURS, YOU KNOW!

BUT FATE HAS SEEN TO IT THAT CONAN IS NOT ALONE THIS NIGHT...

BEEP BEEP

YOU, TOO, ARE A THIEF, THEN. AND AN ABLE ONE, IT WOULD SEEM.

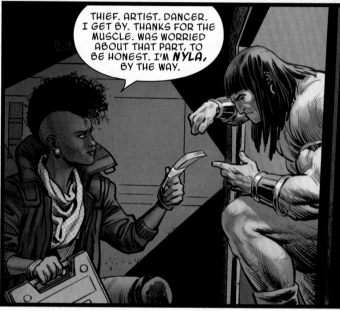

THIEF. ARTIST. DANCER. I GET BY. THANKS FOR THE MUSCLE. WAS WORRIED ABOUT THAT PART, TO BE HONEST. I'M *NYLA*, BY THE WAY.

I AM CALLED CONAN AND--PAPER? WHAT TRICKERY IS THIS? WHERE IS THE GOLD?

UH...THIS IS *MONEY.* WHERE ARE YOU *FROM,* ANYWAY?

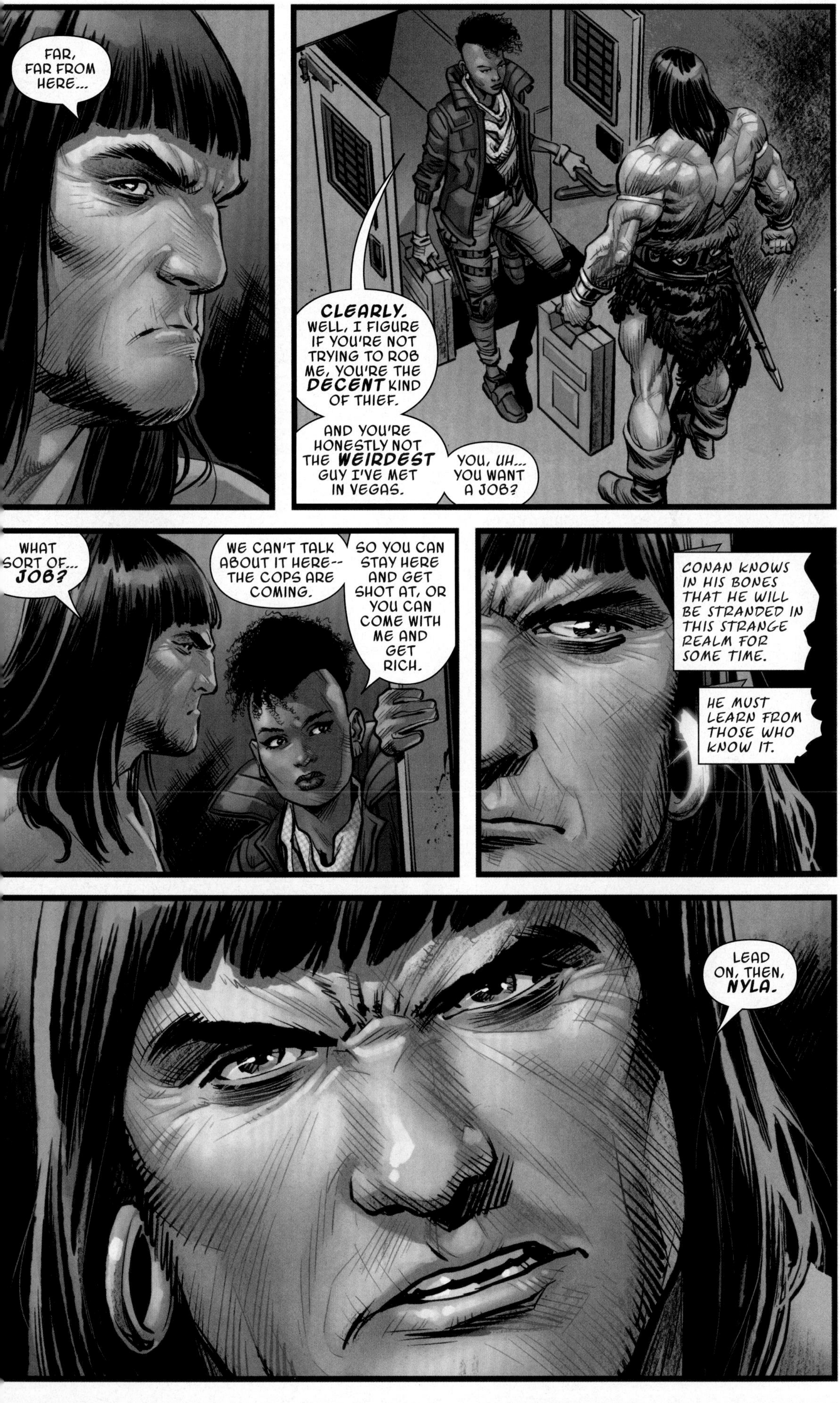
FAR, FAR FROM HERE...
CLEARLY. WELL, I FIGURE IF YOU'RE NOT TRYING TO ROB ME, YOU'RE THE DECENT KIND OF THIEF.
AND YOU'RE HONESTLY NOT THE WEIRDEST GUY I'VE MET IN VEGAS.
YOU, UH... YOU WANT A JOB?
WHAT SORT OF... JOB?
WE CAN'T TALK ABOUT IT HERE-- THE COPS ARE COMING.
SO YOU CAN STAY HERE AND GET SHOT AT, OR YOU CAN COME WITH ME AND GET RICH.
CONAN KNOWS IN HIS BONES THAT HE WILL BE STRANDED IN THIS STRANGE REALM FOR SOME TIME.
HE MUST LEARN FROM THOSE WHO KNOW IT.
LEAD ON, THEN, NYLA.

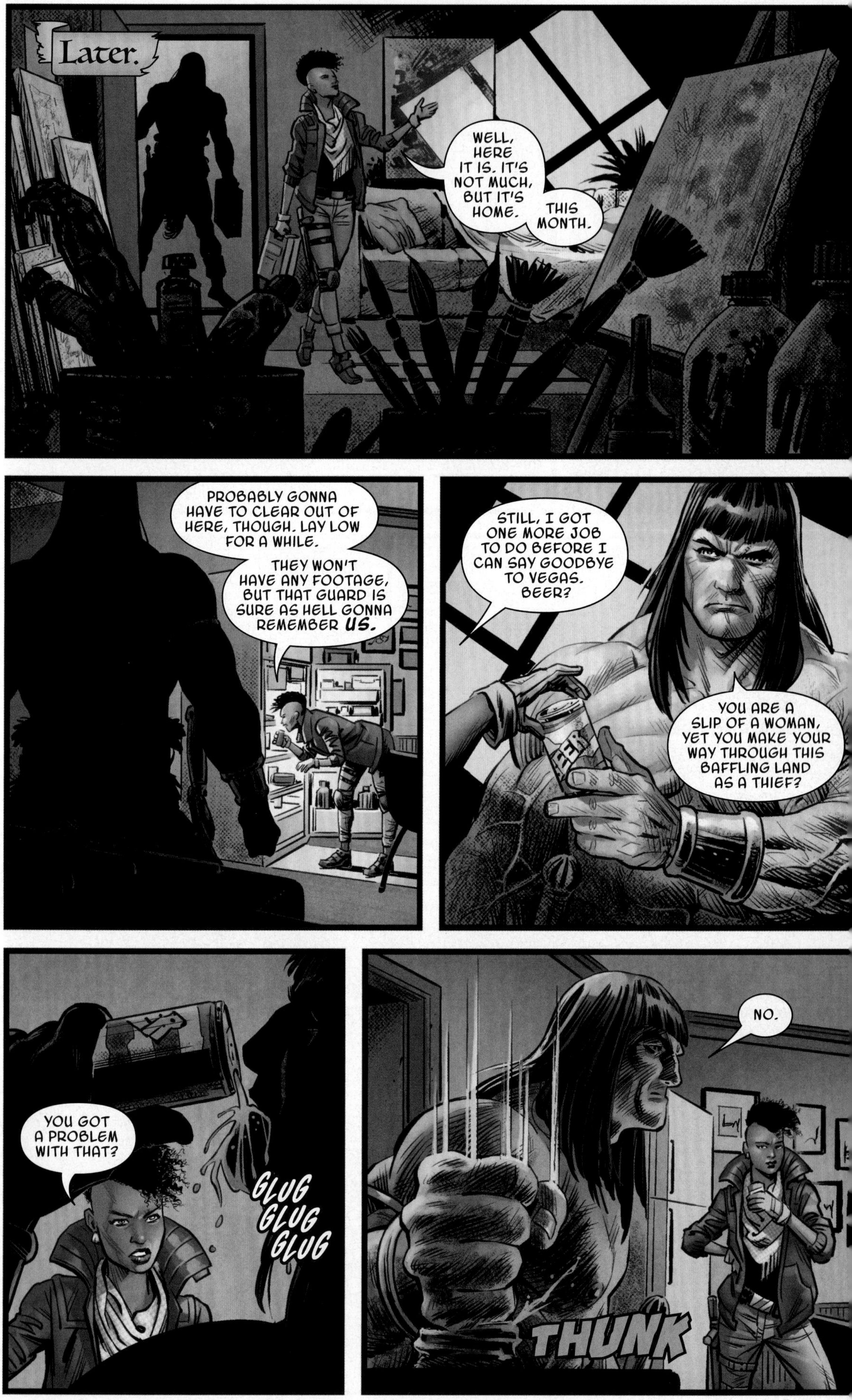

Later.
WELL, HERE IT IS. IT'S NOT MUCH, BUT IT'S HOME.
THIS MONTH.
PROBABLY GONNA HAVE TO CLEAR OUT OF HERE, THOUGH. LAY LOW FOR A WHILE.
THEY WON'T HAVE ANY FOOTAGE, BUT THAT GUARD IS SURE AS HELL GONNA REMEMBER US.
STILL, I GOT ONE MORE JOB TO DO BEFORE I CAN SAY GOODBYE TO VEGAS. BEER?
YOU ARE A SLIP OF A WOMAN, YET YOU MAKE YOUR WAY THROUGH THIS BAFFLING LAND AS A THIEF?
YOU GOT A PROBLEM WITH THAT?
GLUG GLUG GLUG
NO.
THUNK

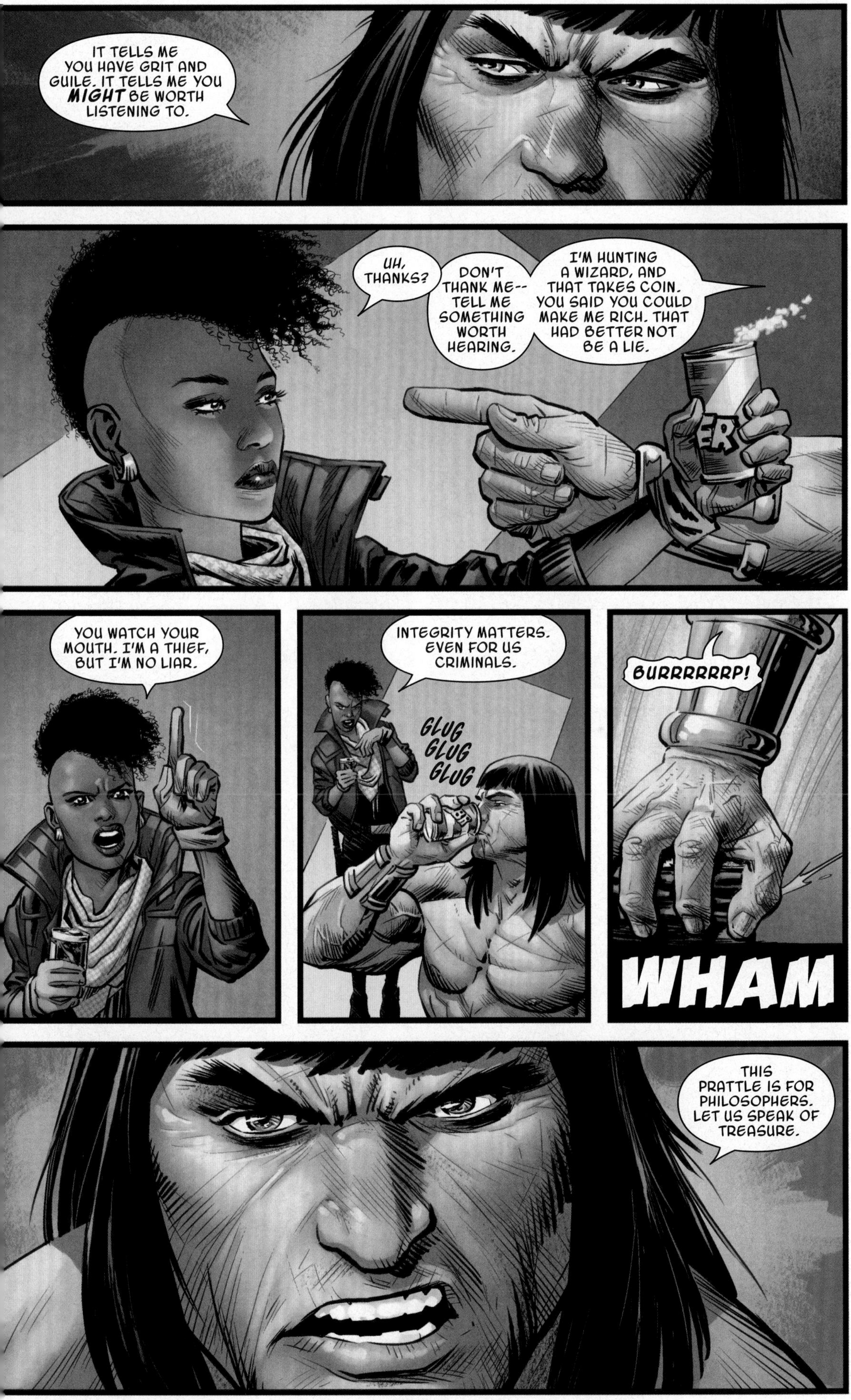
IT TELLS ME YOU HAVE GRIT AND GUILE. IT TELLS ME YOU **MIGHT** BE WORTH LISTENING TO.
UH, THANKS?
DON'T THANK ME-- TELL ME SOMETHING WORTH HEARING.
I'M HUNTING A WIZARD, AND THAT TAKES COIN. YOU SAID YOU COULD MAKE ME RICH. THAT HAD BETTER NOT BE A LIE.
ER
YOU WATCH YOUR MOUTH. I'M A THIEF, BUT I'M NO LIAR.
INTEGRITY MATTERS. EVEN FOR US CRIMINALS.
GLUG GLUG GLUG
BURRRRRRP!
WHAM
THIS PRATTLE IS FOR PHILOSOPHERS. LET US SPEAK OF TREASURE.

ALL RIGHT, I'LL MAKE IT SIMPLE--WE'RE GOING TO BREAK INTO A HOTEL AND ROB A VERY BAD MAN.

IMUS CHAMPION. A CRIMINALLY RICH BASTARD WHO KILLED MY FRIEND AND STOLE SOMETHING FROM HIM. I NEED TO STEAL IT BACK.

A SAD TALE. BUT SAD TALES ARE NO RARE THING. AND AVENGING YOUR FRIEND WON'T MAKE ME RICH.

IN CASE YOU FORGOT, PAL, I SAVED YOUR FURRY UNDERWEAR-COVERED ASS BACK THERE AT THE ARMORED CAR.

YOU OWE ME!

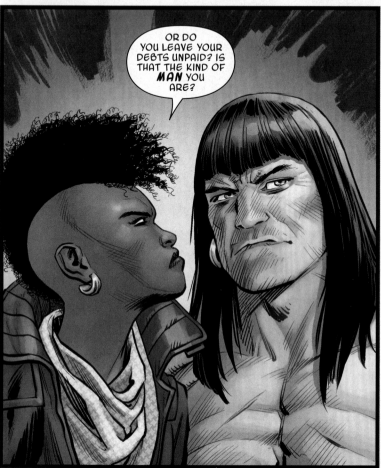

OR DO YOU LEAVE YOUR DEBTS UNPAID? IS THAT THE KIND OF MAN YOU ARE?

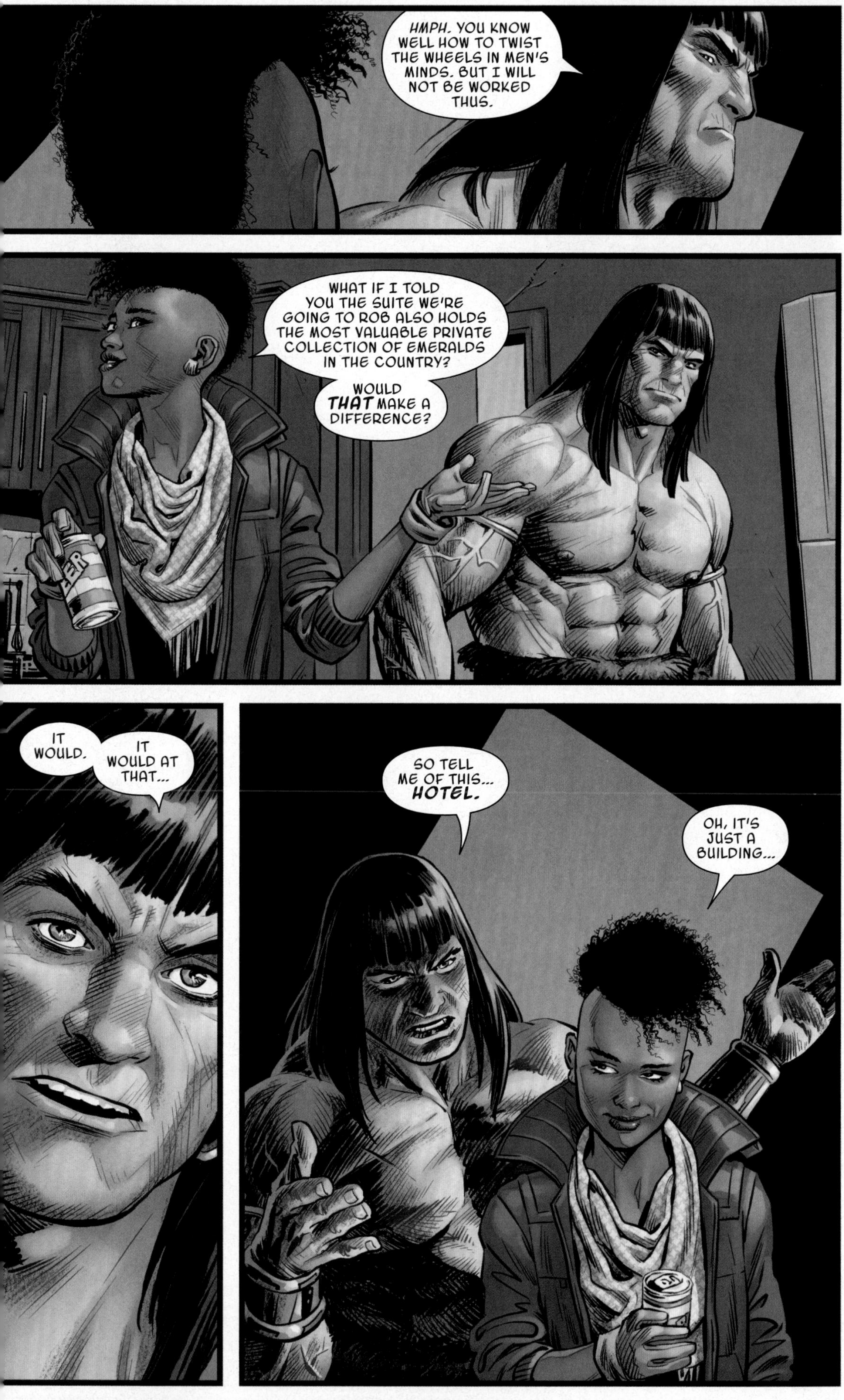

HMPH. YOU KNOW WELL HOW TO TWIST THE WHEELS IN MEN'S MINDS. BUT I WILL NOT BE WORKED THUS.
WHAT IF I TOLD YOU THE SUITE WE'RE GOING TO ROB ALSO HOLDS THE MOST VALUABLE PRIVATE COLLECTION OF EMERALDS IN THE COUNTRY?
WOULD THAT MAKE A DIFFERENCE?
IT WOULD.
IT WOULD AT THAT...
SO TELL ME OF THIS... HOTEL.
OH, IT'S JUST A BUILDING...

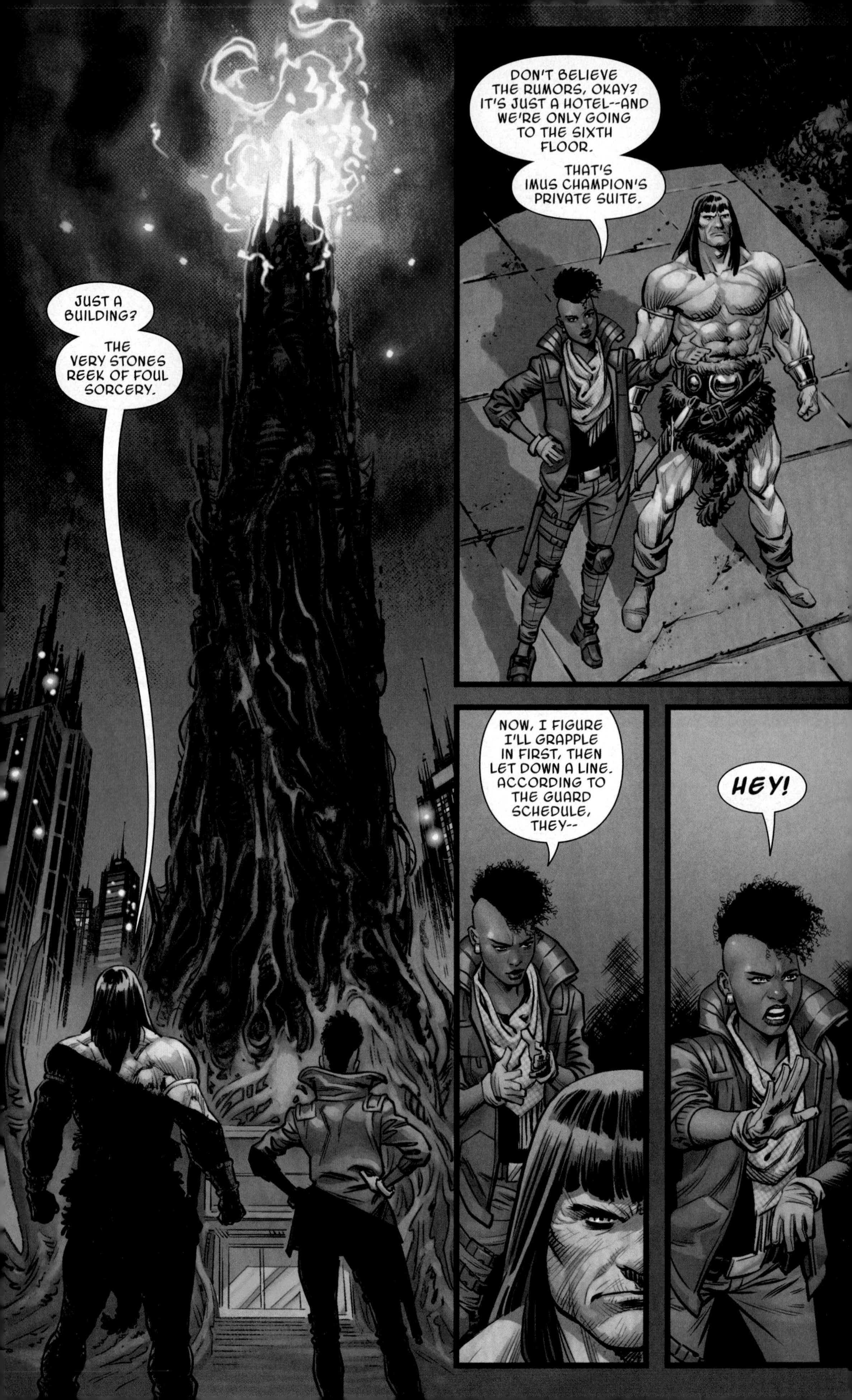
JUST A BUILDING?
THE VERY STONES REEK OF FOUL SORCERY.
DON'T BELIEVE THE RUMORS, OKAY? IT'S JUST A HOTEL--AND WE'RE ONLY GOING TO THE SIXTH FLOOR.
THAT'S IMUS CHAMPION'S PRIVATE SUITE.
NOW, I FIGURE I'LL GRAPPLE IN FIRST, THEN LET DOWN A LINE. ACCORDING TO THE GUARD SCHEDULE, THEY--
HEY!

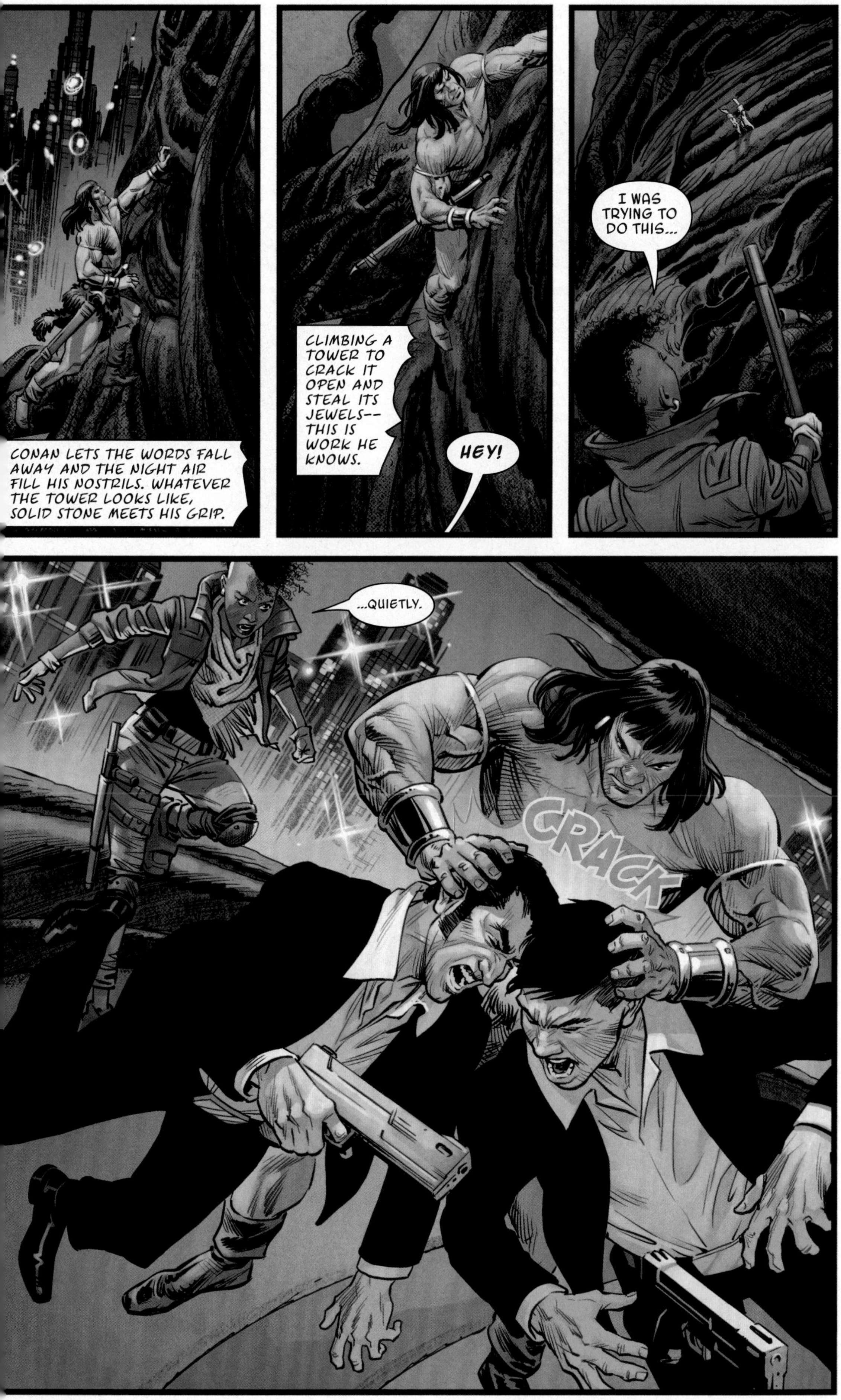
CONAN LETS THE WORDS FALL AWAY AND THE NIGHT AIR FILL HIS NOSTRILS. WHATEVER THE TOWER LOOKS LIKE, SOLID STONE MEETS HIS GRIP.
CLIMBING A TOWER TO CRACK IT OPEN AND STEAL ITS JEWELS-- THIS IS WORK HE KNOWS.
HEY!
I WAS TRYING TO DO THIS...
...QUIETLY.
CRACK

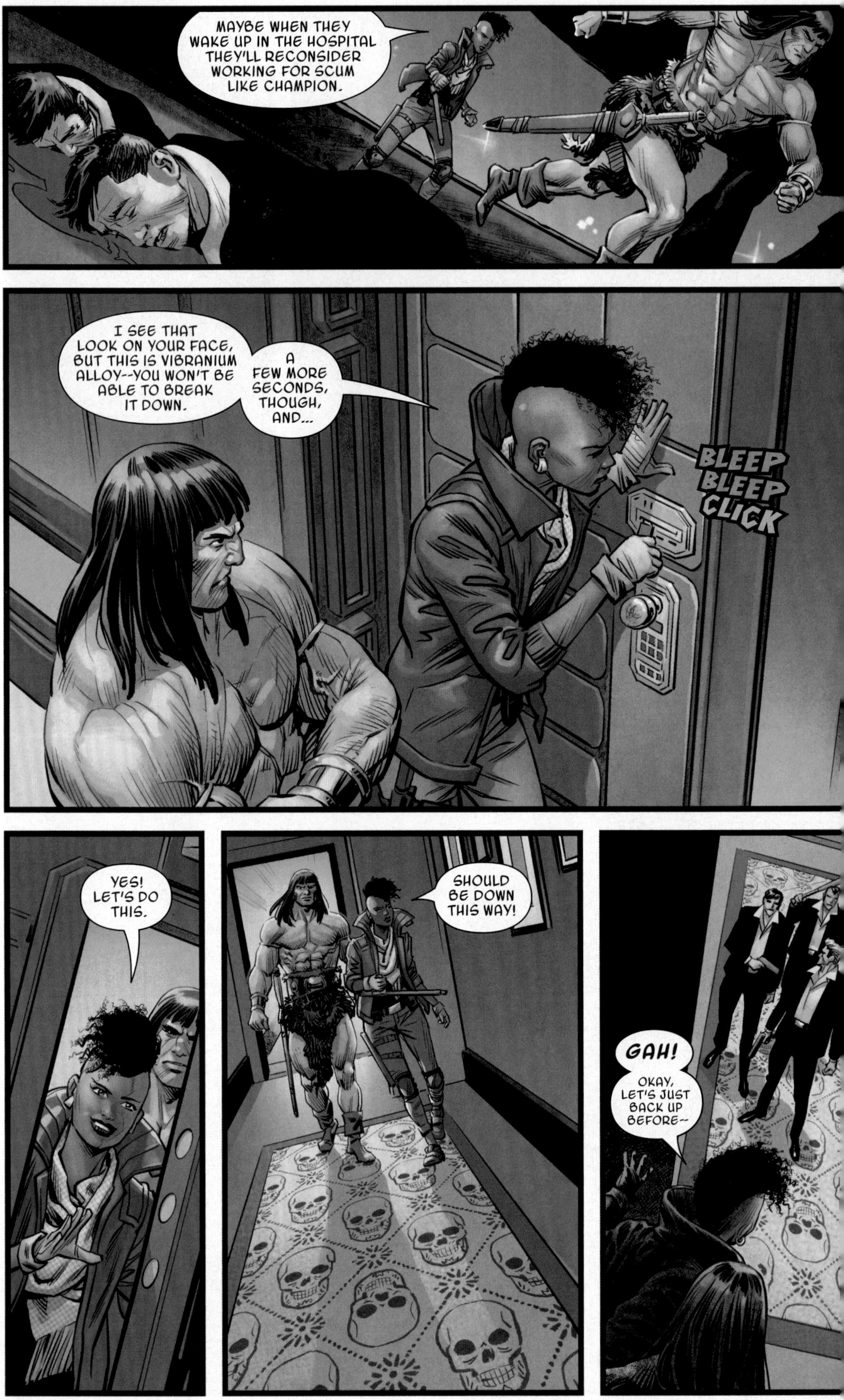
MAYBE WHEN THEY WAKE UP IN THE HOSPITAL THEY'LL RECONSIDER WORKING FOR SCUM LIKE CHAMPION.
I SEE THAT LOOK ON YOUR FACE, BUT THIS IS VIBRANIUM ALLOY--YOU WON'T BE ABLE TO BREAK IT DOWN.
A FEW MORE SECONDS, THOUGH, AND...
BLEEP BLEEP CLICK
YES! LET'S DO THIS.
SHOULD BE DOWN THIS WAY!
GAH!
OKAY, LET'S JUST BACK UP BEFORE--

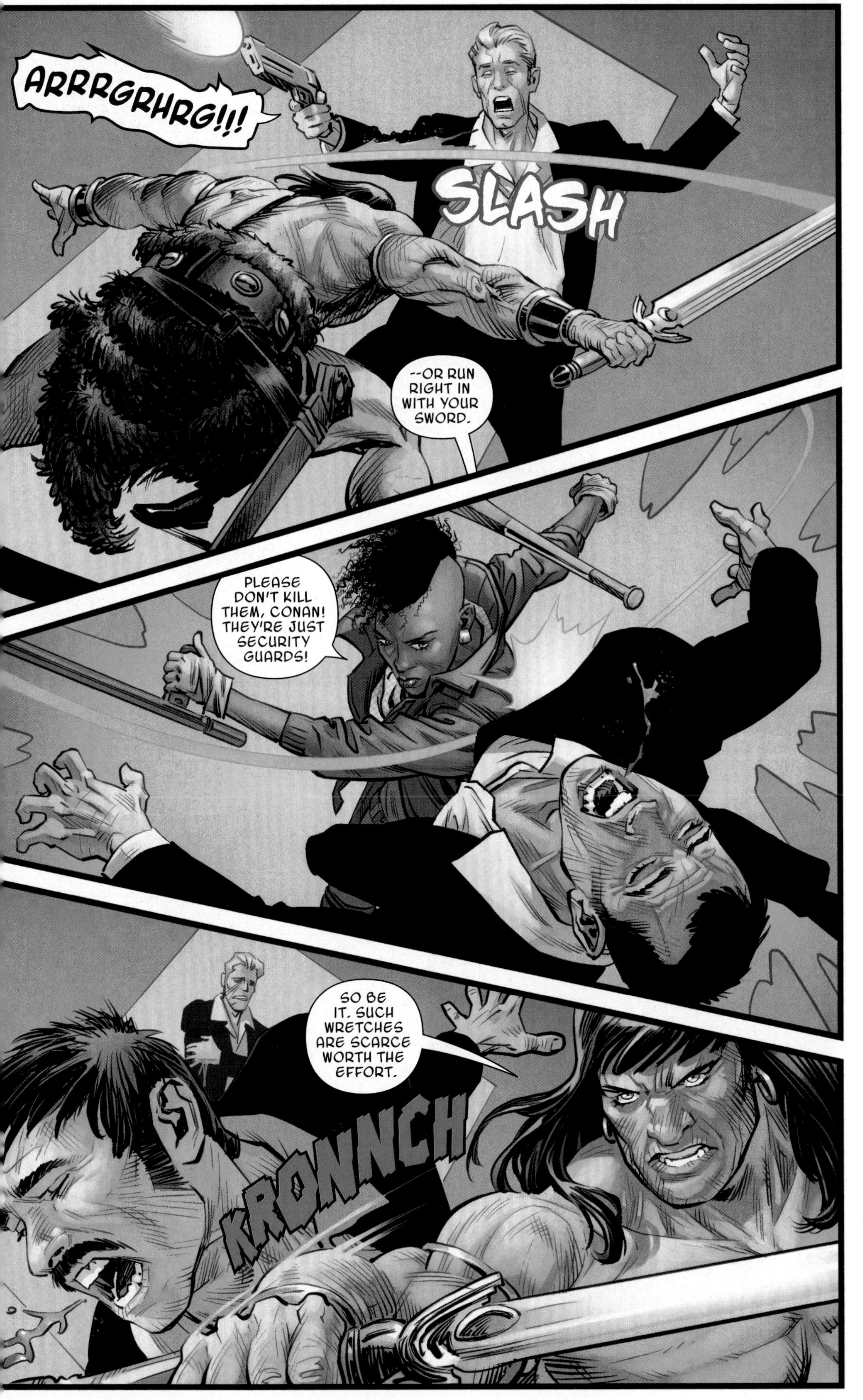
ARRRGRHRG!!!
SLASH
--OR RUN RIGHT IN WITH YOUR SWORD.
PLEASE DON'T KILL THEM, CONAN! THEY'RE JUST SECURITY GUARDS!
SO BE IT. SUCH WRETCHES ARE SCARCE WORTH THE EFFORT.
KRONNCH

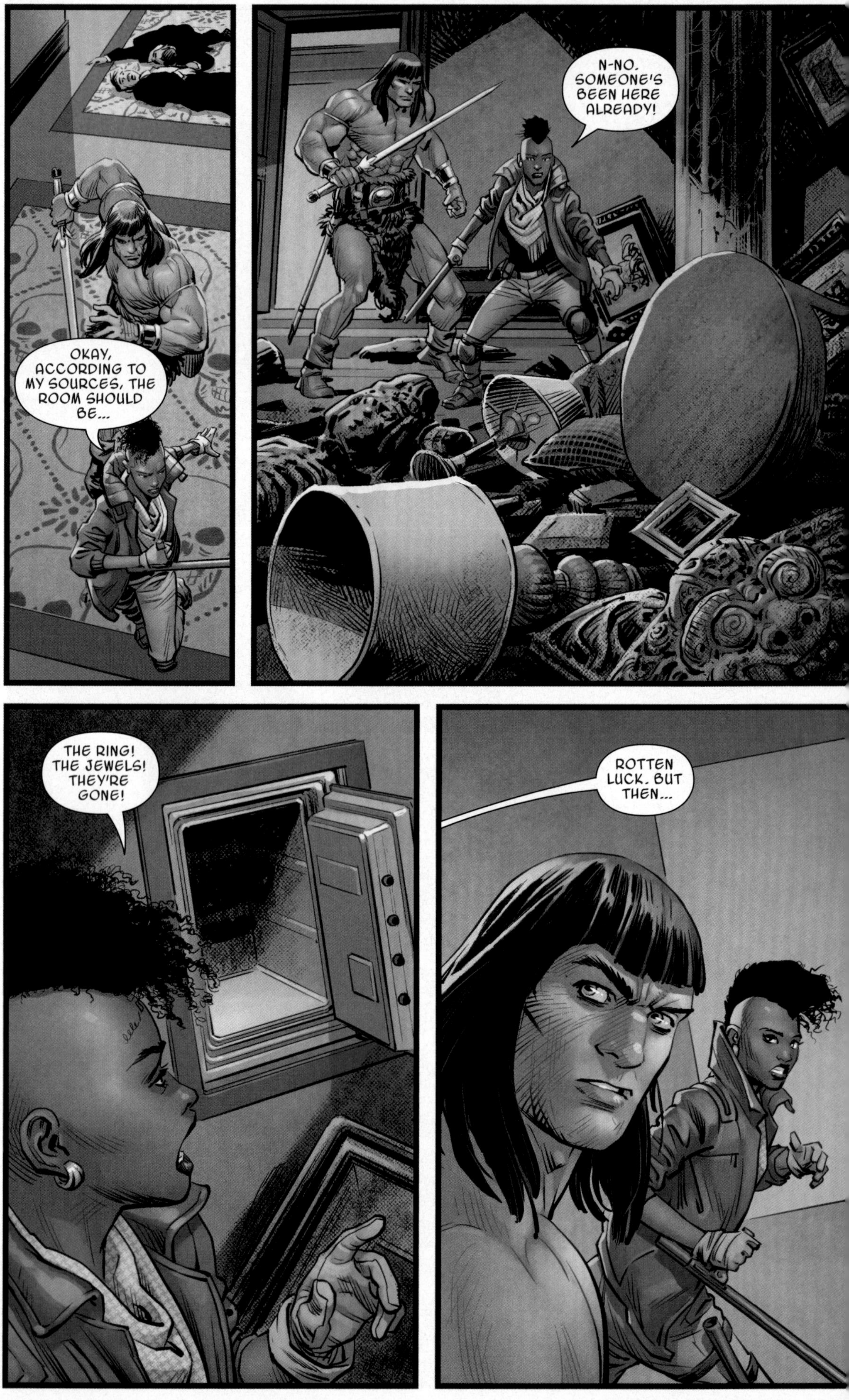
OKAY, ACCORDING TO MY SOURCES, THE ROOM SHOULD BE...
N-NO. SOMEONE'S BEEN HERE ALREADY!
THE RING! THE JEWELS! THEY'RE GONE!
ROTTEN LUCK. BUT THEN...

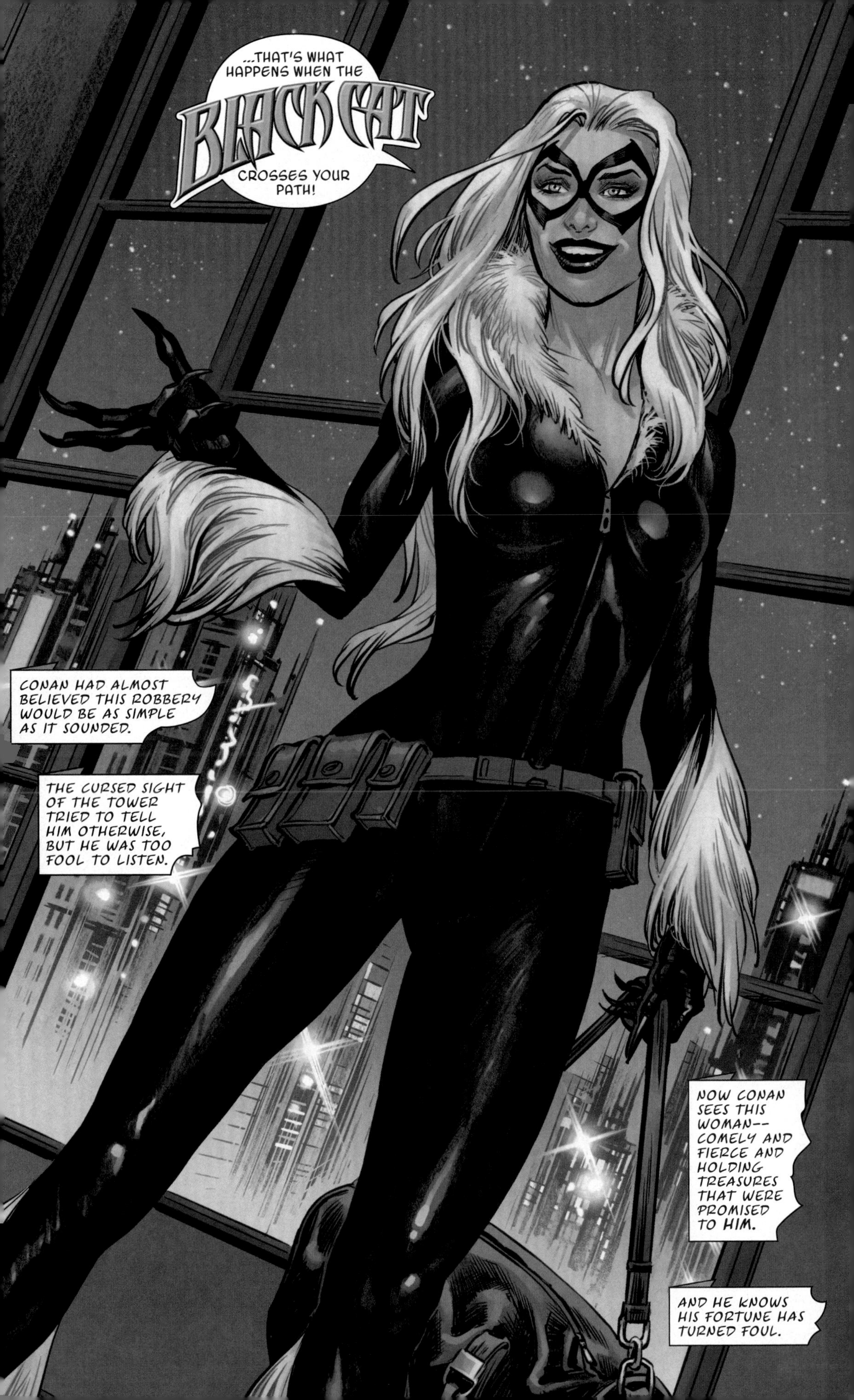

...THAT'S WHAT HAPPENS WHEN THE BLACK CAT CROSSES YOUR PATH!
CONAN HAD ALMOST BELIEVED THIS ROBBERY WOULD BE AS SIMPLE AS IT SOUNDED.
THE CURSED SIGHT OF THE TOWER TRIED TO TELL HIM OTHERWISE, BUT HE WAS TOO FOOL TO LISTEN.
NOW CONAN SEES THIS WOMAN-- COMELY AND FIERCE AND HOLDING TREASURES THAT WERE PROMISED TO HIM.
AND HE KNOWS HIS FORTUNE HAS TURNED FOUL.

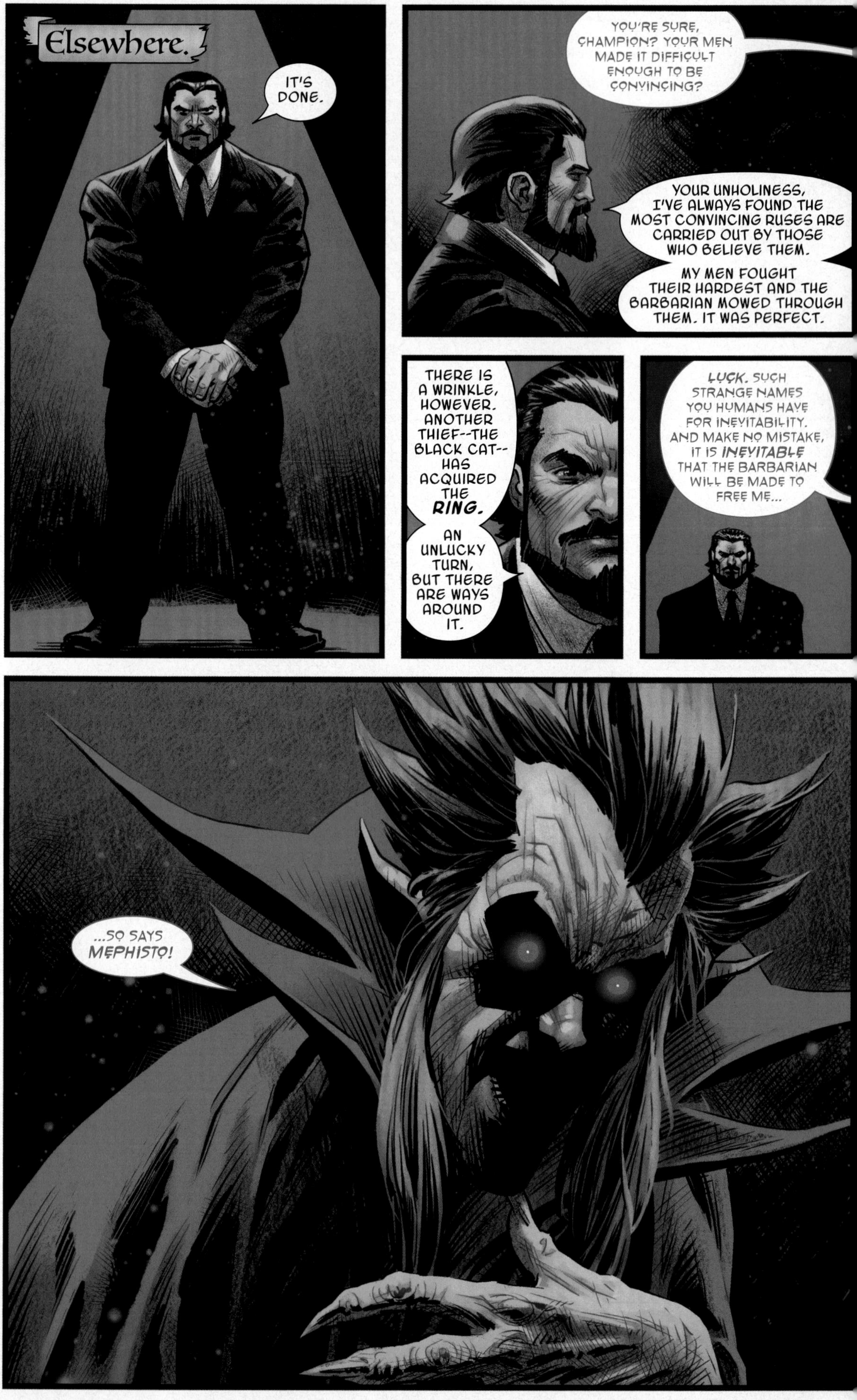
Elsewhere.
IT'S DONE.
YOU'RE SURE, CHAMPION? YOUR MEN MADE IT DIFFICULT ENOUGH TO BE CONVINCING?
YOUR UNHOLINESS, I'VE ALWAYS FOUND THE MOST CONVINCING RUSES ARE CARRIED OUT BY THOSE WHO BELIEVE THEM.
MY MEN FOUGHT THEIR HARDEST AND THE BARBARIAN MOWED THROUGH THEM. IT WAS PERFECT.
THERE IS A WRINKLE, HOWEVER. ANOTHER THIEF--THE BLACK CAT--HAS ACQUIRED THE RING.
AN UNLUCKY TURN, BUT THERE ARE WAYS AROUND IT.
LUCK. SUCH STRANGE NAMES YOU HUMANS HAVE FOR INEVITABILITY. AND MAKE NO MISTAKE, IT IS INEVITABLE THAT THE BARBARIAN WILL BE MADE TO FREE ME...
...SO SAYS MEPHISTO!

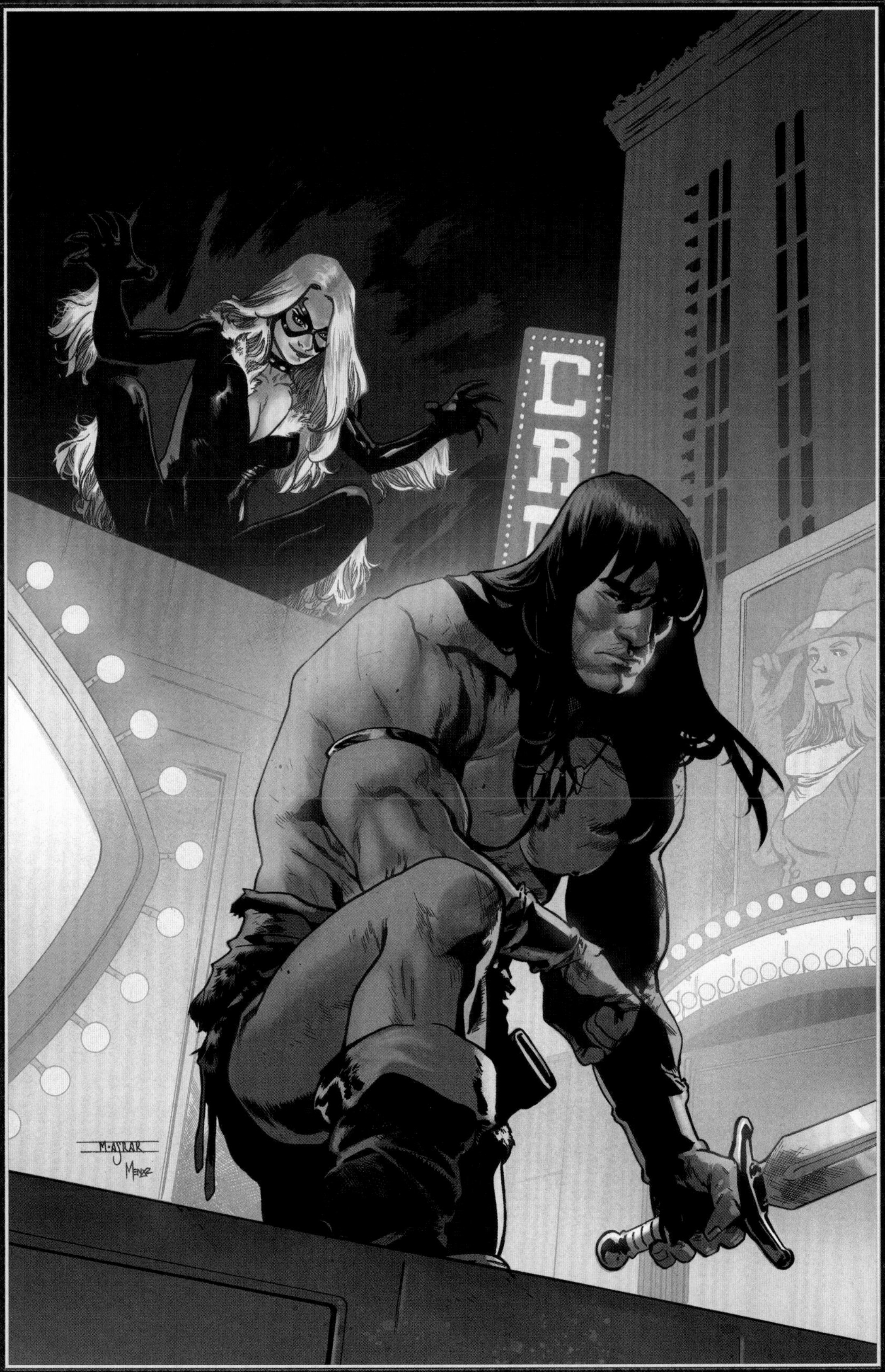

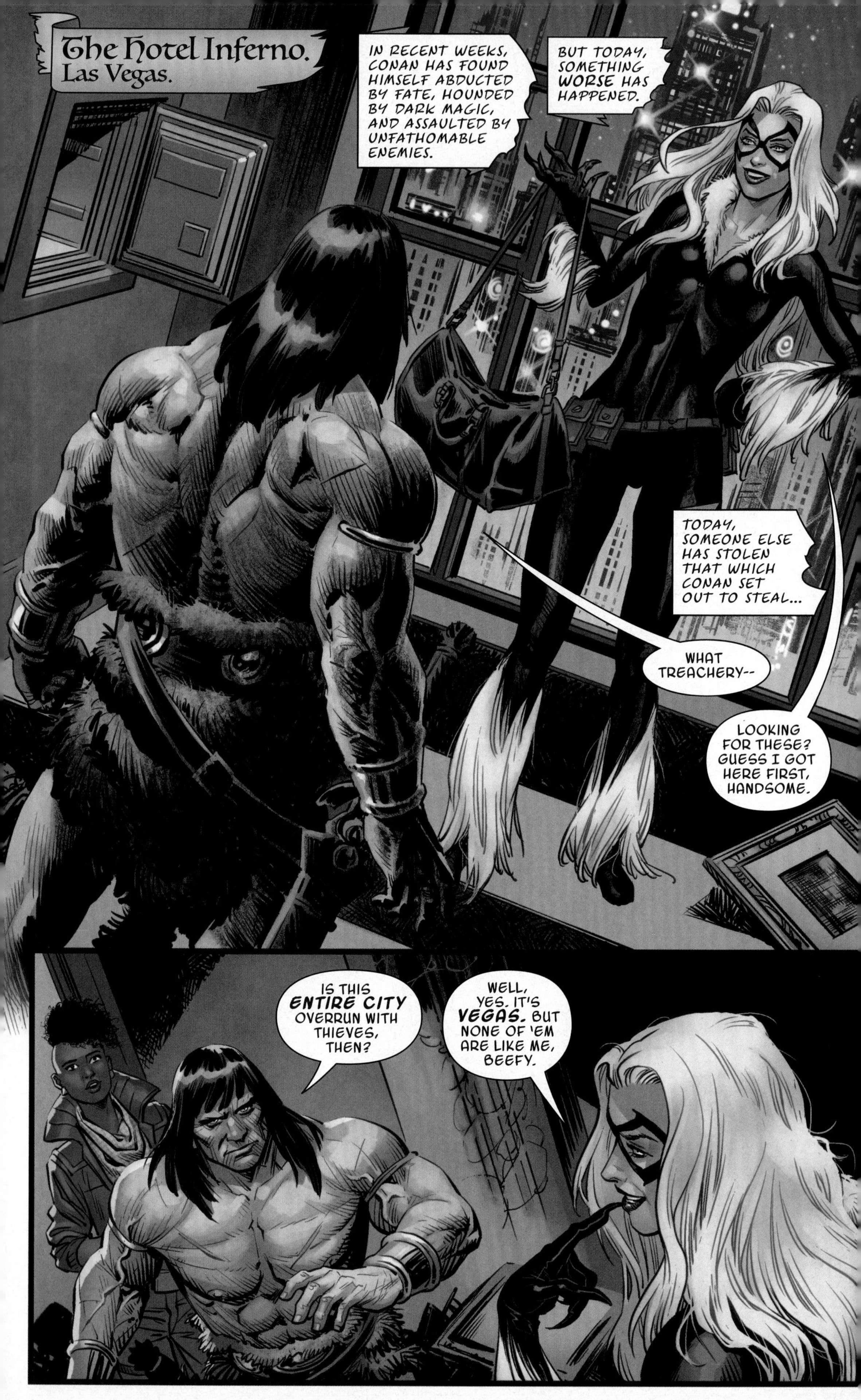
The Hotel Inferno.
Las Vegas.
IN RECENT WEEKS, CONAN HAS FOUND HIMSELF ABDUCTED BY FATE, HOUNDED BY DARK MAGIC, AND ASSAULTED BY UNFATHOMABLE ENEMIES.
BUT TODAY, SOMETHING WORSE HAS HAPPENED.
TODAY, SOMEONE ELSE HAS STOLEN THAT WHICH CONAN SET OUT TO STEAL...
WHAT TREACHERY--
LOOKING FOR THESE? GUESS I GOT HERE FIRST, HANDSOME.
IS THIS ENTIRE CITY OVERRUN WITH THIEVES, THEN?
WELL, YES. IT'S VEGAS. BUT NONE OF 'EM ARE LIKE ME, BEEFY.

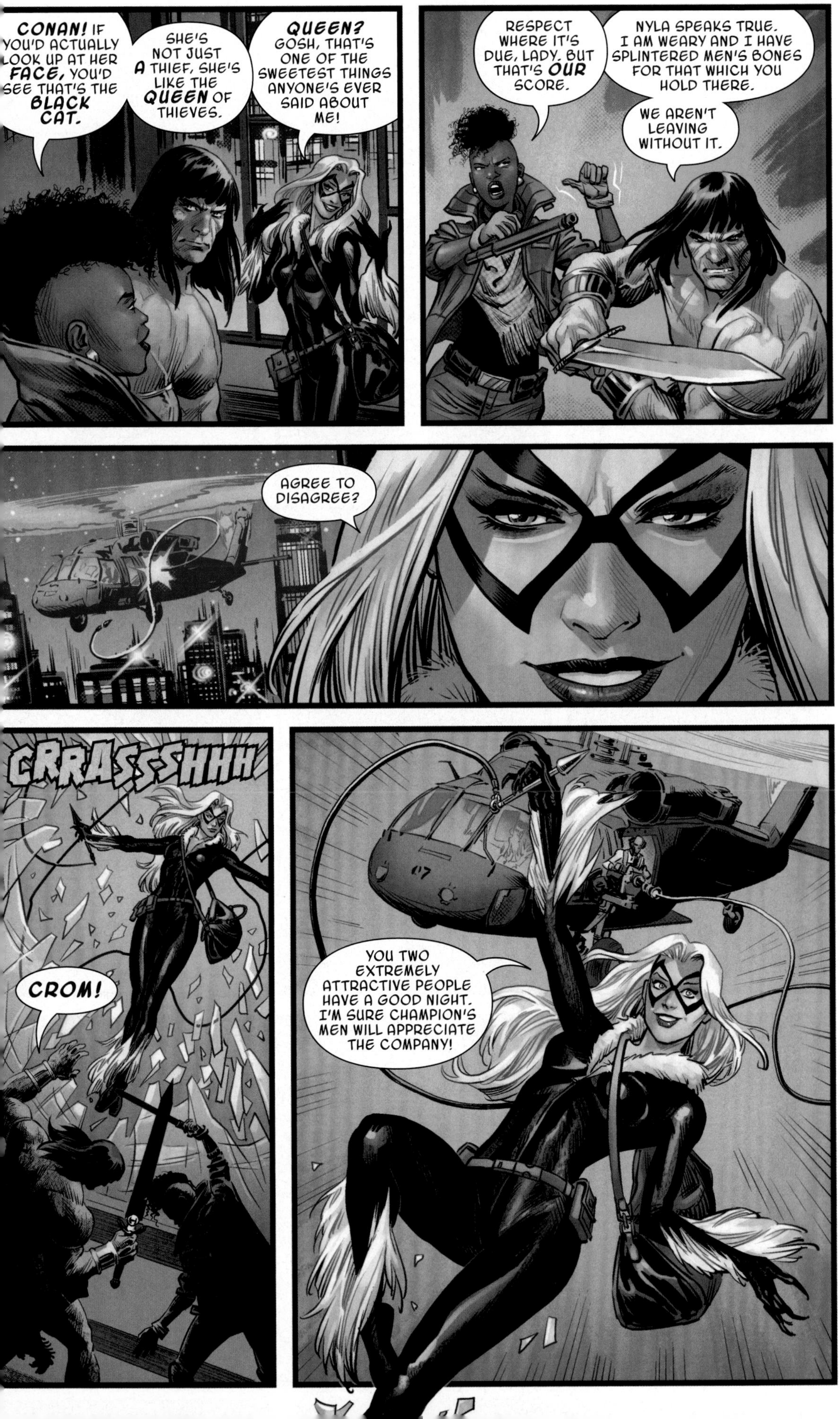

CONAN! IF YOU'D ACTUALLY LOOK UP AT HER FACE, YOU'D SEE THAT'S THE BLACK CAT.
SHE'S NOT JUST A THIEF, SHE'S LIKE THE QUEEN OF THIEVES.
QUEEN? GOSH, THAT'S ONE OF THE SWEETEST THINGS ANYONE'S EVER SAID ABOUT ME!
RESPECT WHERE IT'S DUE, LADY. BUT THAT'S OUR SCORE.
NYLA SPEAKS TRUE. I AM WEARY AND I HAVE SPLINTERED MEN'S BONES FOR THAT WHICH YOU HOLD THERE.
WE AREN'T LEAVING WITHOUT IT.
AGREE TO DISAGREE?
CRRASSSHHH
CROM!
YOU TWO EXTREMELY ATTRACTIVE PEOPLE HAVE A GOOD NIGHT. I'M SURE CHAMPION'S MEN WILL APPRECIATE THE COMPANY!

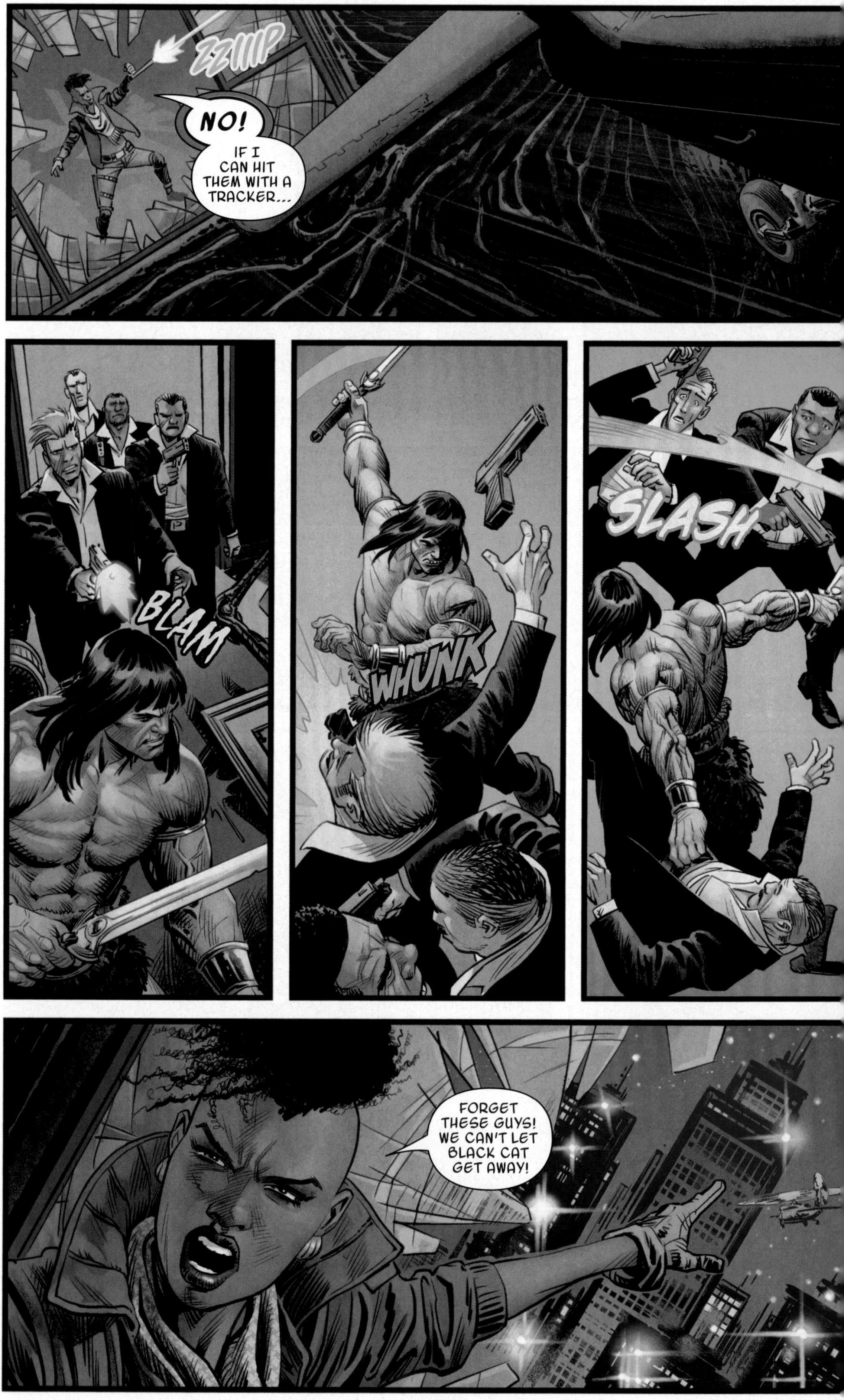
ZZIIIIP
NO!
IF I CAN HIT THEM WITH A TRACKER...
BLAM
WHUNK
SLASH
FORGET THESE GUYS! WE CAN'T LET BLACK CAT GET AWAY!

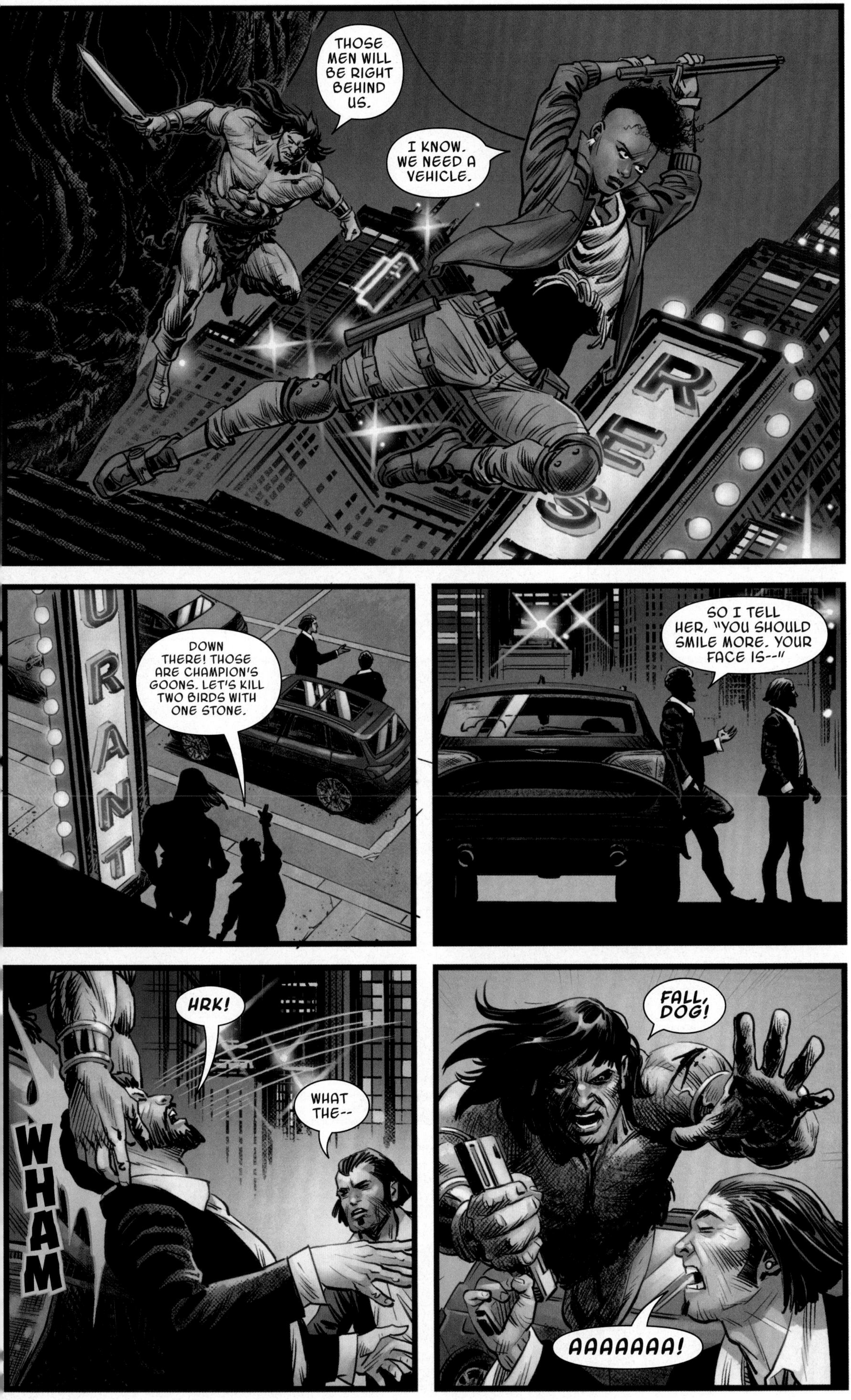
THOSE MEN WILL BE RIGHT BEHIND US.
I KNOW. WE NEED A VEHICLE.
DOWN THERE! THOSE ARE CHAMPION'S GOONS. LET'S KILL TWO BIRDS WITH ONE STONE.
SO I TELL HER, "YOU SHOULD SMILE MORE. YOUR FACE IS--"
HRK!
WHAT THE--
WHAM
FALL, DOG!
AAAAAAA!

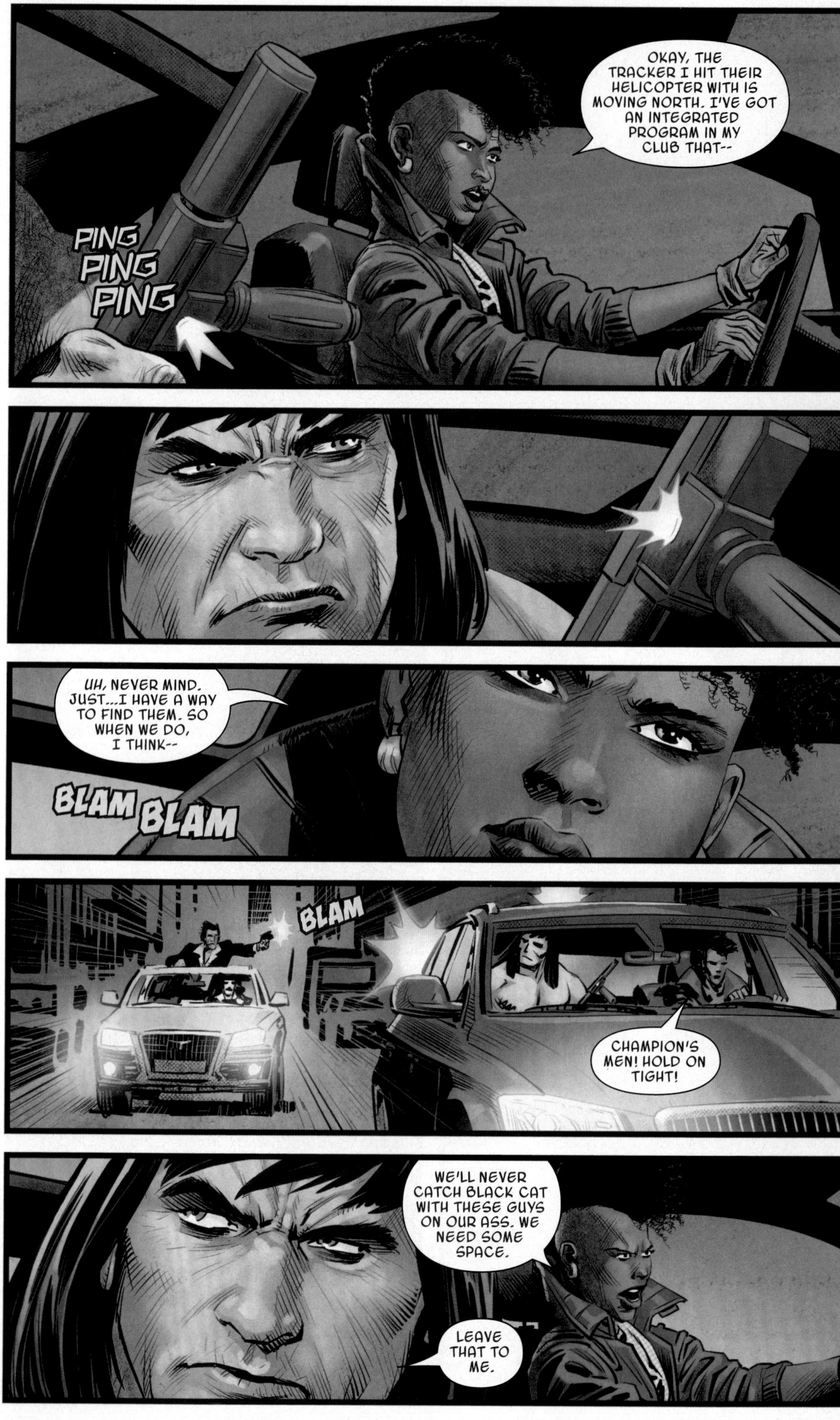
OKAY, THE TRACKER I HIT THEIR HELICOPTER WITH IS MOVING NORTH. I'VE GOT AN INTEGRATED PROGRAM IN MY CLUB THAT--
PING PING PING
UH, NEVER MIND. JUST...I HAVE A WAY TO FIND THEM. SO WHEN WE DO, I THINK--
BLAM BLAM
BLAM
CHAMPION'S MEN! HOLD ON TIGHT!
WE'LL NEVER CATCH BLACK CAT WITH THESE GUYS ON OUR ASS. WE NEED SOME SPACE.
LEAVE THAT TO ME.

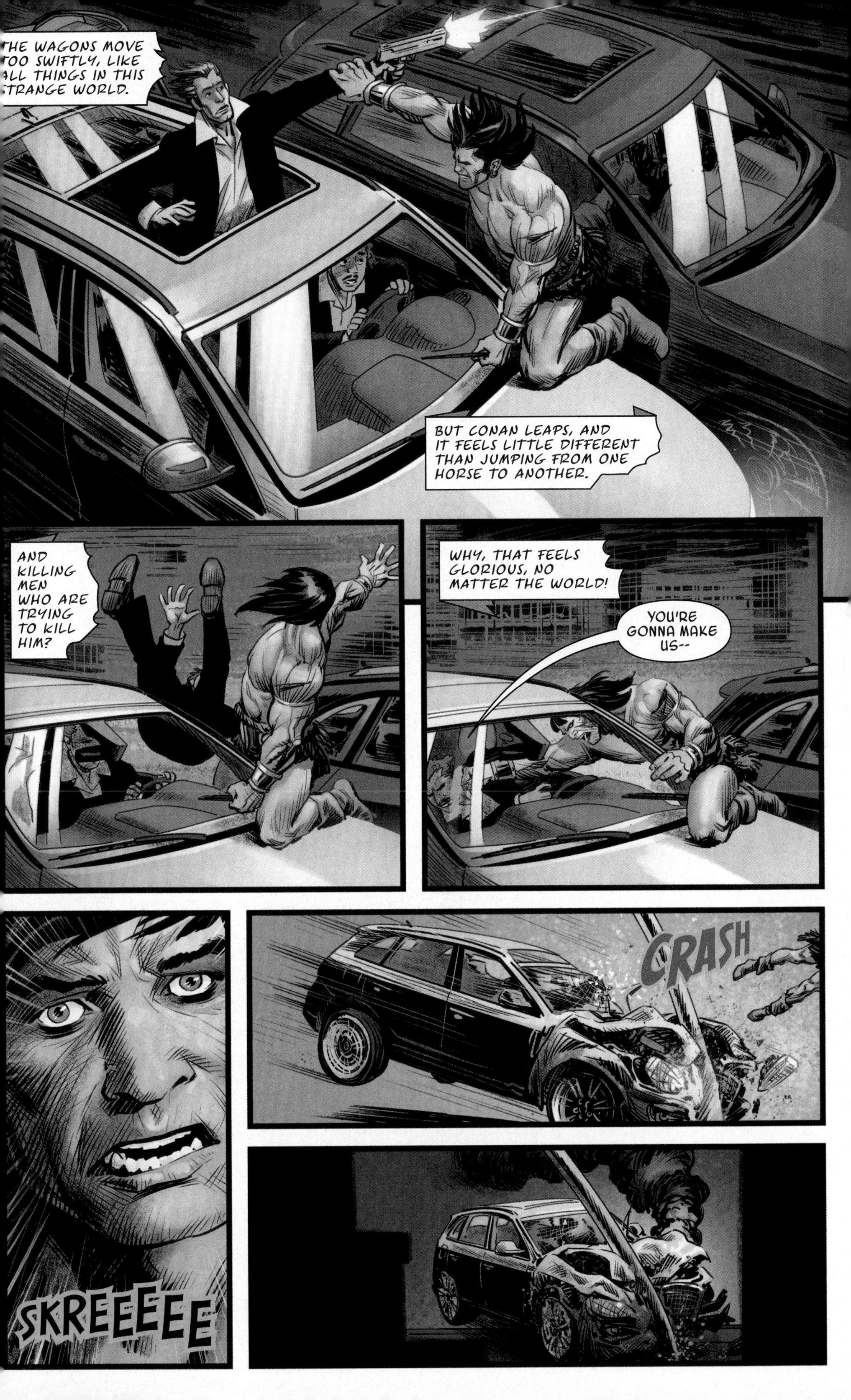
THE WAGONS MOVE TOO SWIFTLY, LIKE ALL THINGS IN THIS STRANGE WORLD.
BUT CONAN LEAPS, AND IT FEELS LITTLE DIFFERENT THAN JUMPING FROM ONE HORSE TO ANOTHER.
AND KILLING MEN WHO ARE TRYING TO KILL HIM?
WHY, THAT FEELS GLORIOUS, NO MATTER THE WORLD!
YOU'RE GONNA MAKE US--
SKREEEEEE
CRASH

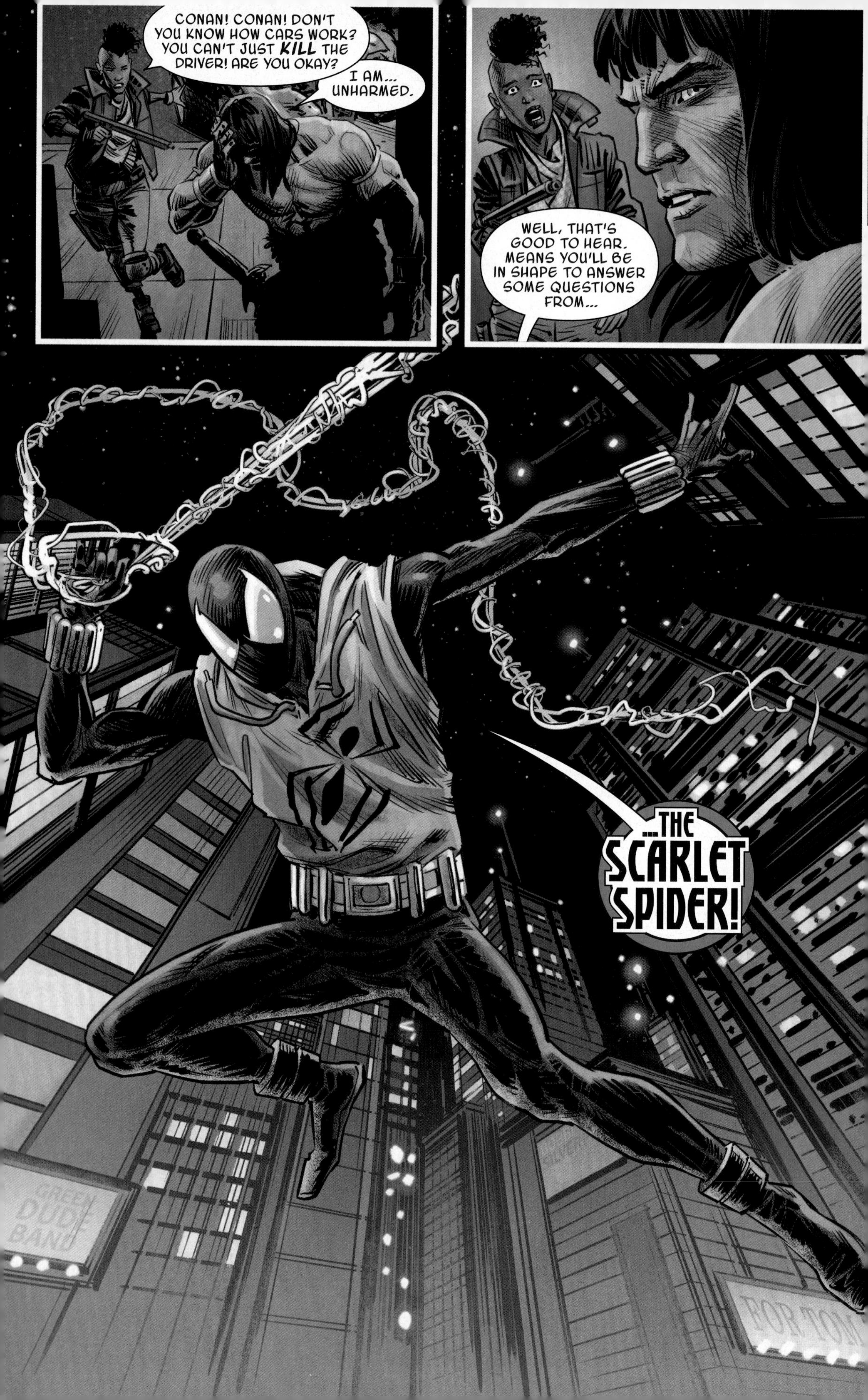
CONAN! CONAN! DON'T YOU KNOW HOW CARS WORK? YOU CAN'T JUST KILL THE DRIVER! ARE YOU OKAY?
I AM... UNHARMED.
WELL, THAT'S GOOD TO HEAR. MEANS YOU'LL BE IN SHAPE TO ANSWER SOME QUESTIONS FROM...
...THE SCARLET SPIDER!
GREEN DUDE BAND

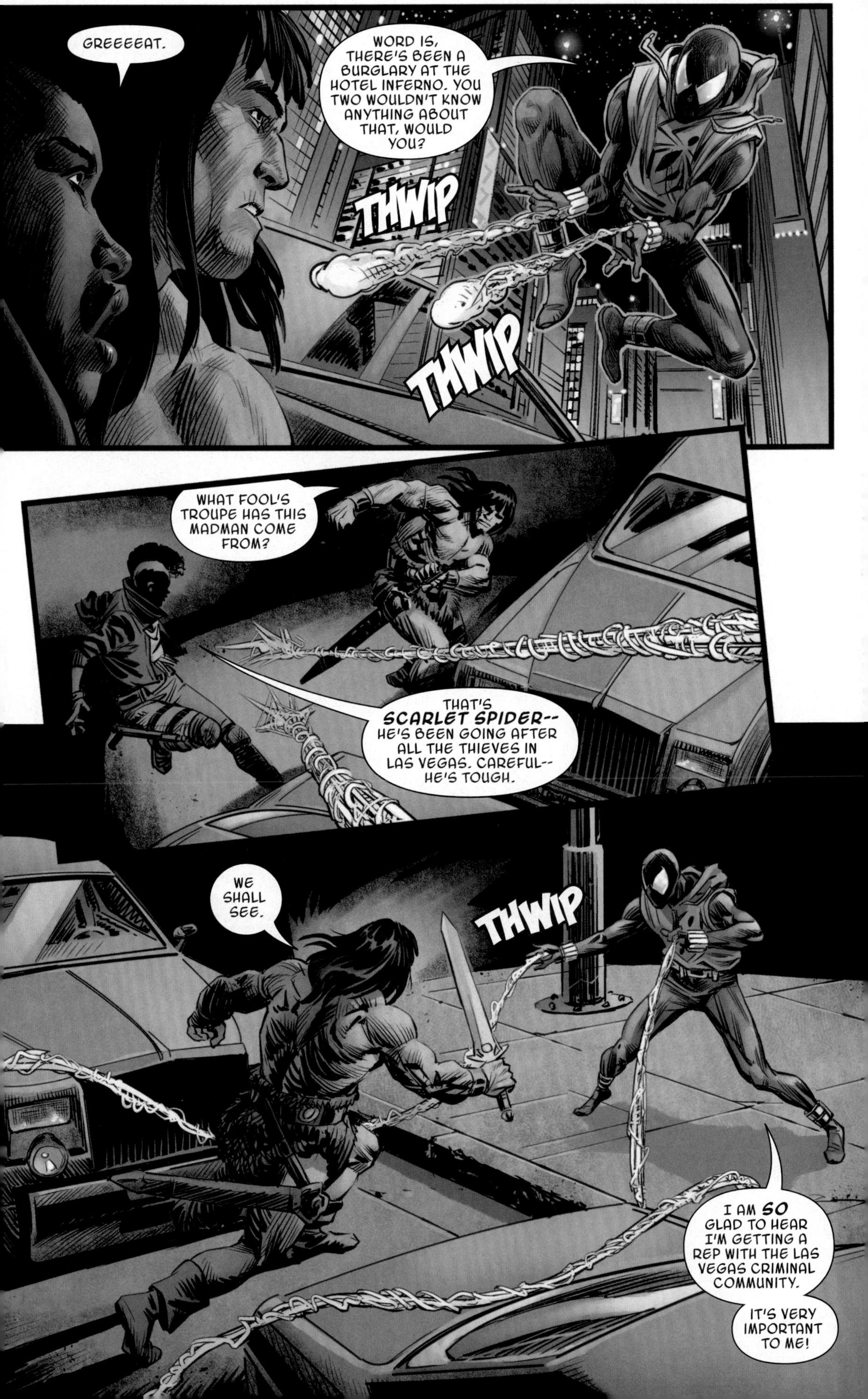
GREEEEAT.
WORD IS, THERE'S BEEN A BURGLARY AT THE HOTEL INFERNO. YOU TWO WOULDN'T KNOW ANYTHING ABOUT THAT, WOULD YOU?
THWIP
THWIP
WHAT FOOL'S TROUPE HAS THIS MADMAN COME FROM?
THAT'S SCARLET SPIDER-- HE'S BEEN GOING AFTER ALL THE THIEVES IN LAS VEGAS. CAREFUL-- HE'S TOUGH.
WE SHALL SEE.
THWIP
I AM SO GLAD TO HEAR I'M GETTING A REP WITH THE LAS VEGAS CRIMINAL COMMUNITY.
IT'S VERY IMPORTANT TO ME!

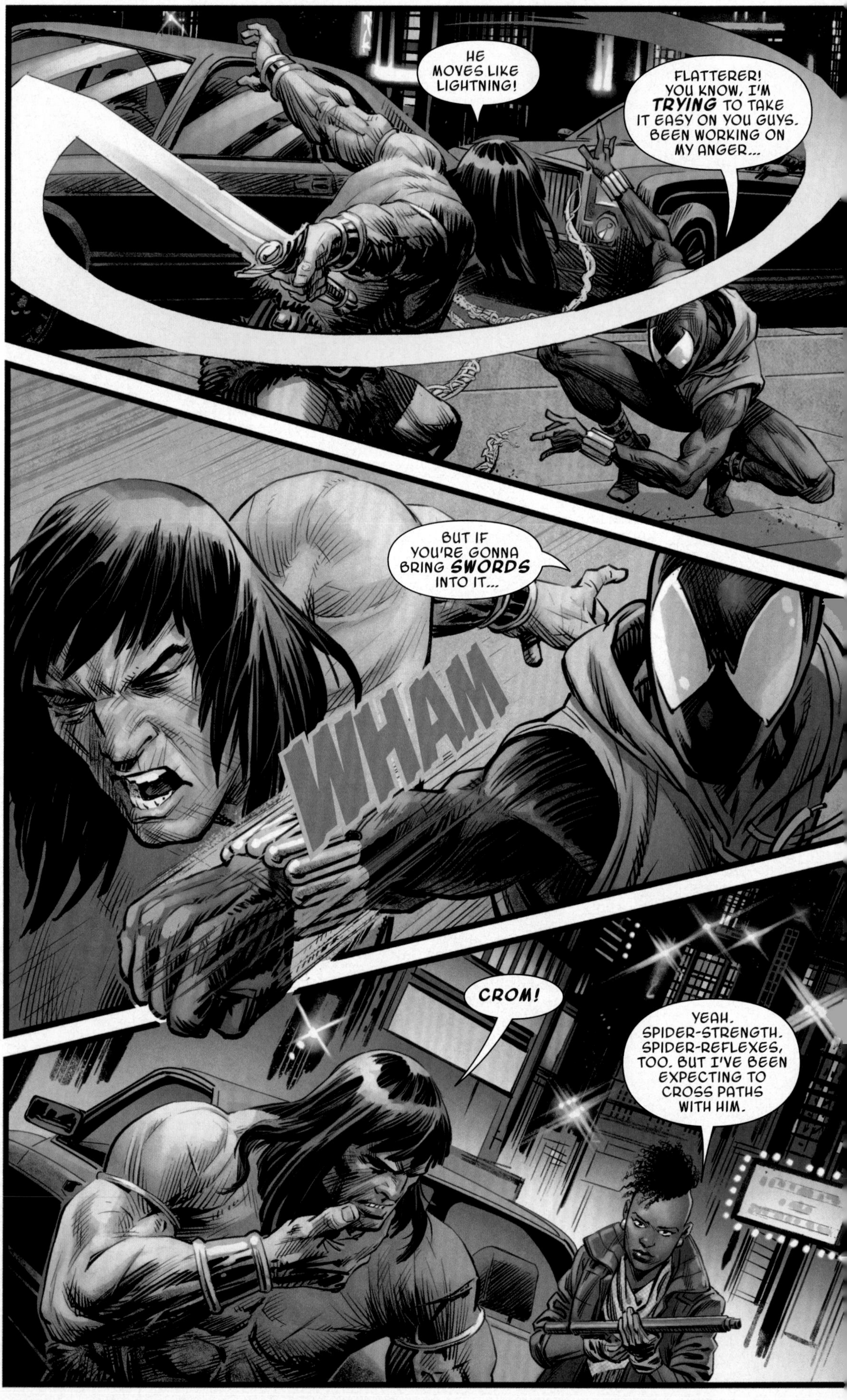

HE MOVES LIKE LIGHTNING!
FLATTERER! YOU KNOW, I'M TRYING TO TAKE IT EASY ON YOU GUYS. BEEN WORKING ON MY ANGER...
BUT IF YOU'RE GONNA BRING SWORDS INTO IT...
WHAM
CROM!
YEAH. SPIDER-STRENGTH. SPIDER-REFLEXES, TOO. BUT I'VE BEEN EXPECTING TO CROSS PATHS WITH HIM.

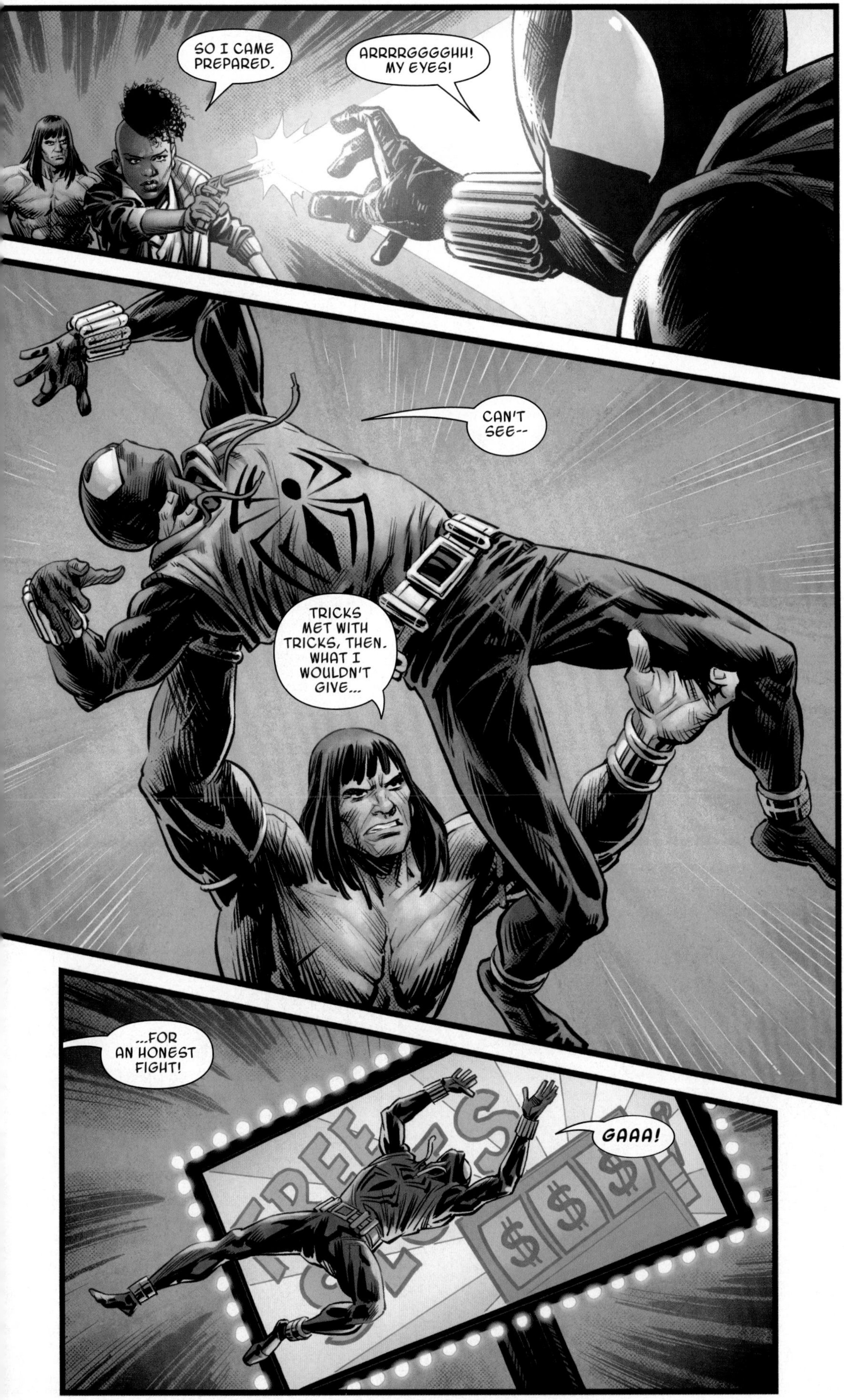
SO I CAME PREPARED.
ARRRRGGGGHH! MY EYES!
CAN'T SEE--
TRICKS MET WITH TRICKS, THEN. WHAT I WOULDN'T GIVE...
...FOR AN HONEST FIGHT!
GAAA!

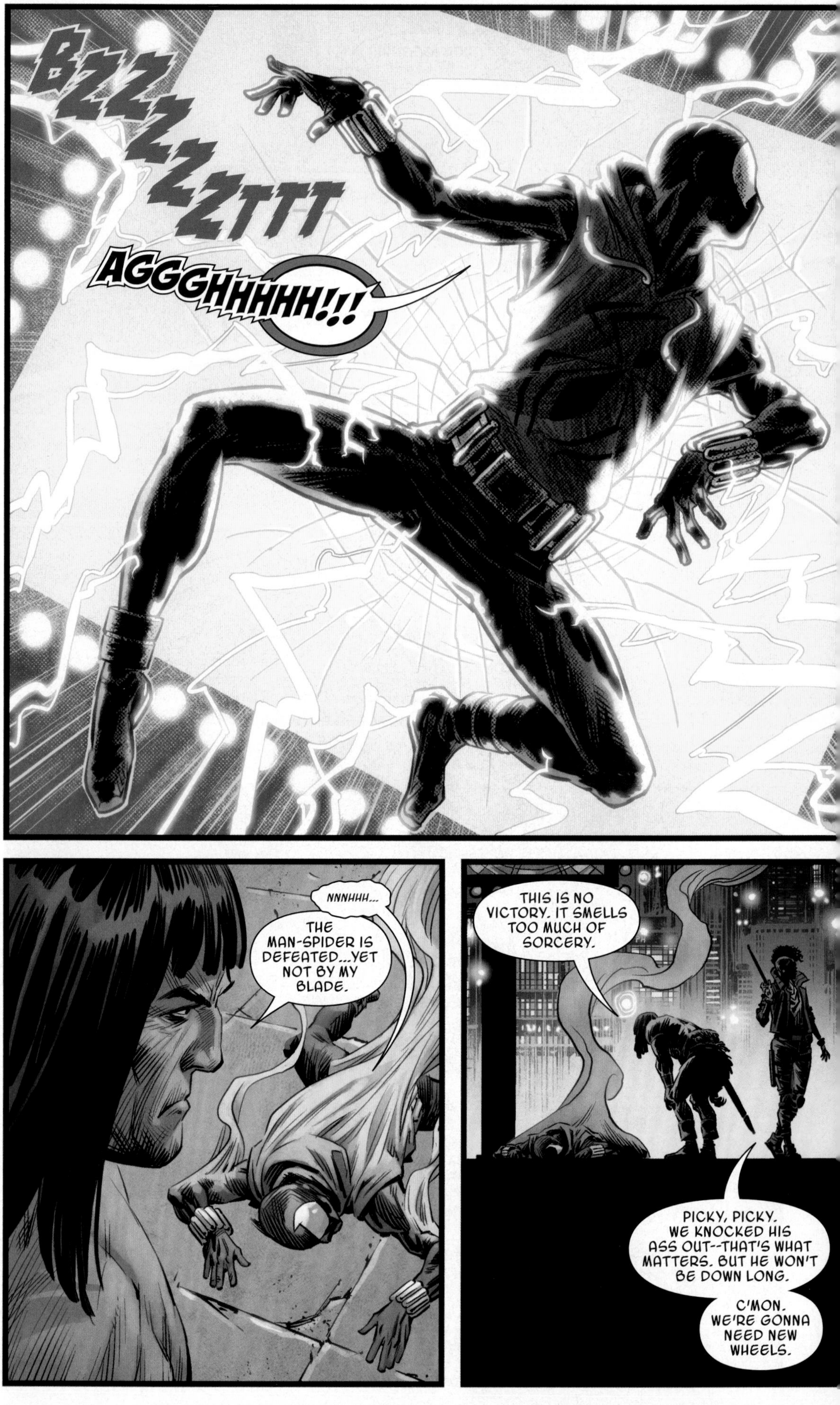
BZZZZZTTT
AGGGHHHHH!!!
NNNHHH...
THE MAN-SPIDER IS DEFEATED...YET NOT BY MY BLADE.
THIS IS NO VICTORY. IT SMELLS TOO MUCH OF SORCERY.
PICKY, PICKY. WE KNOCKED HIS ASS OUT--THAT'S WHAT MATTERS. BUT HE WON'T BE DOWN LONG.
C'MON. WE'RE GONNA NEED NEW WHEELS.

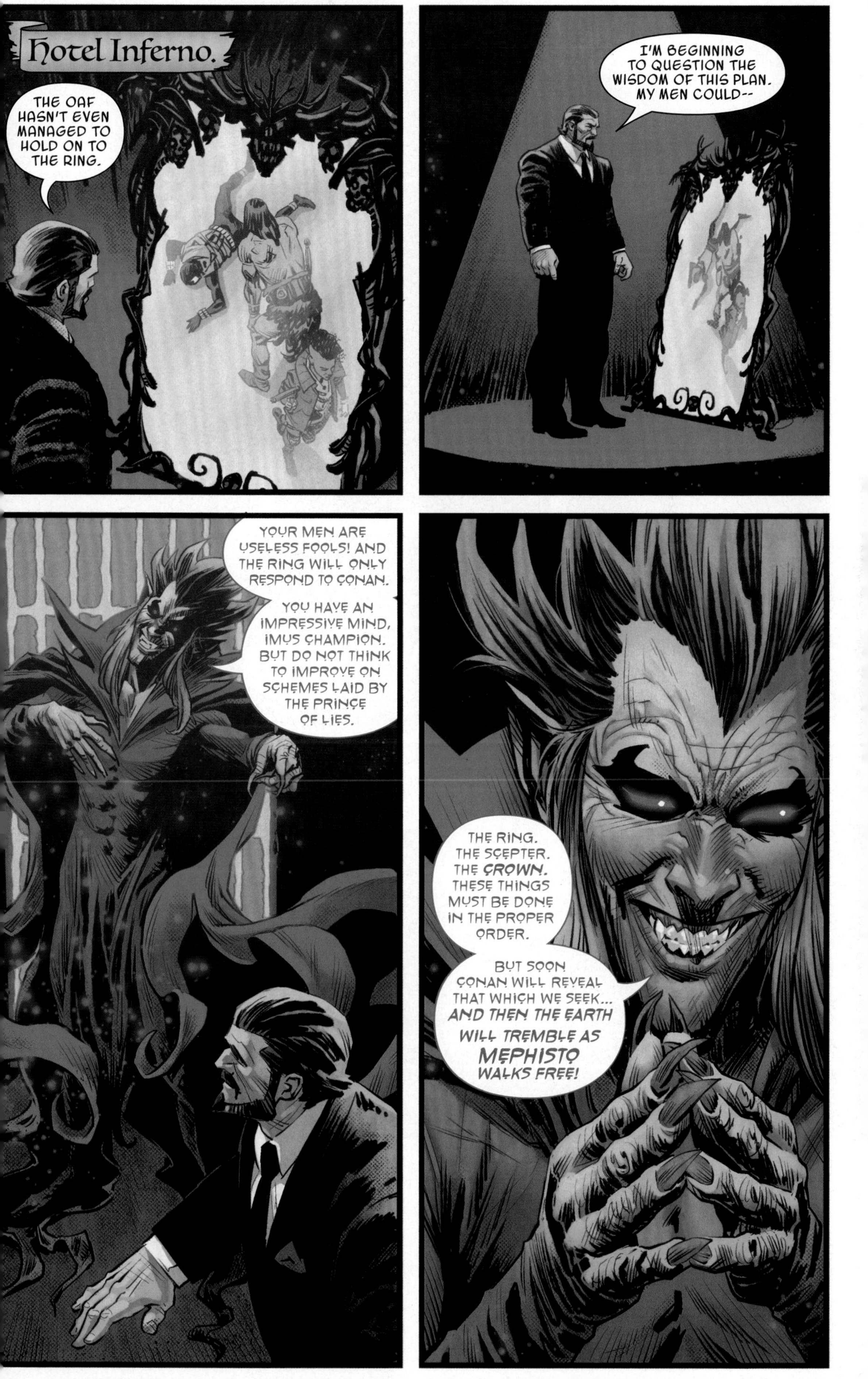
Hotel Inferno.
THE OAF HASN'T EVEN MANAGED TO HOLD ON TO THE RING.
I'M BEGINNING TO QUESTION THE WISDOM OF THIS PLAN. MY MEN COULD--
YOUR MEN ARE USELESS FOOLS! AND THE RING WILL ONLY RESPOND TO CONAN.
YOU HAVE AN IMPRESSIVE MIND, IMUS CHAMPION. BUT DO NOT THINK TO IMPROVE ON SCHEMES LAID BY THE PRINCE OF LIES.
THE RING. THE SCEPTER. THE CROWN. THESE THINGS MUST BE DONE IN THE PROPER ORDER.
BUT SOON CONAN WILL REVEAL THAT WHICH WE SEEK... AND THEN THE EARTH WILL TREMBLE AS MEPHISTO WALKS FREE!

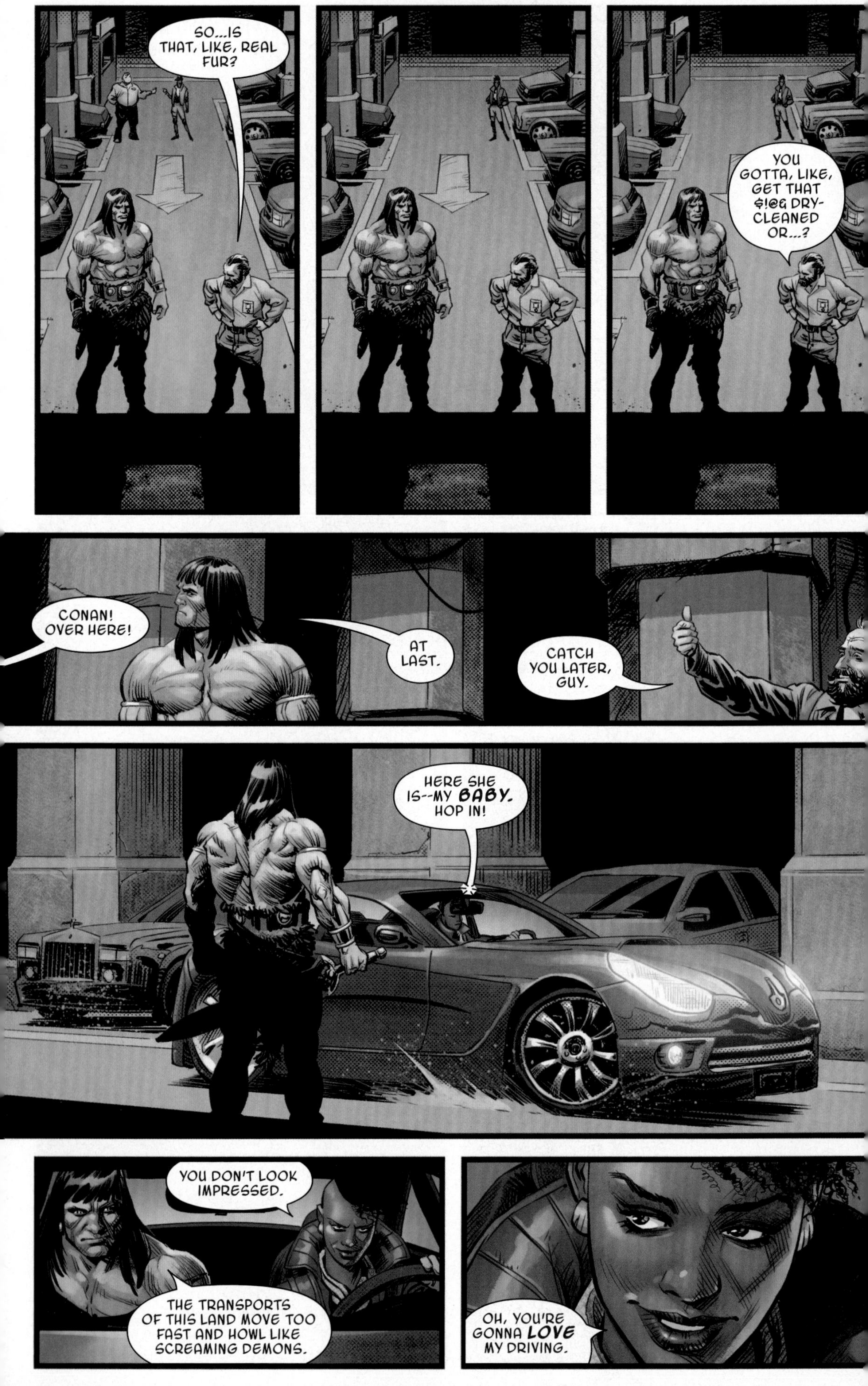
SO...IS THAT, LIKE, REAL FUR?
YOU GOTTA, LIKE, GET THAT $!@G DRY-CLEANED OR...?
CONAN! OVER HERE!
AT LAST.
CATCH YOU LATER, GUY.
HERE SHE IS--MY BABY. HOP IN!
YOU DON'T LOOK IMPRESSED.
THE TRANSPORTS OF THIS LAND MOVE TOO FAST AND HOWL LIKE SCREAMING DEMONS.
OH, YOU'RE GONNA LOVE MY DRIVING.

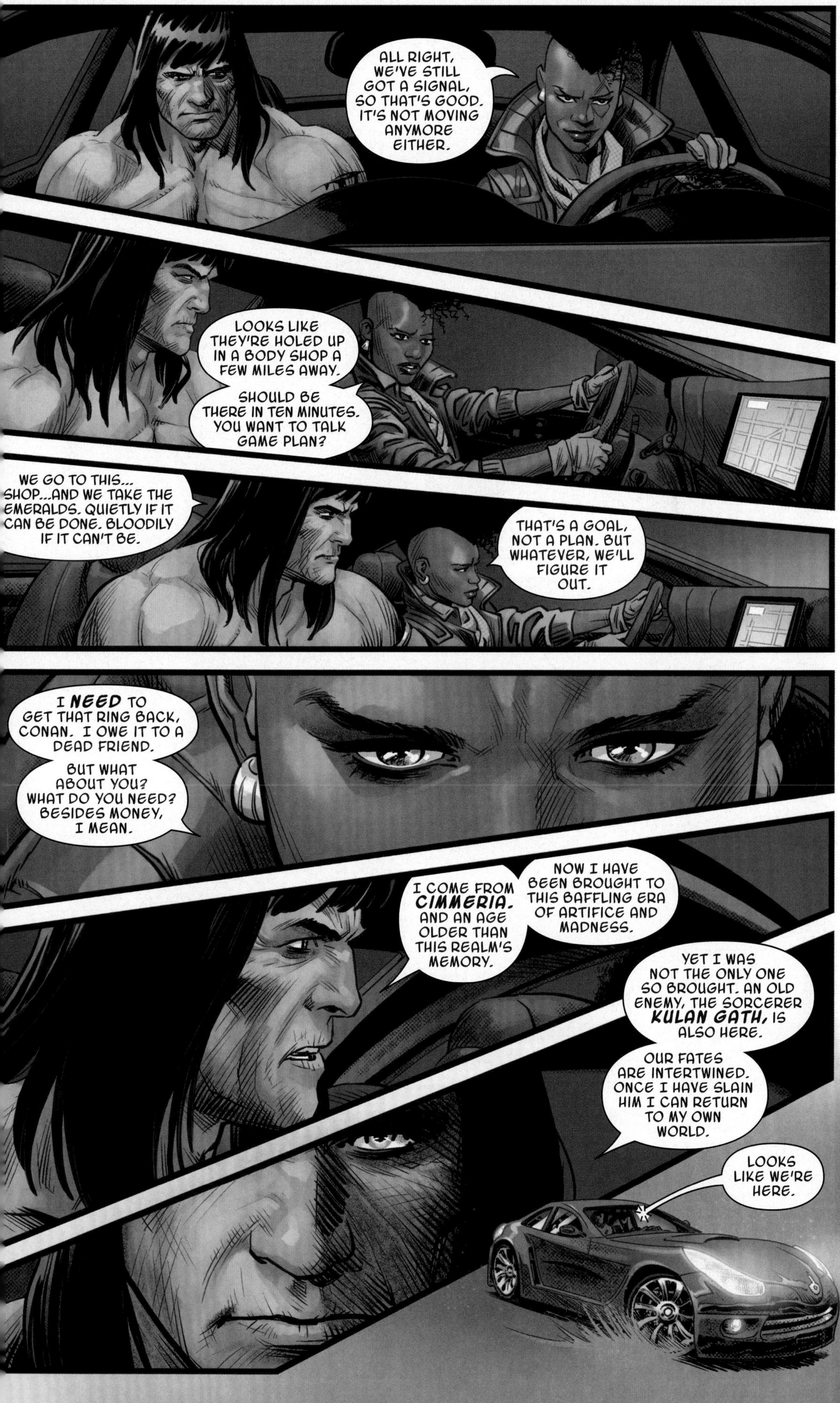
ALL RIGHT, WE'VE STILL GOT A SIGNAL, SO THAT'S GOOD. IT'S NOT MOVING ANYMORE EITHER.
LOOKS LIKE THEY'RE HOLED UP IN A BODY SHOP A FEW MILES AWAY.
SHOULD BE THERE IN TEN MINUTES. YOU WANT TO TALK GAME PLAN?
WE GO TO THIS... SHOP...AND WE TAKE THE EMERALDS. QUIETLY IF IT CAN BE DONE. BLOODILY IF IT CAN'T BE.
THAT'S A GOAL, NOT A PLAN. BUT WHATEVER, WE'LL FIGURE IT OUT.
I NEED TO GET THAT RING BACK, CONAN. I OWE IT TO A DEAD FRIEND.
BUT WHAT ABOUT YOU? WHAT DO YOU NEED? BESIDES MONEY, I MEAN.
I COME FROM CIMMERIA. AND AN AGE OLDER THAN THIS REALM'S MEMORY.
NOW I HAVE BEEN BROUGHT TO THIS BAFFLING ERA OF ARTIFICE AND MADNESS.
YET I WAS NOT THE ONLY ONE SO BROUGHT. AN OLD ENEMY, THE SORCERER KULAN GATH, IS ALSO HERE.
OUR FATES ARE INTERTWINED. ONCE I HAVE SLAIN HIM I CAN RETURN TO MY OWN WORLD.
LOOKS LIKE WE'RE HERE.

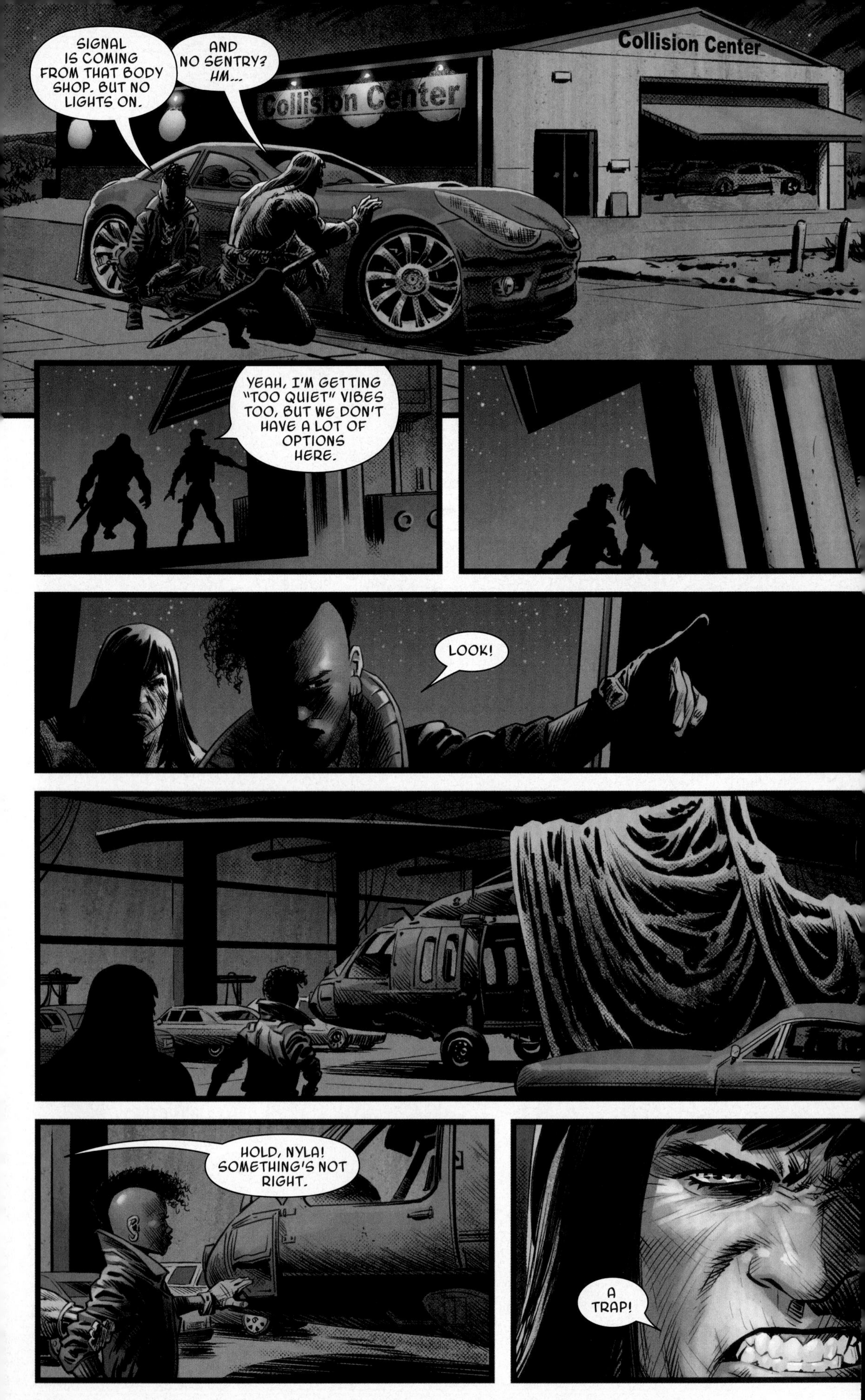
Collision Center
Collision Center
SIGNAL IS COMING FROM THAT BODY SHOP. BUT NO LIGHTS ON.
AND NO SENTRY? HM...
YEAH, I'M GETTING "TOO QUIET" VIBES TOO, BUT WE DON'T HAVE A LOT OF OPTIONS HERE.
LOOK!
HOLD, NYLA! SOMETHING'S NOT RIGHT.
A TRAP!

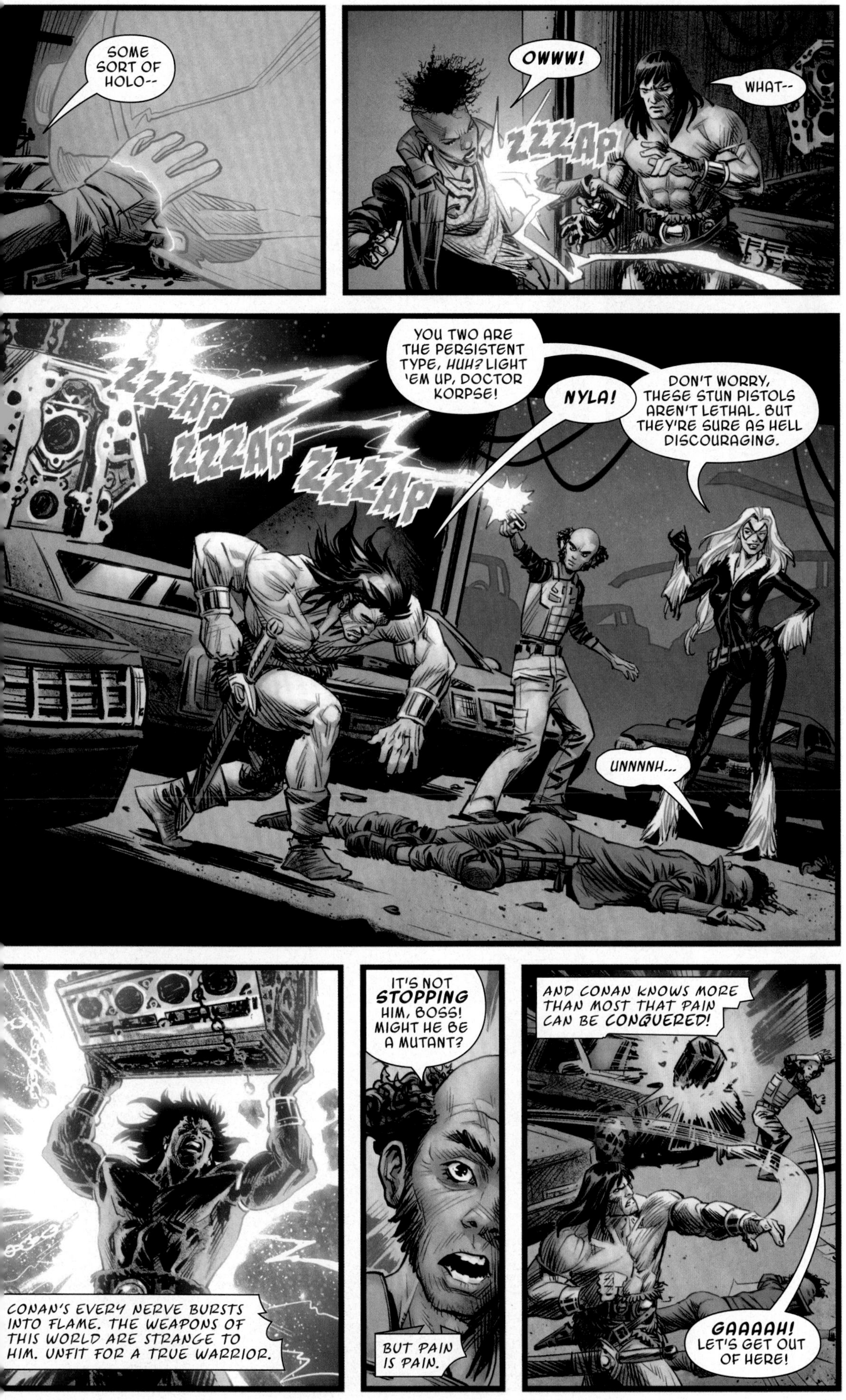
SOME SORT OF HOLO--
OWWW!
ZZZAP
WHAT--
ZZZAP
ZZZAP
ZZZAP
YOU TWO ARE THE PERSISTENT TYPE, HUH? LIGHT 'EM UP, DOCTOR KORPSE!
NYLA!
DON'T WORRY, THESE STUN PISTOLS AREN'T LETHAL. BUT THEY'RE SURE AS HELL DISCOURAGING.
UNNNNH...
CONAN'S EVERY NERVE BURSTS INTO FLAME. THE WEAPONS OF THIS WORLD ARE STRANGE TO HIM. UNFIT FOR A TRUE WARRIOR.
IT'S NOT STOPPING HIM, BOSS! MIGHT HE BE A MUTANT?
BUT PAIN IS PAIN.
AND CONAN KNOWS MORE THAN MOST THAT PAIN CAN BE CONQUERED!
GAAAAH! LET'S GET OUT OF HERE!

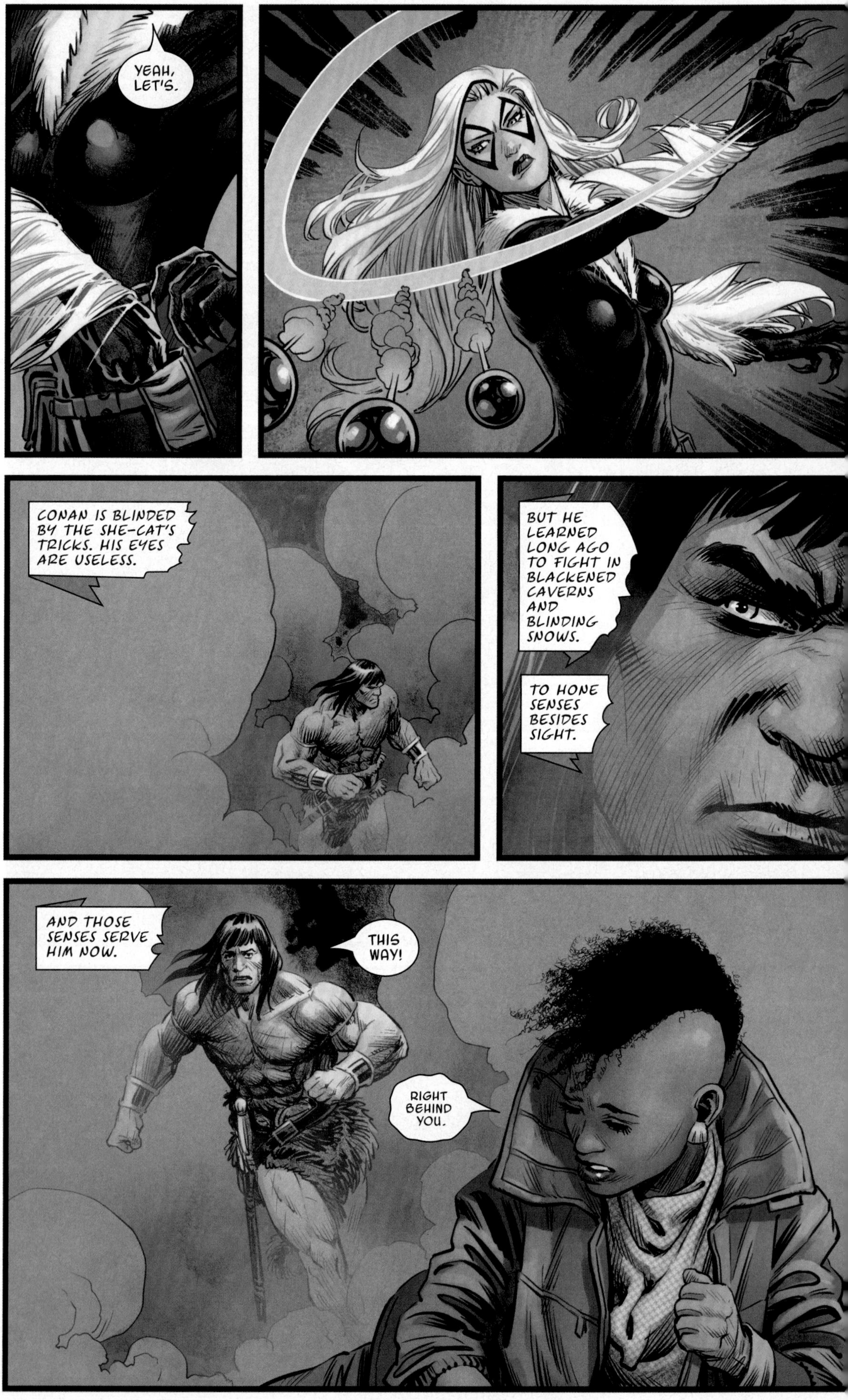
YEAH, LET'S.
CONAN IS BLINDED BY THE SHE-CAT'S TRICKS. HIS EYES ARE USELESS.
BUT HE LEARNED LONG AGO TO FIGHT IN BLACKENED CAVERNS AND BLINDING SNOWS.
TO HONE SENSES BESIDES SIGHT.
AND THOSE SENSES SERVE HIM NOW.
THIS WAY!
RIGHT BEHIND YOU.

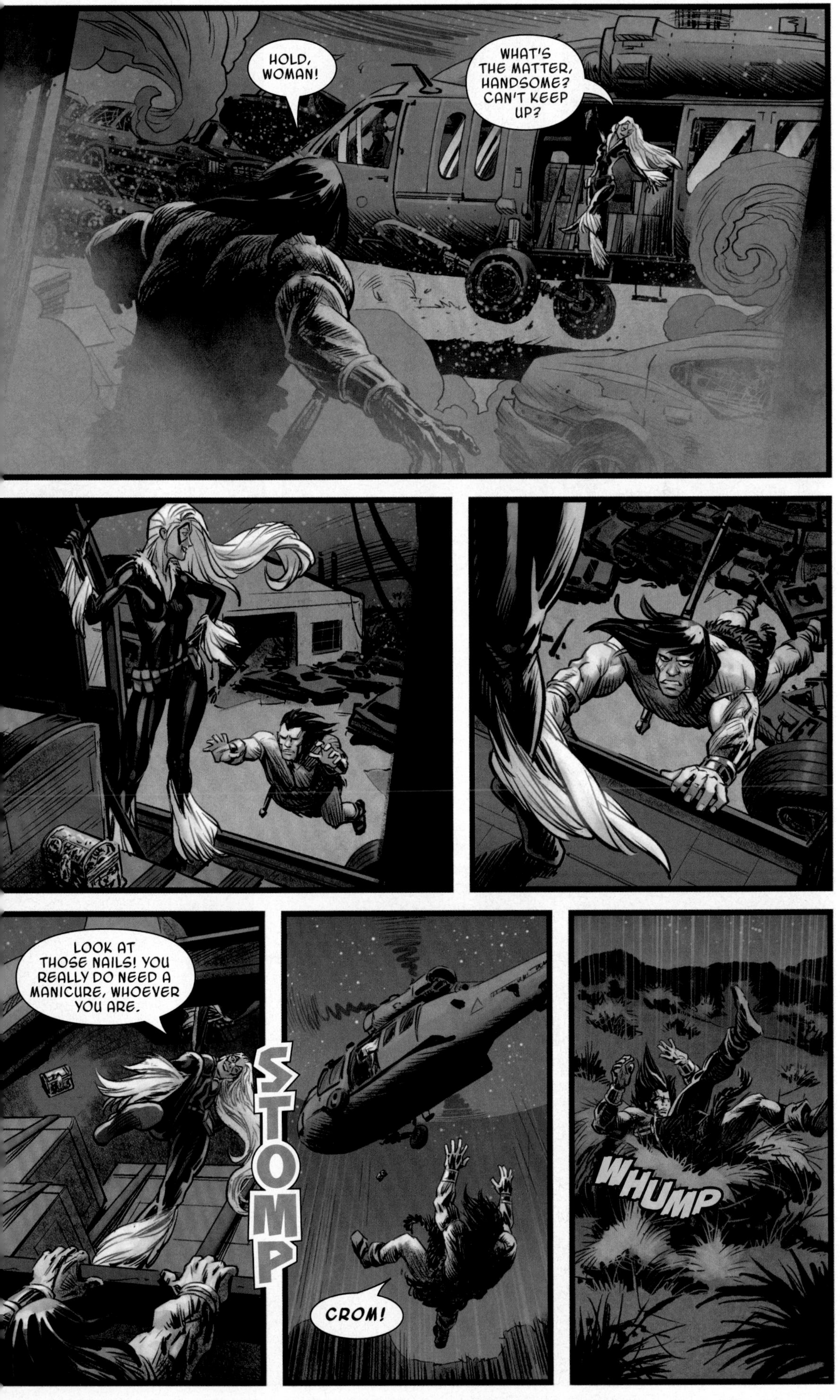
HOLD, WOMAN!
WHAT'S THE MATTER, HANDSOME? CAN'T KEEP UP?
LOOK AT THOSE NAILS! YOU REALLY DO NEED A MANICURE, WHOEVER YOU ARE.
STOMP
CROM!
WHUMP

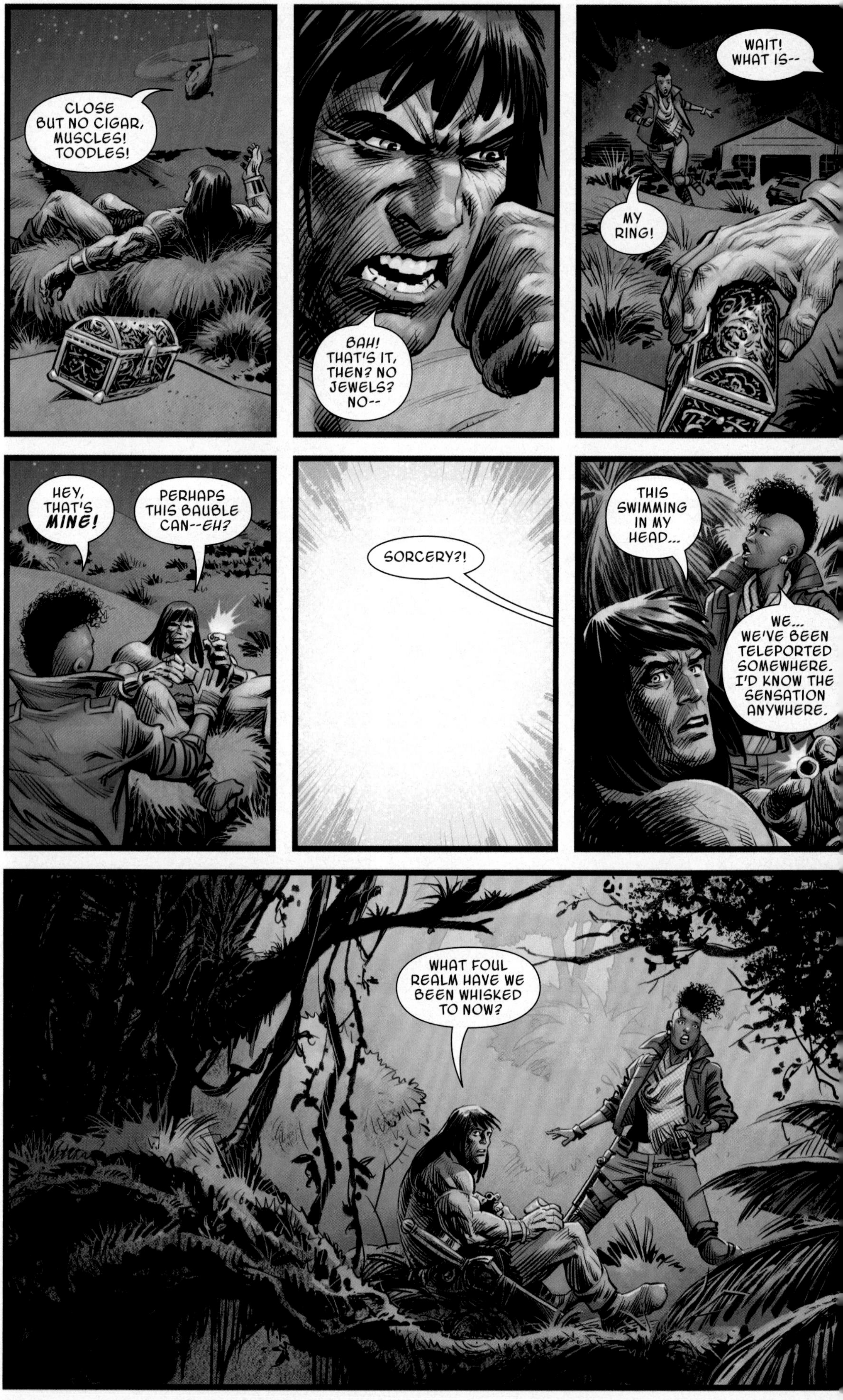

CLOSE BUT NO CIGAR, MUSCLES! TOODLES!
BAH! THAT'S IT, THEN? NO JEWELS? NO--
WAIT! WHAT IS--
MY RING!
HEY, THAT'S **MINE!**
PERHAPS THIS BAUBLE CAN--EH?
SORCERY?!
THIS SWIMMING IN MY HEAD...
WE... WE'VE BEEN TELEPORTED SOMEWHERE. I'D KNOW THE SENSATION ANYWHERE.
WHAT FOUL REALM HAVE WE BEEN WHISKED TO NOW?

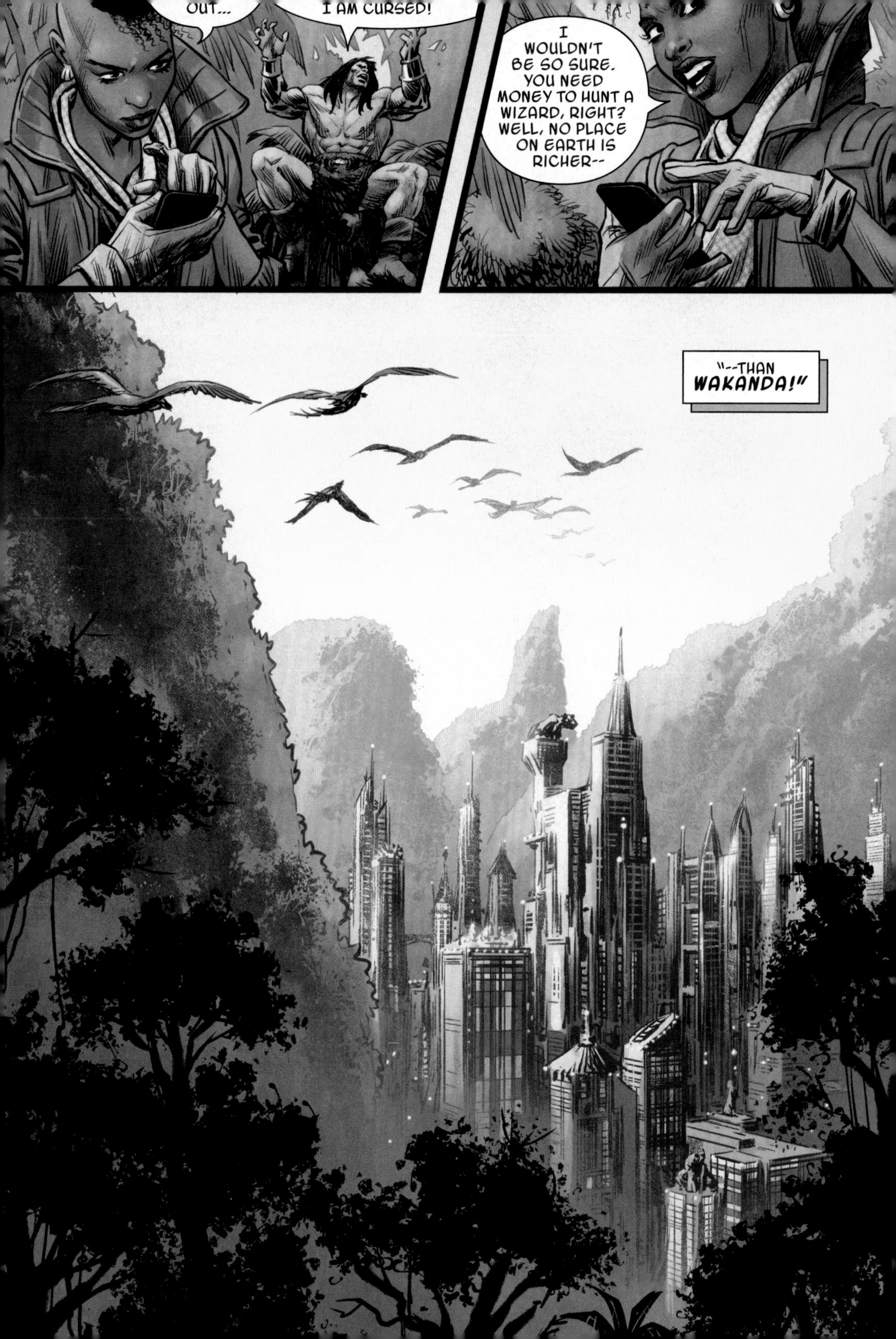
OUT...
I AM CURSED!
I WOULDN'T BE SO SURE. YOU NEED MONEY TO HUNT A WIZARD, RIGHT? WELL, NO PLACE ON EARTH IS RICHER--
"--THAN WAKANDA!"

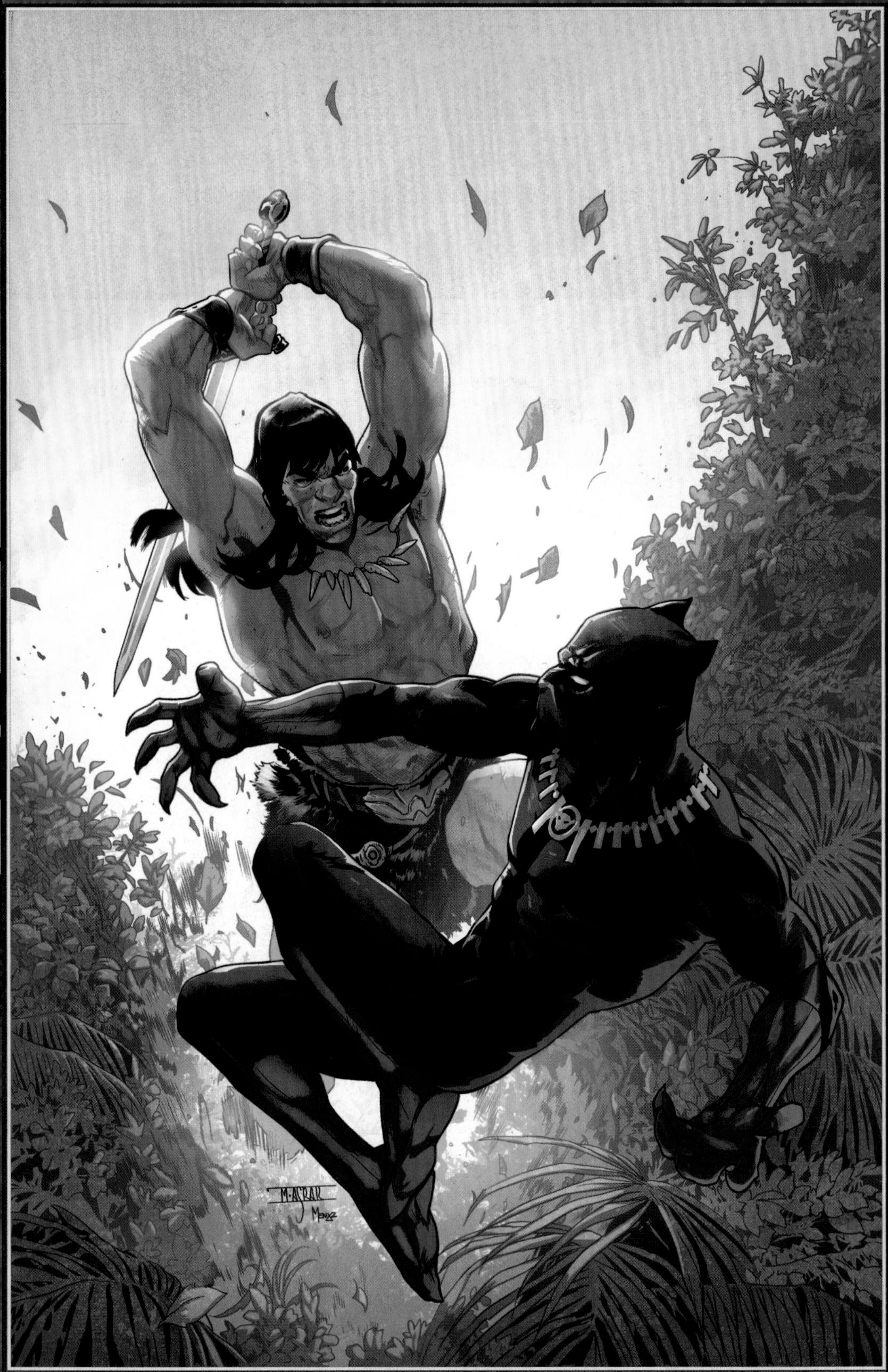
M·ASRAR

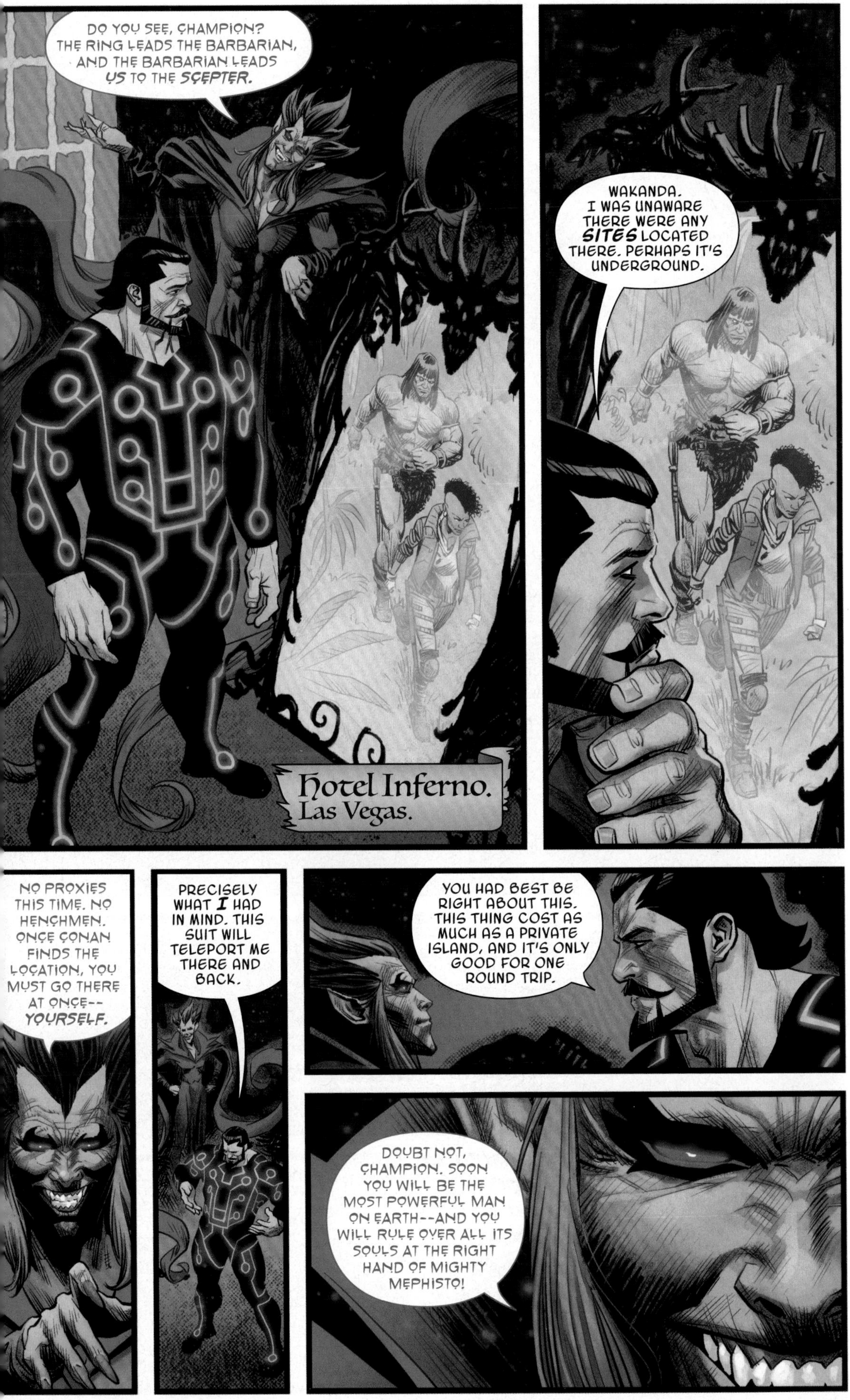

DO YOU SEE, CHAMPION? THE RING LEADS THE BARBARIAN, AND THE BARBARIAN LEADS US TO THE SCEPTER.
Hotel Inferno. Las Vegas.
WAKANDA. I WAS UNAWARE THERE WERE ANY SITES LOCATED THERE. PERHAPS IT'S UNDERGROUND.
NO PROXIES THIS TIME. NO HENCHMEN. ONCE CONAN FINDS THE LOCATION, YOU MUST GO THERE AT ONCE-- YOURSELF.
PRECISELY WHAT I HAD IN MIND. THIS SUIT WILL TELEPORT ME THERE AND BACK.
YOU HAD BEST BE RIGHT ABOUT THIS. THIS THING COST AS MUCH AS A PRIVATE ISLAND, AND IT'S ONLY GOOD FOR ONE ROUND TRIP.
DOUBT NOT, CHAMPION. SOON YOU WILL BE THE MOST POWERFUL MAN ON EARTH--AND YOU WILL RULE OVER ALL ITS SOULS AT THE RIGHT HAND OF MIGHTY MEPHISTO!

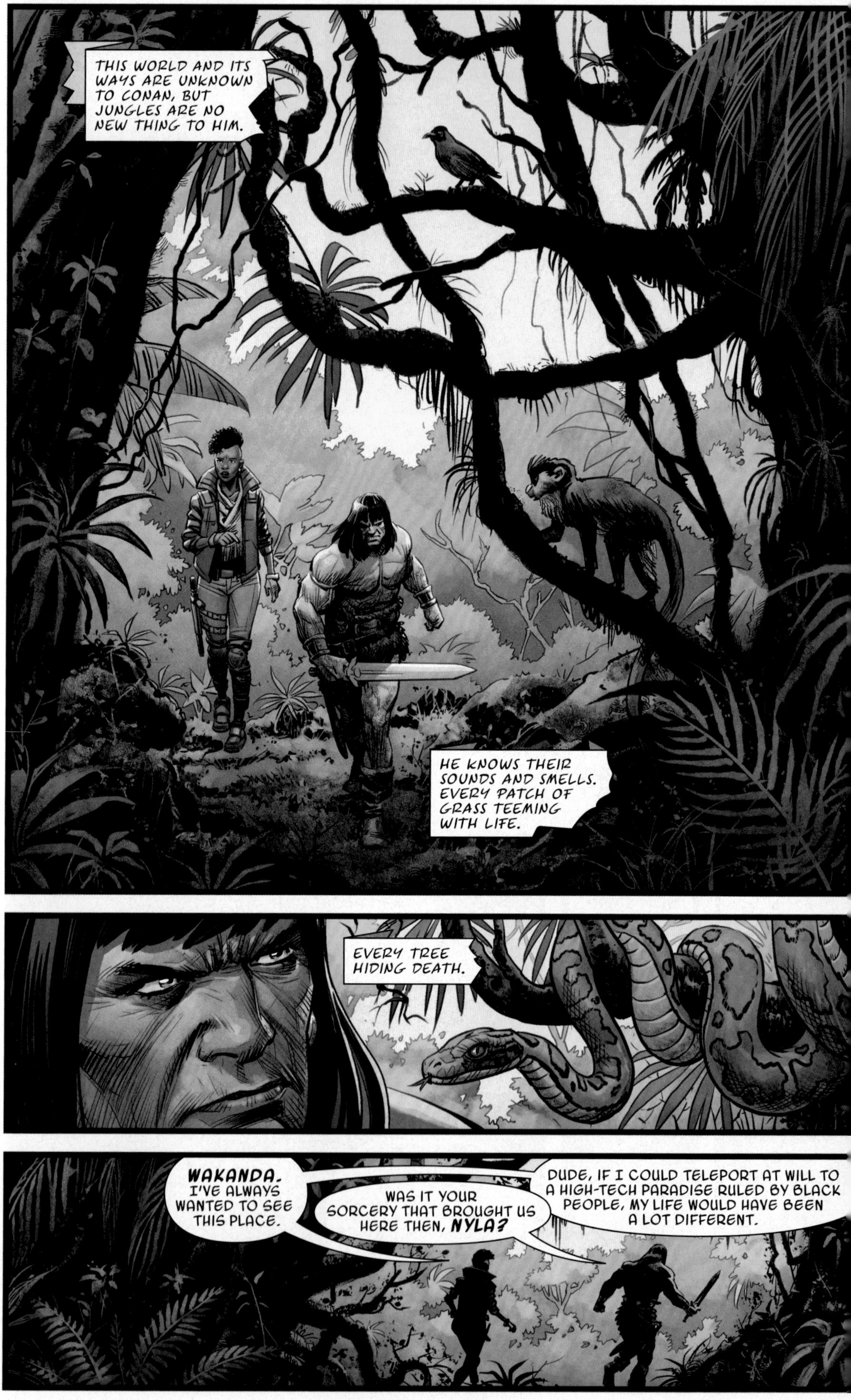
THIS WORLD AND ITS WAYS ARE UNKNOWN TO CONAN, BUT JUNGLES ARE NO NEW THING TO HIM.
HE KNOWS THEIR SOUNDS AND SMELLS. EVERY PATCH OF GRASS TEEMING WITH LIFE.
EVERY TREE HIDING DEATH.
WAKANDA. I'VE ALWAYS WANTED TO SEE THIS PLACE.
WAS IT YOUR SORCERY THAT BROUGHT US HERE THEN, NYLA?
DUDE, IF I COULD TELEPORT AT WILL TO A HIGH-TECH PARADISE RULED BY BLACK PEOPLE, MY LIFE WOULD HAVE BEEN A LOT DIFFERENT.

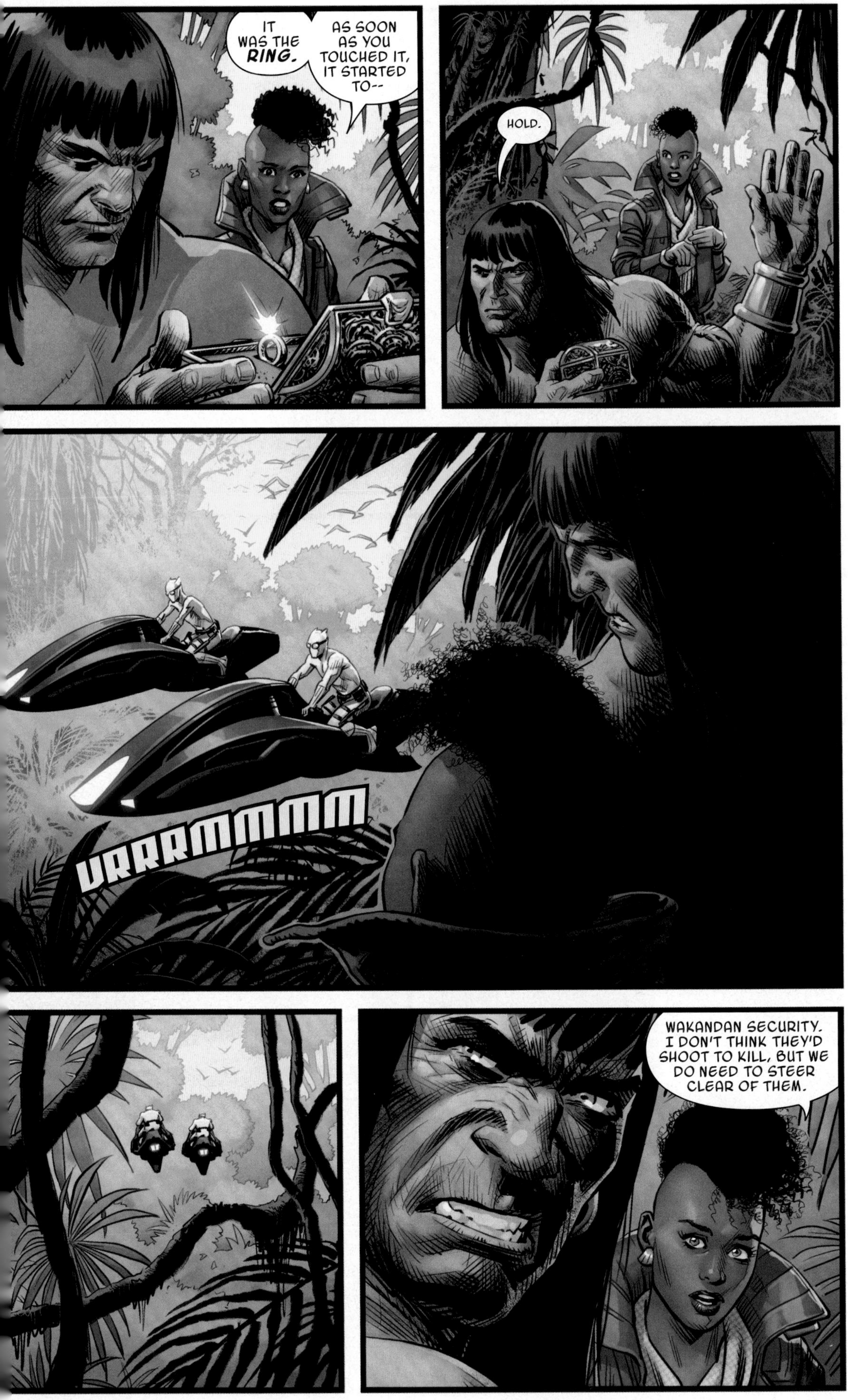
IT WAS THE **RING.**
AS SOON AS YOU TOUCHED IT, IT STARTED TO--
HOLD.
VRRRMMMMM
WAKANDAN SECURITY. I DON'T THINK THEY'D SHOOT TO KILL, BUT WE DO NEED TO STEER CLEAR OF THEM.

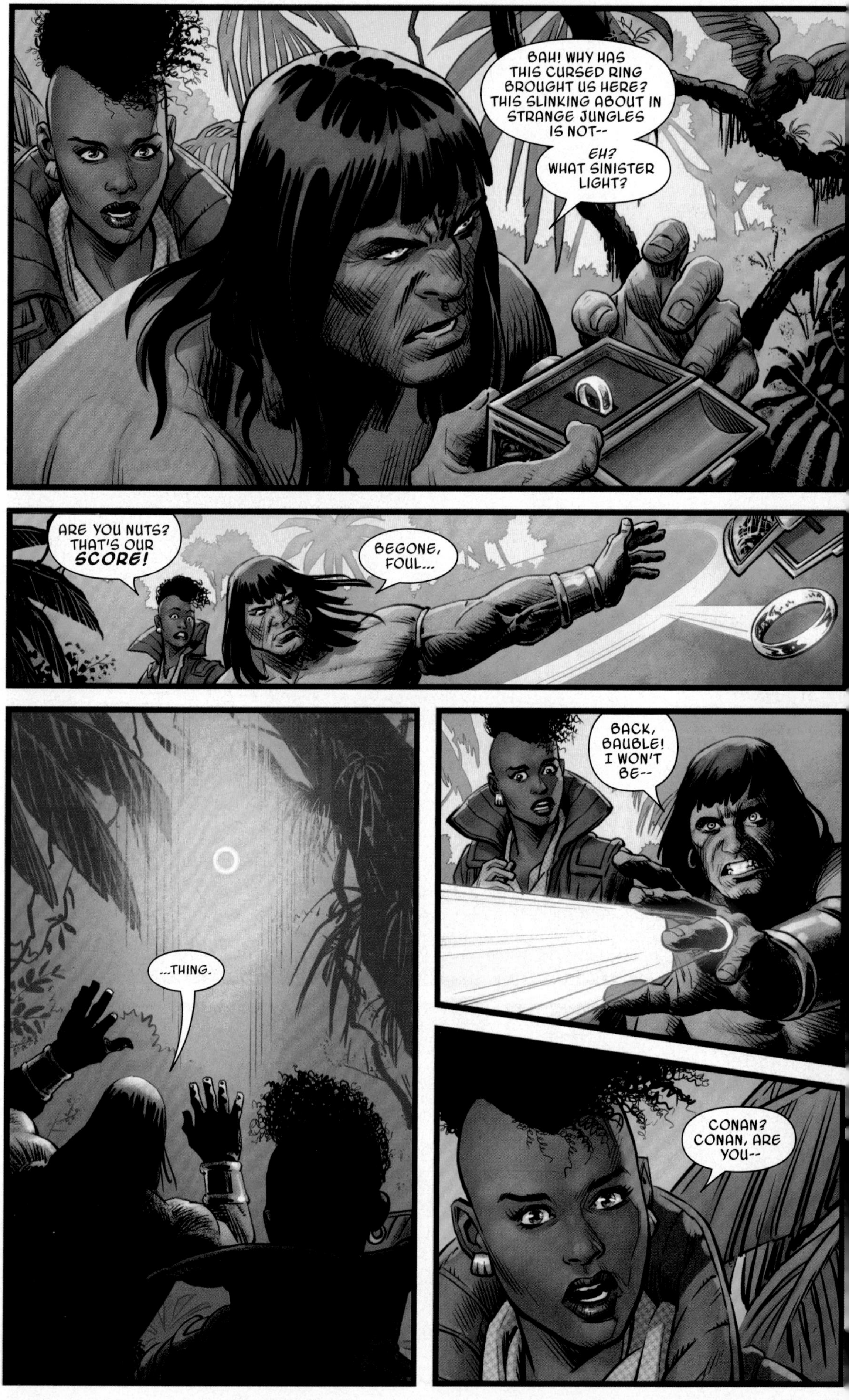

BAH! WHY HAS THIS CURSED RING BROUGHT US HERE? THIS SLINKING ABOUT IN STRANGE JUNGLES IS NOT--
EH? WHAT SINISTER LIGHT?
ARE YOU NUTS? THAT'S OUR **SCORE!**
BEGONE, FOUL...
...THING.
BACK, BAUBLE! I WON'T BE--
CONAN? CONAN, ARE YOU--

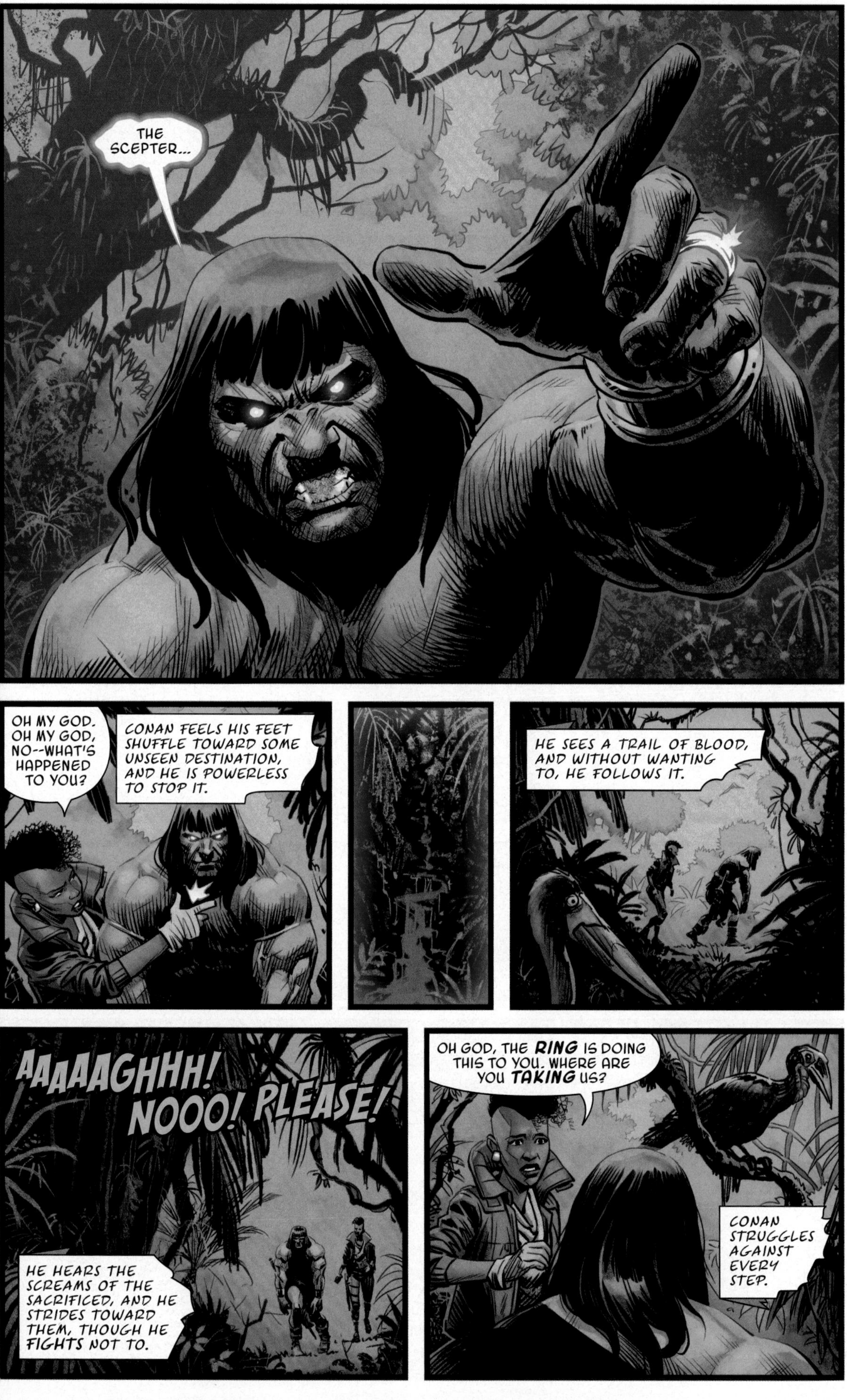
THE SCEPTER...
OH MY GOD. OH MY GOD, NO--WHAT'S HAPPENED TO YOU?
CONAN FEELS HIS FEET SHUFFLE TOWARD SOME UNSEEN DESTINATION, AND HE IS POWERLESS TO STOP IT.
HE SEES A TRAIL OF BLOOD, AND WITHOUT WANTING TO, HE FOLLOWS IT.
AAAAAGHHH! NOOO! PLEASE!
HE HEARS THE SCREAMS OF THE SACRIFICED, AND HE STRIDES TOWARD THEM, THOUGH HE FIGHTS NOT TO.
OH GOD, THE RING IS DOING THIS TO YOU. WHERE ARE YOU TAKING US?
CONAN STRUGGLES AGAINST EVERY STEP.

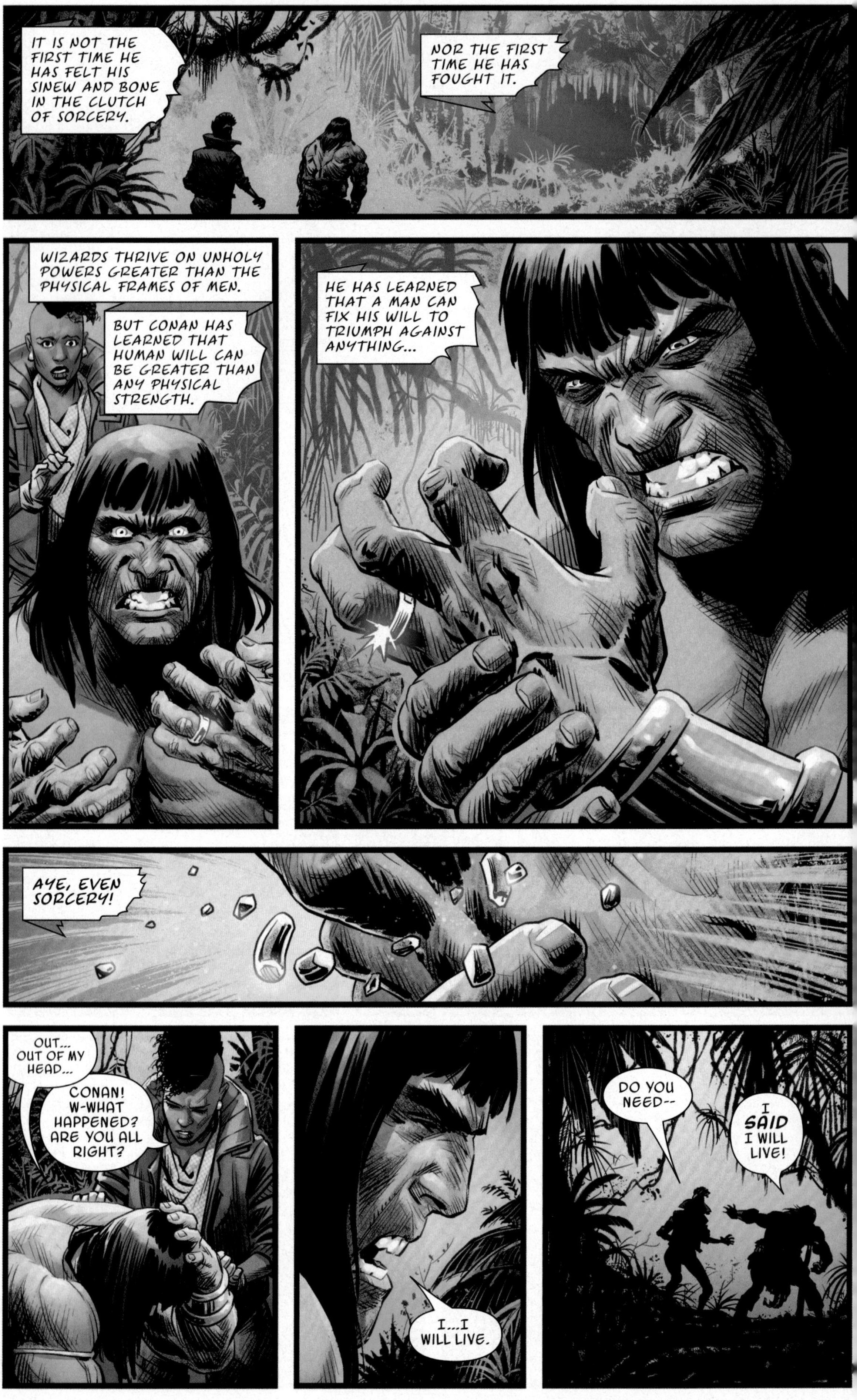
IT IS NOT THE FIRST TIME HE HAS FELT HIS SINEW AND BONE IN THE CLUTCH OF SORCERY.
NOR THE FIRST TIME HE HAS FOUGHT IT.
WIZARDS THRIVE ON UNHOLY POWERS GREATER THAN THE PHYSICAL FRAMES OF MEN.
BUT CONAN HAS LEARNED THAT HUMAN WILL CAN BE GREATER THAN ANY PHYSICAL STRENGTH.
HE HAS LEARNED THAT A MAN CAN FIX HIS WILL TO TRIUMPH AGAINST ANYTHING...
AYE, EVEN SORCERY!
OUT... OUT OF MY HEAD...
CONAN! W-WHAT HAPPENED? ARE YOU ALL RIGHT?
I...I WILL LIVE.
DO YOU NEED--
I SAID I WILL LIVE!

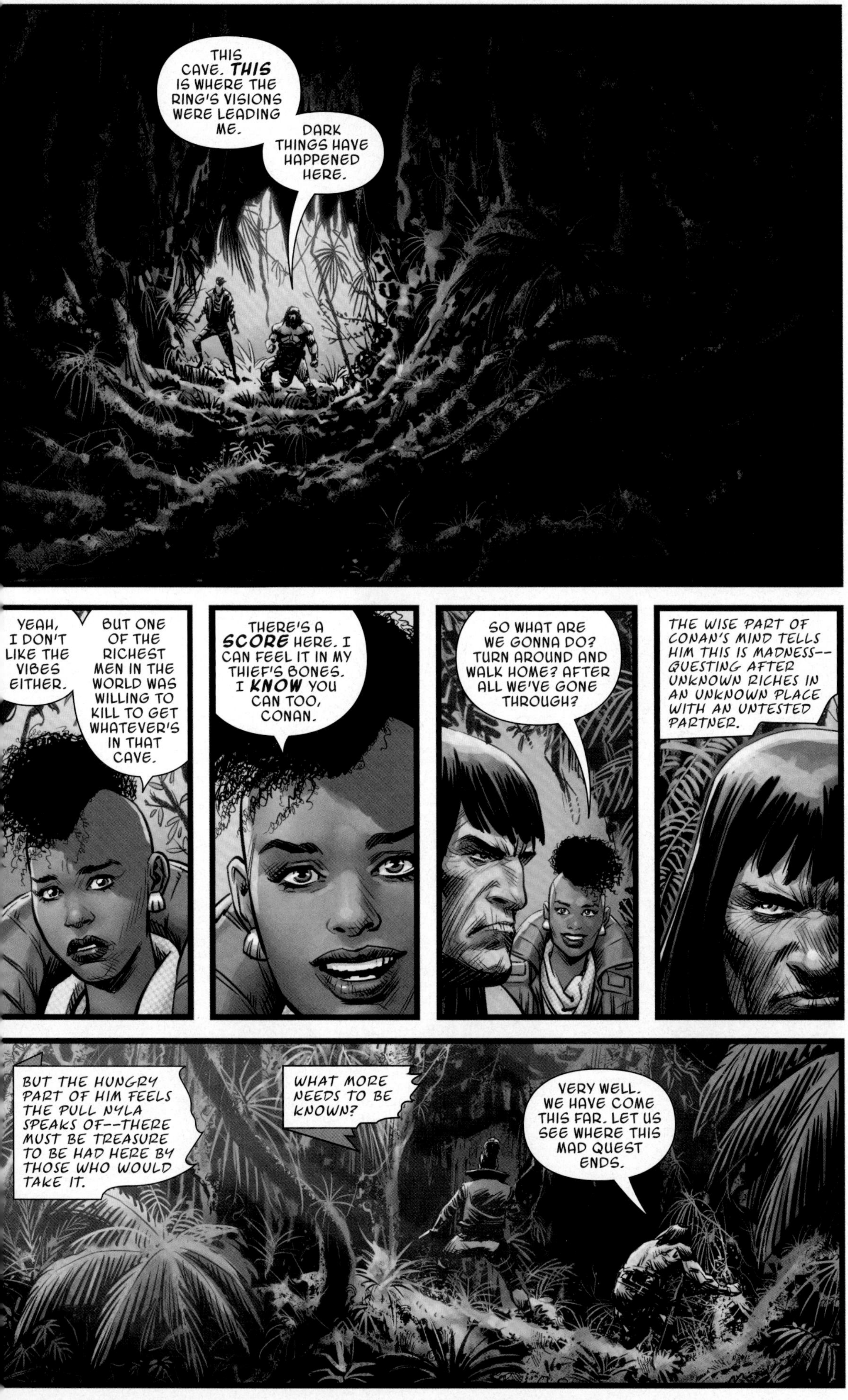
THIS CAVE. THIS IS WHERE THE RING'S VISIONS WERE LEADING ME.
DARK THINGS HAVE HAPPENED HERE.
YEAH, I DON'T LIKE THE VIBES EITHER.
BUT ONE OF THE RICHEST MEN IN THE WORLD WAS WILLING TO KILL TO GET WHATEVER'S IN THAT CAVE.
THERE'S A SCORE HERE. I CAN FEEL IT IN MY THIEF'S BONES. I KNOW YOU CAN TOO, CONAN.
SO WHAT ARE WE GONNA DO? TURN AROUND AND WALK HOME? AFTER ALL WE'VE GONE THROUGH?
THE WISE PART OF CONAN'S MIND TELLS HIM THIS IS MADNESS-- QUESTING AFTER UNKNOWN RICHES IN AN UNKNOWN PLACE WITH AN UNTESTED PARTNER.
BUT THE HUNGRY PART OF HIM FEELS THE PULL NYLA SPEAKS OF--THERE MUST BE TREASURE TO BE HAD HERE BY THOSE WHO WOULD TAKE IT.
WHAT MORE NEEDS TO BE KNOWN?
VERY WELL. WE HAVE COME THIS FAR. LET US SEE WHERE THIS MAD QUEST ENDS.

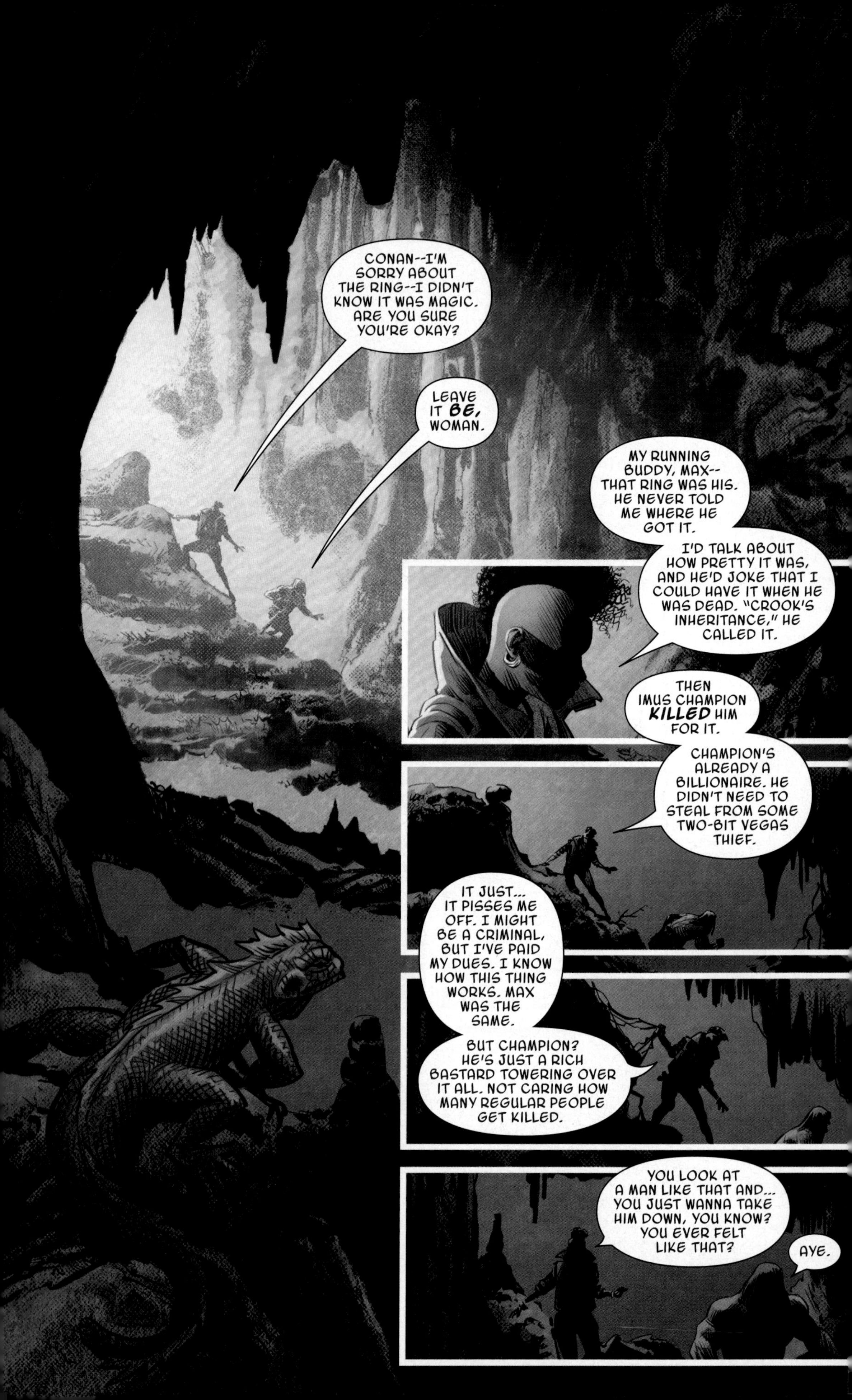
CONAN--I'M SORRY ABOUT THE RING--I DIDN'T KNOW IT WAS MAGIC. ARE YOU SURE YOU'RE OKAY?
LEAVE IT BE, WOMAN.
MY RUNNING BUDDY, MAX--THAT RING WAS HIS. HE NEVER TOLD ME WHERE HE GOT IT.
I'D TALK ABOUT HOW PRETTY IT WAS, AND HE'D JOKE THAT I COULD HAVE IT WHEN HE WAS DEAD. "CROOK'S INHERITANCE," HE CALLED IT.
THEN IMUS CHAMPION KILLED HIM FOR IT.
CHAMPION'S ALREADY A BILLIONAIRE. HE DIDN'T NEED TO STEAL FROM SOME TWO-BIT VEGAS THIEF.
IT JUST... IT PISSES ME OFF. I MIGHT BE A CRIMINAL, BUT I'VE PAID MY DUES. I KNOW HOW THIS THING WORKS. MAX WAS THE SAME.
BUT CHAMPION? HE'S JUST A RICH BASTARD TOWERING OVER IT ALL. NOT CARING HOW MANY REGULAR PEOPLE GET KILLED.
YOU LOOK AT A MAN LIKE THAT AND... YOU JUST WANNA TAKE HIM DOWN, YOU KNOW? YOU EVER FELT LIKE THAT?
AYE.

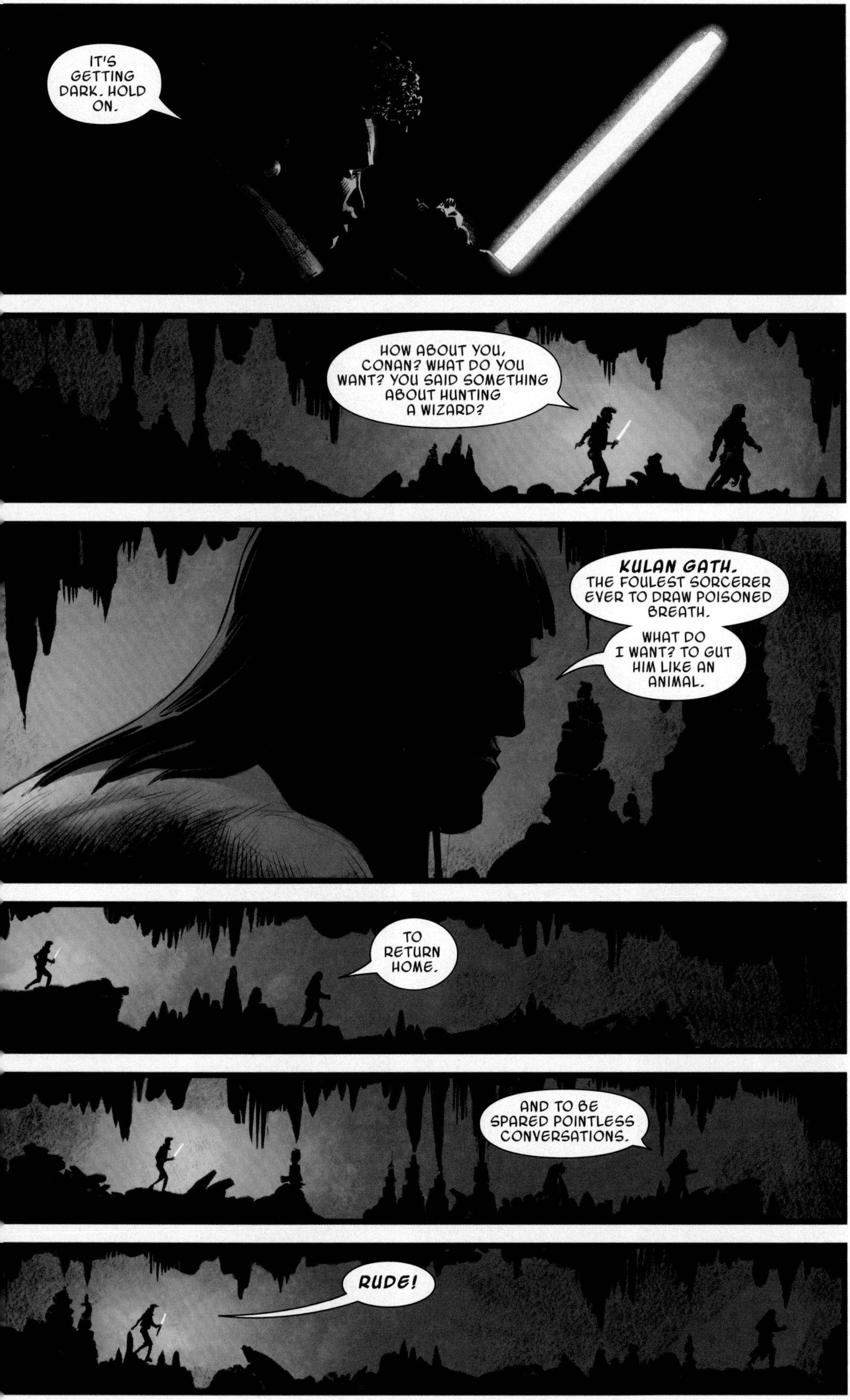
IT'S GETTING DARK. HOLD ON.
HOW ABOUT YOU, CONAN? WHAT DO YOU WANT? YOU SAID SOMETHING ABOUT HUNTING A WIZARD?
KULAN GATH. THE FOULEST SORCERER EVER TO DRAW POISONED BREATH.
WHAT DO I WANT? TO GUT HIM LIKE AN ANIMAL.
TO RETURN HOME.
AND TO BE SPARED POINTLESS CONVERSATIONS.
RUDE!

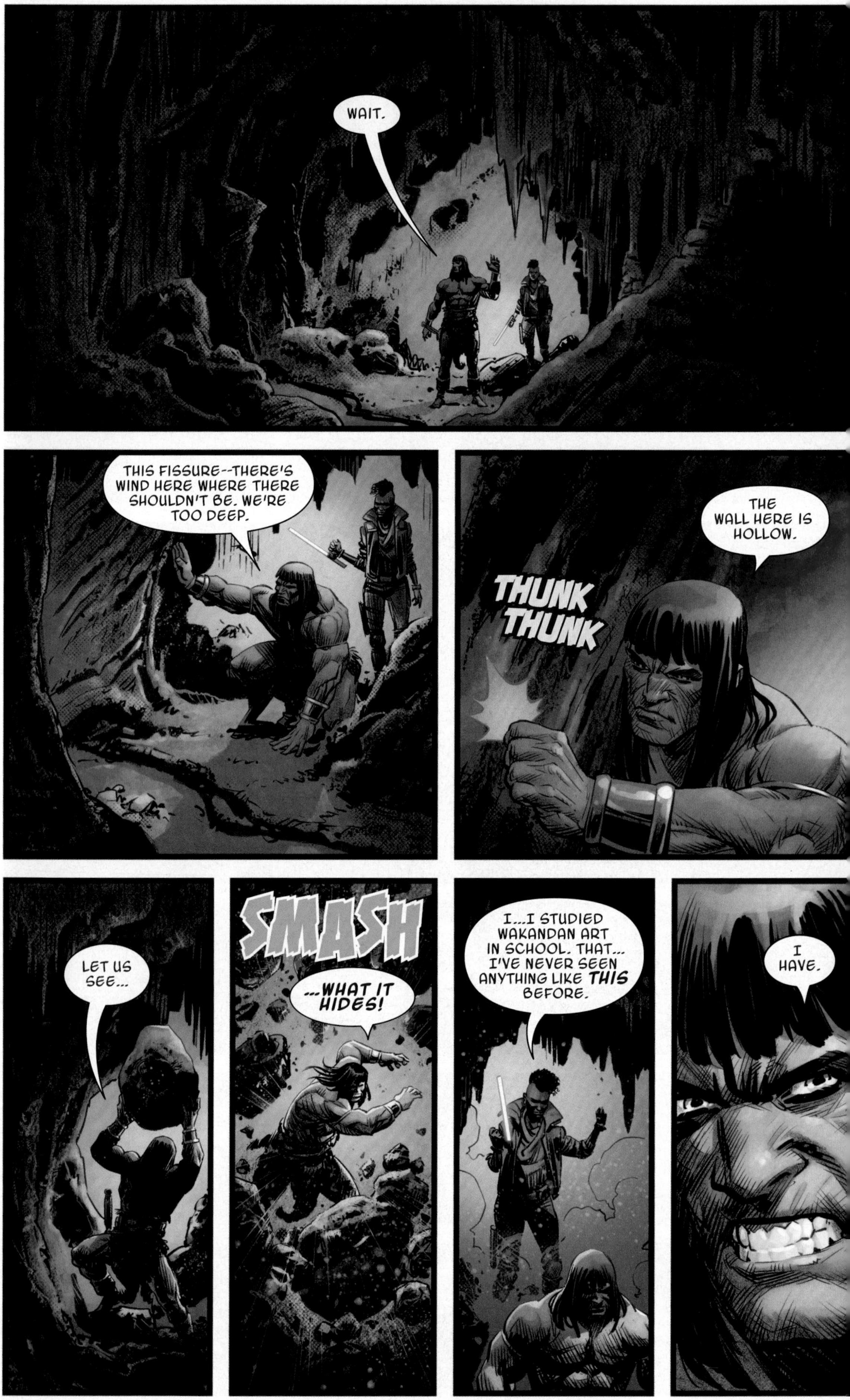
WAIT.
THIS FISSURE--THERE'S WIND HERE WHERE THERE SHOULDN'T BE. WE'RE TOO DEEP.
THUNK THUNK
THE WALL HERE IS HOLLOW.
LET US SEE...
SMASH
...WHAT IT HIDES!
I...I STUDIED WAKANDAN ART IN SCHOOL. THAT... I'VE NEVER SEEN ANYTHING LIKE THIS BEFORE.
I HAVE.

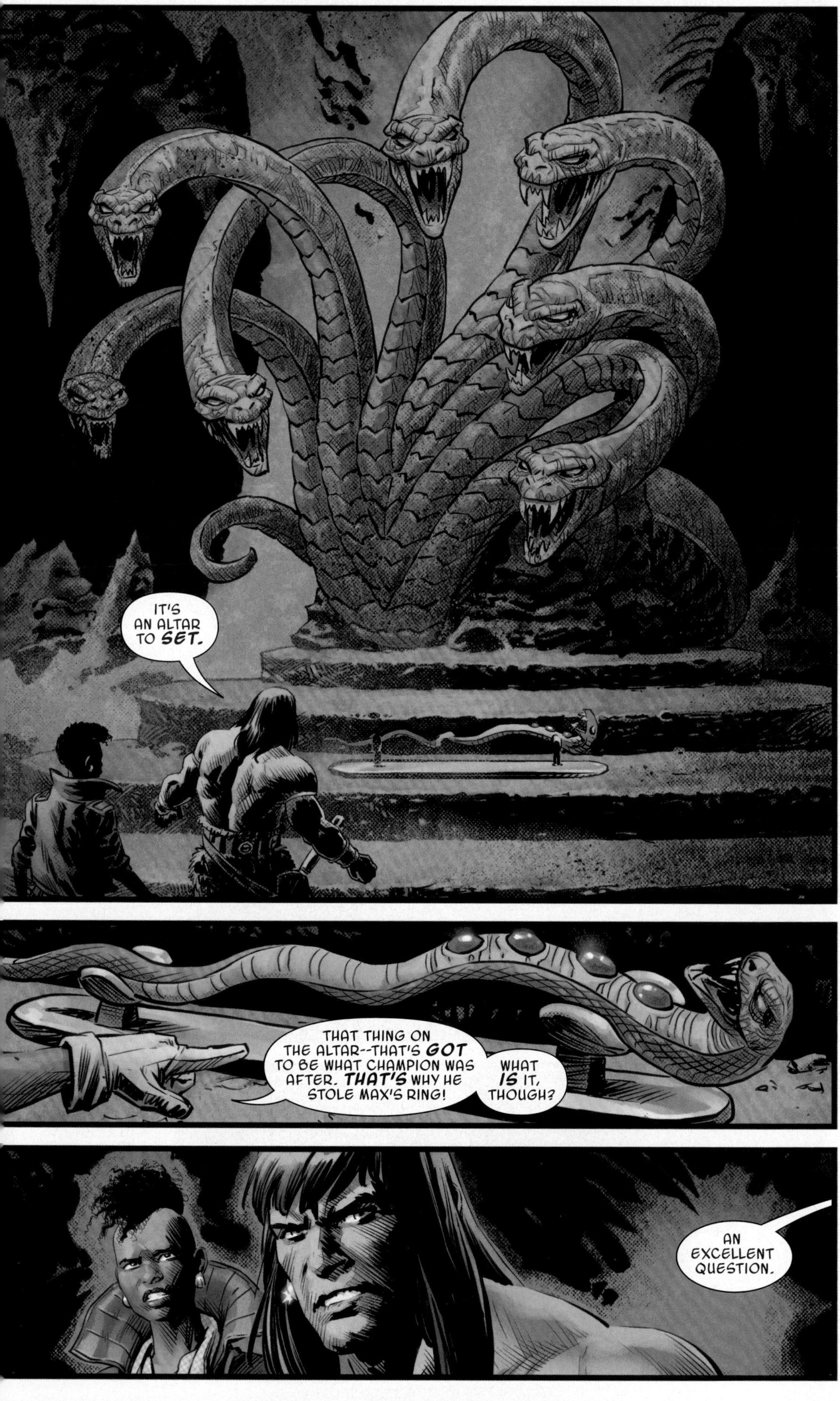
IT'S AN ALTAR TO **SET.**
THAT THING ON THE ALTAR--THAT'S **GOT** TO BE WHAT CHAMPION WAS AFTER. **THAT'S** WHY HE STOLE MAX'S RING!
WHAT **IS** IT, THOUGH?
AN EXCELLENT QUESTION.

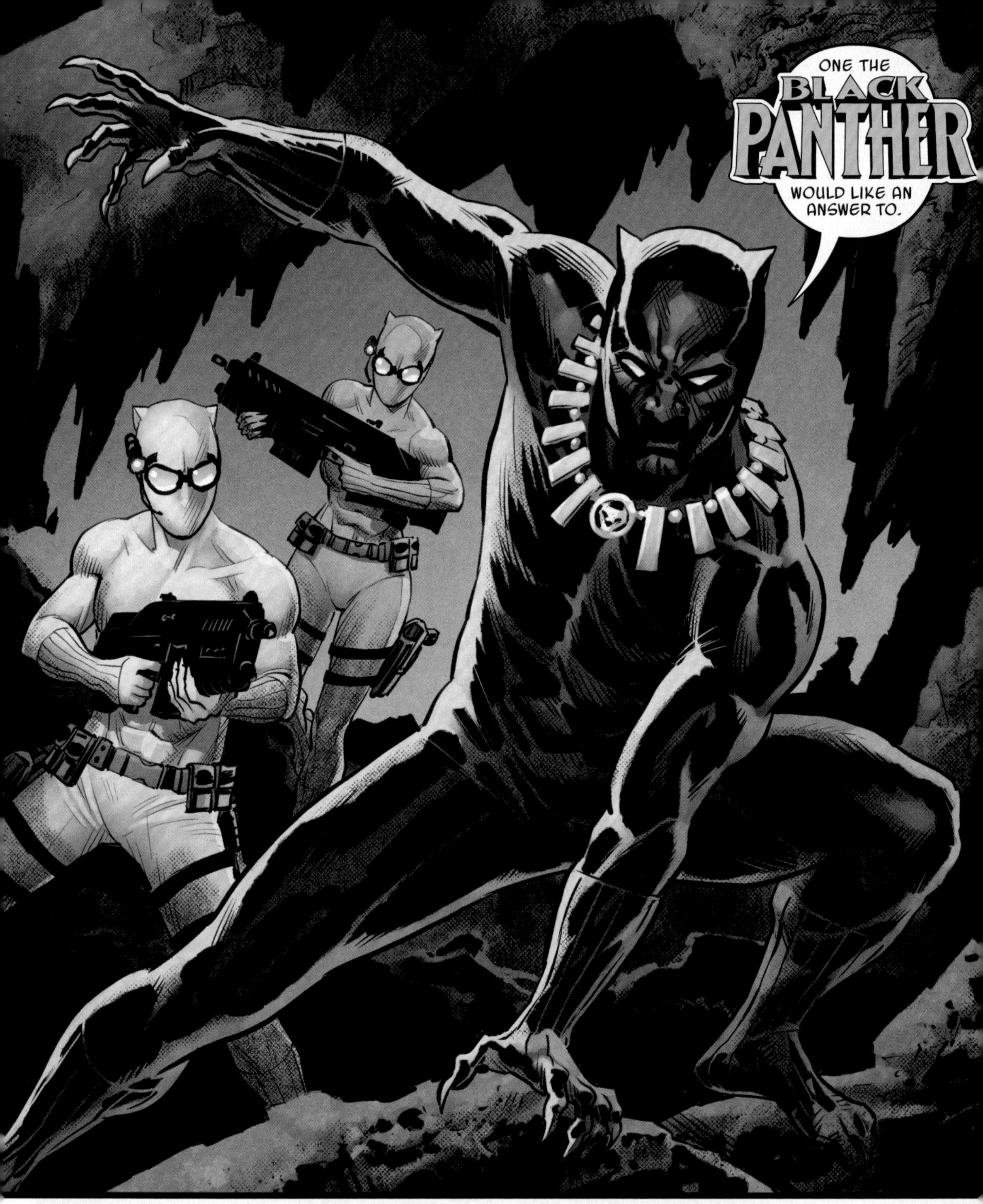
ONE THE BLACK PANTHER WOULD LIKE AN ANSWER TO.

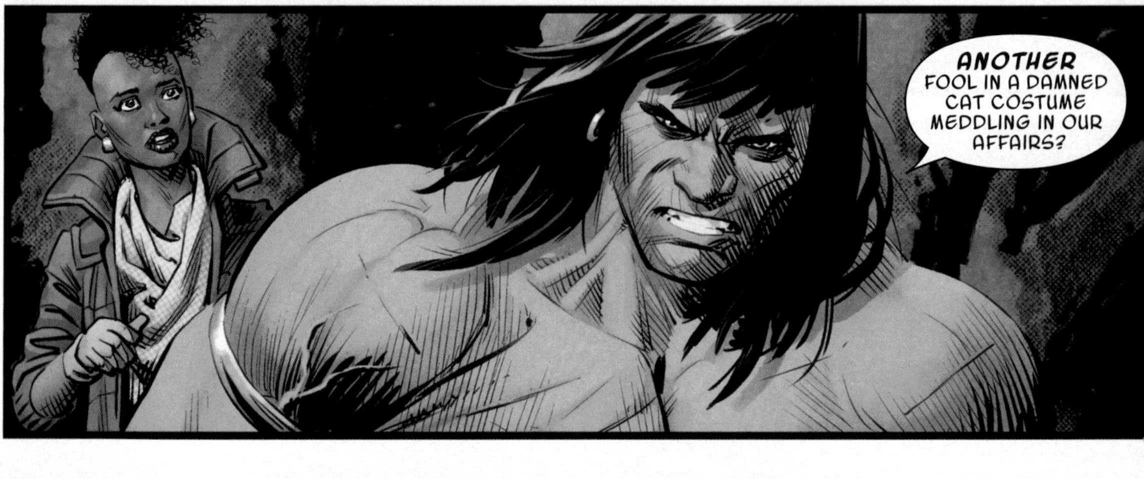
ANOTHER FOOL IN A DAMNED CAT COSTUME MEDDLING IN OUR AFFAIRS?

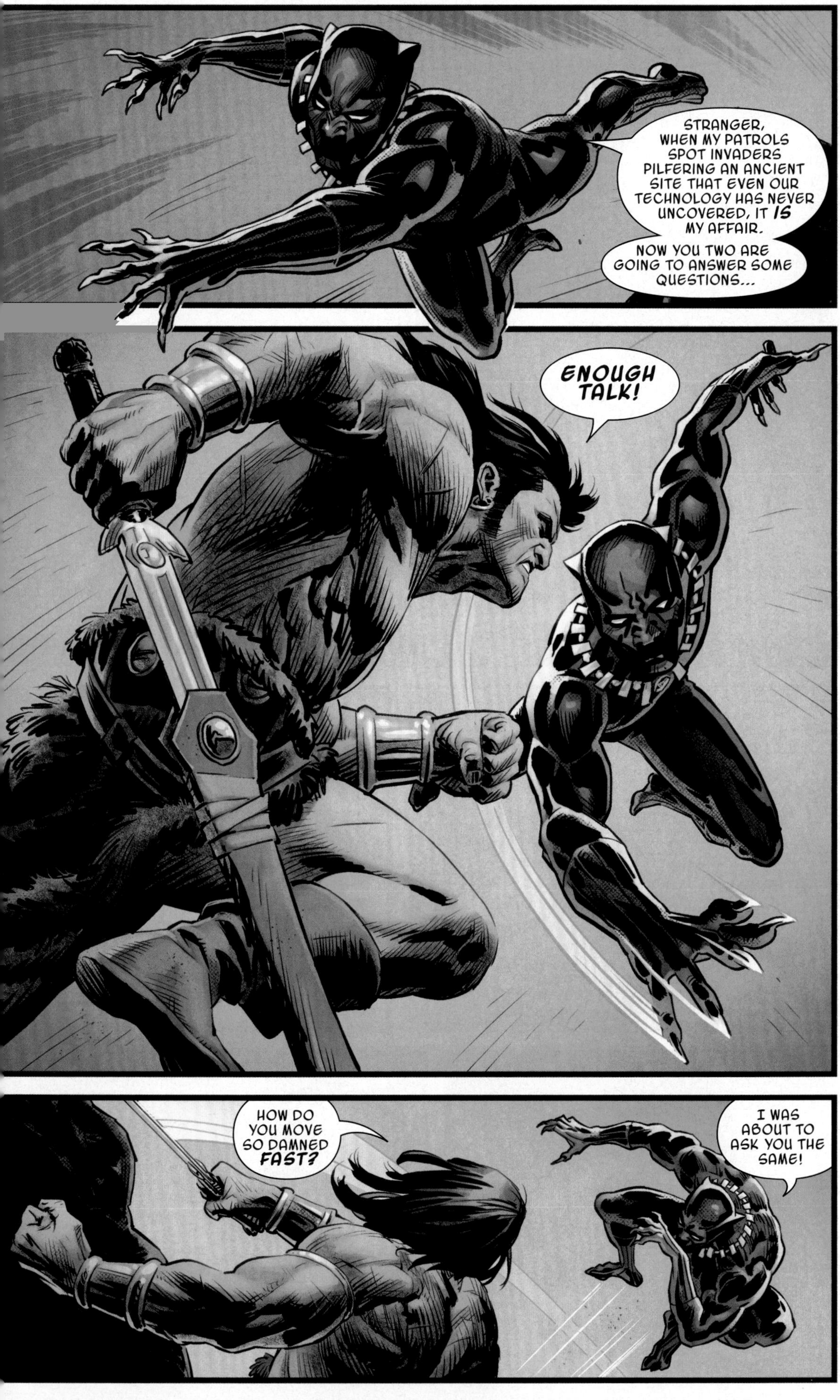
STRANGER, WHEN MY PATROLS SPOT INVADERS PILFERING AN ANCIENT SITE THAT EVEN OUR TECHNOLOGY HAS NEVER UNCOVERED, IT IS MY AFFAIR.
NOW YOU TWO ARE GOING TO ANSWER SOME QUESTIONS...
ENOUGH TALK!
HOW DO YOU MOVE SO DAMNED FAST?
I WAS ABOUT TO ASK YOU THE SAME!

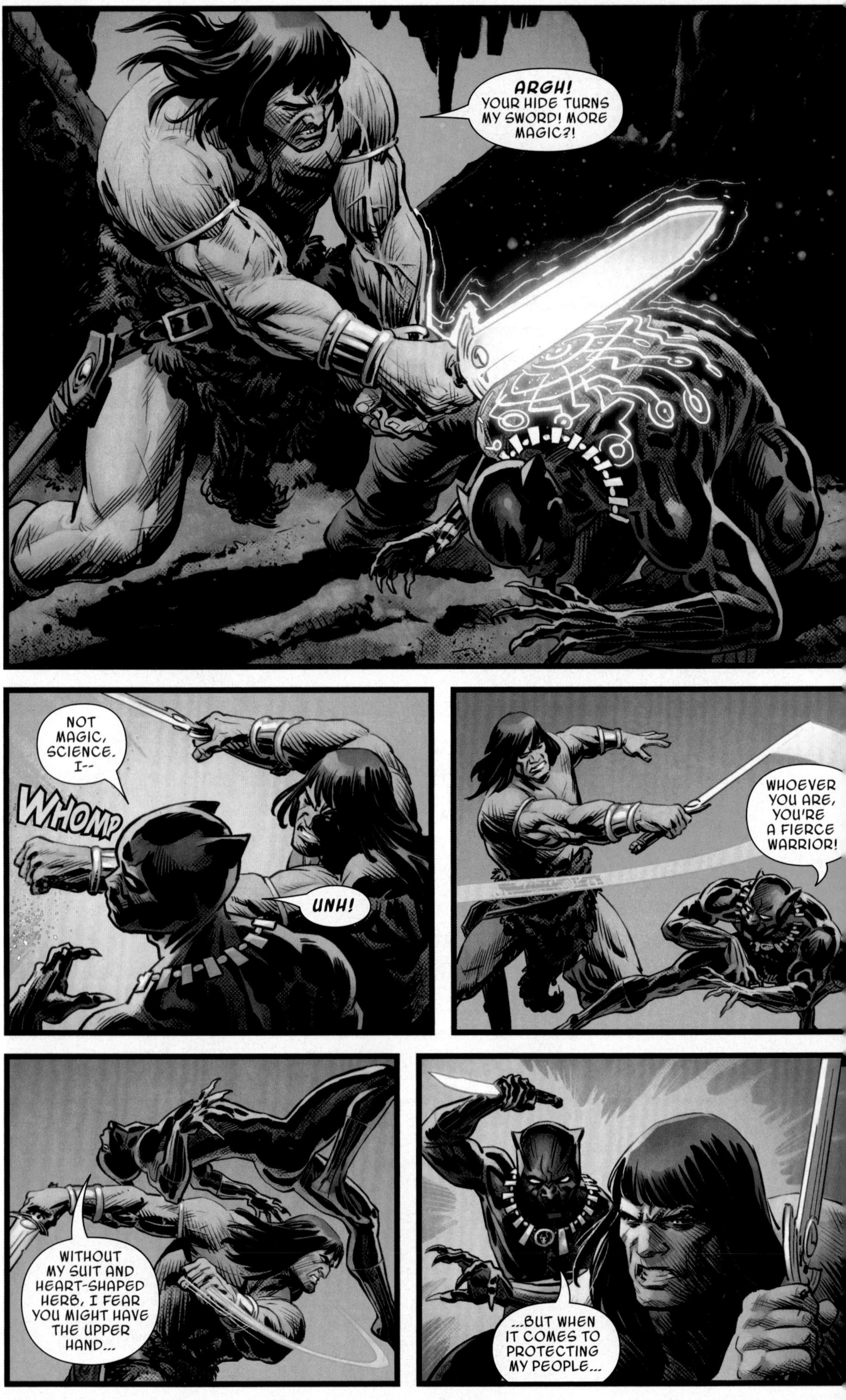
ARGH!
YOUR HIDE TURNS MY SWORD! MORE MAGIC?!
NOT MAGIC, SCIENCE. I--
WHOMP
UNH!
WHOEVER YOU ARE, YOU'RE A FIERCE WARRIOR!
WITHOUT MY SUIT AND HEART-SHAPED HERB, I FEAR YOU MIGHT HAVE THE UPPER HAND...
...BUT WHEN IT COMES TO PROTECTING MY PEOPLE...

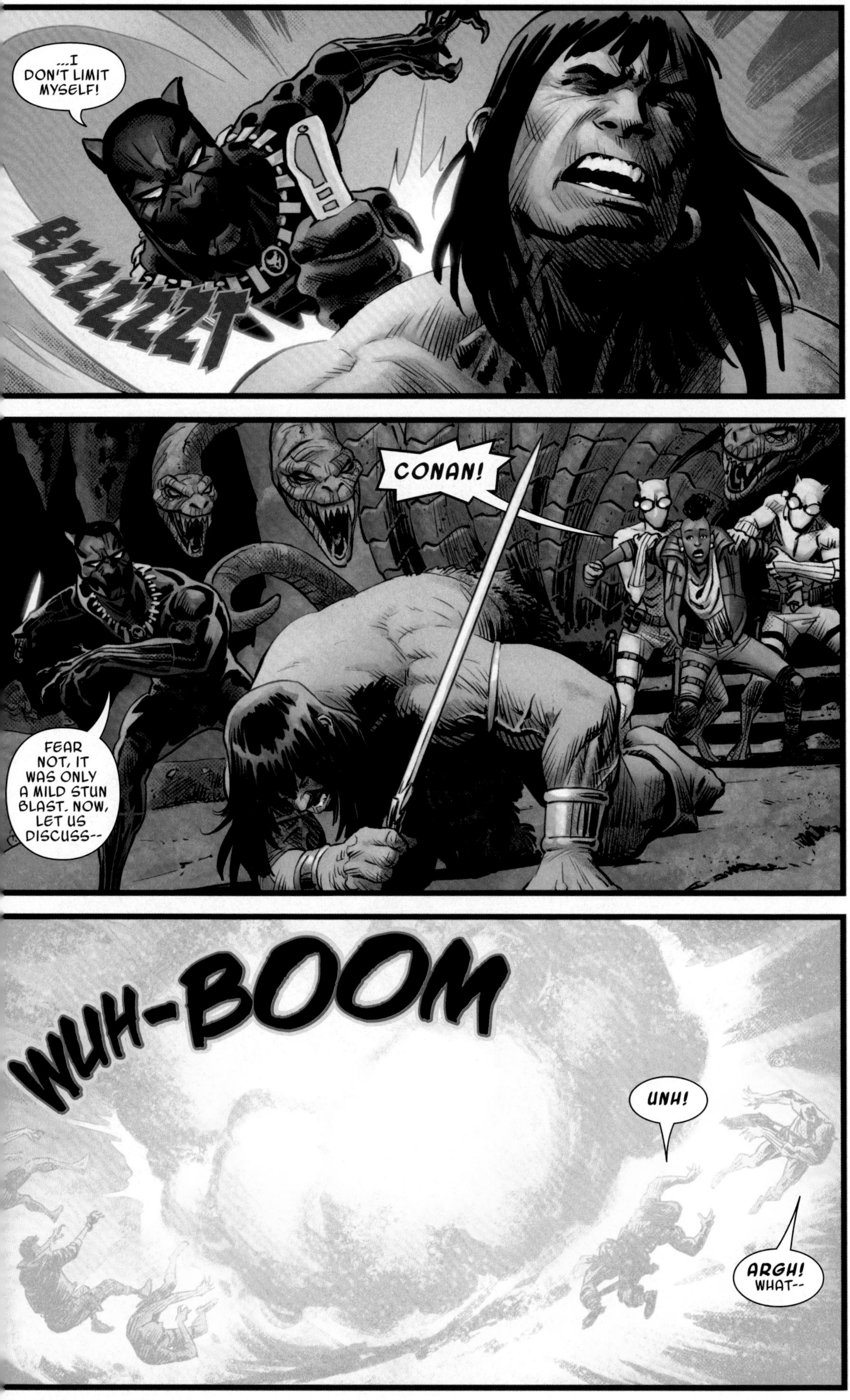
...I DON'T LIMIT MYSELF!
BZZZZZT
CONAN!
FEAR NOT, IT WAS ONLY A MILD STUN BLAST. NOW, LET US DISCUSS--
WUH-BOOM
UNH!
ARGH! WHAT--

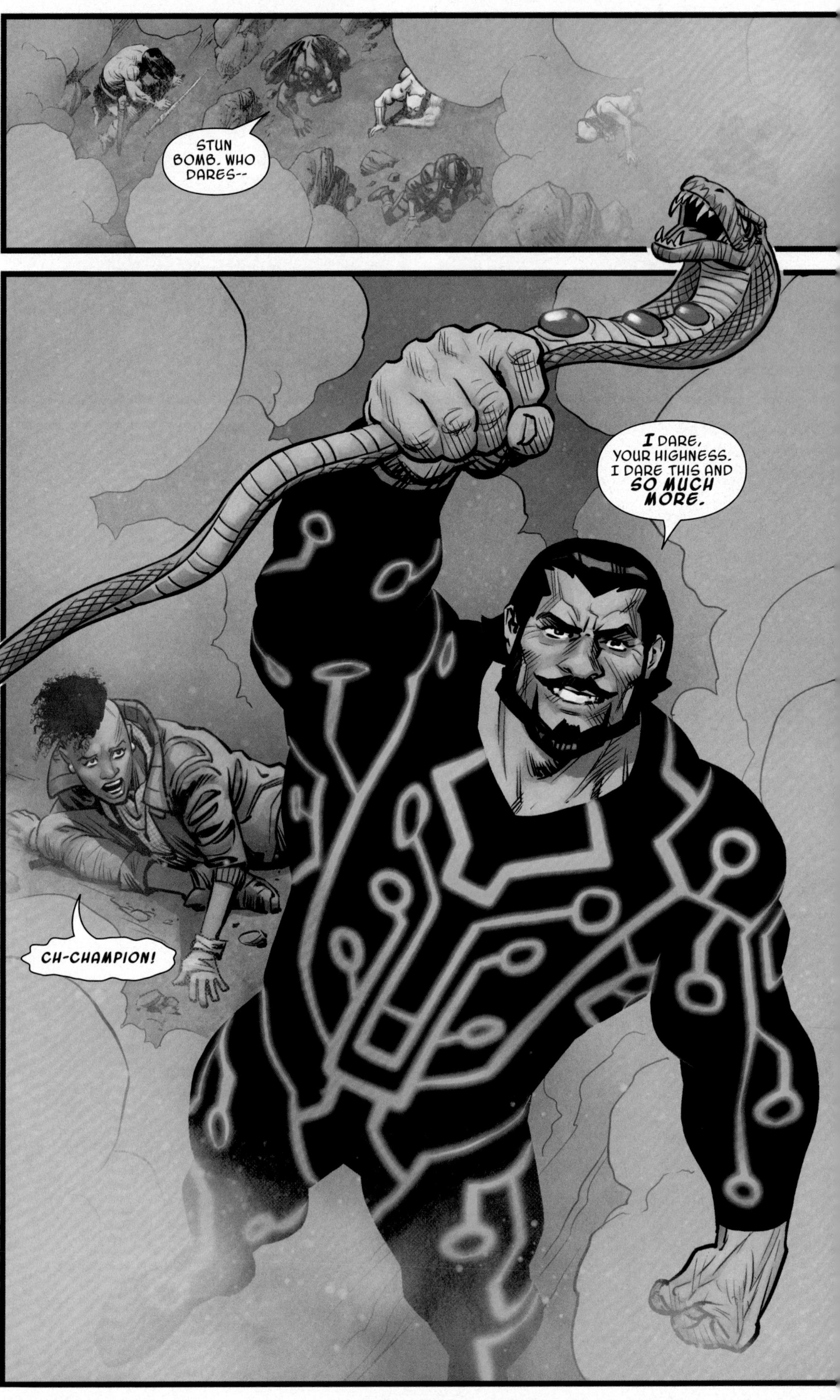
STUN BOMB. WHO DARES--
I DARE, YOUR HIGHNESS. I DARE THIS AND SO MUCH MORE.
CH-CHAMPION!

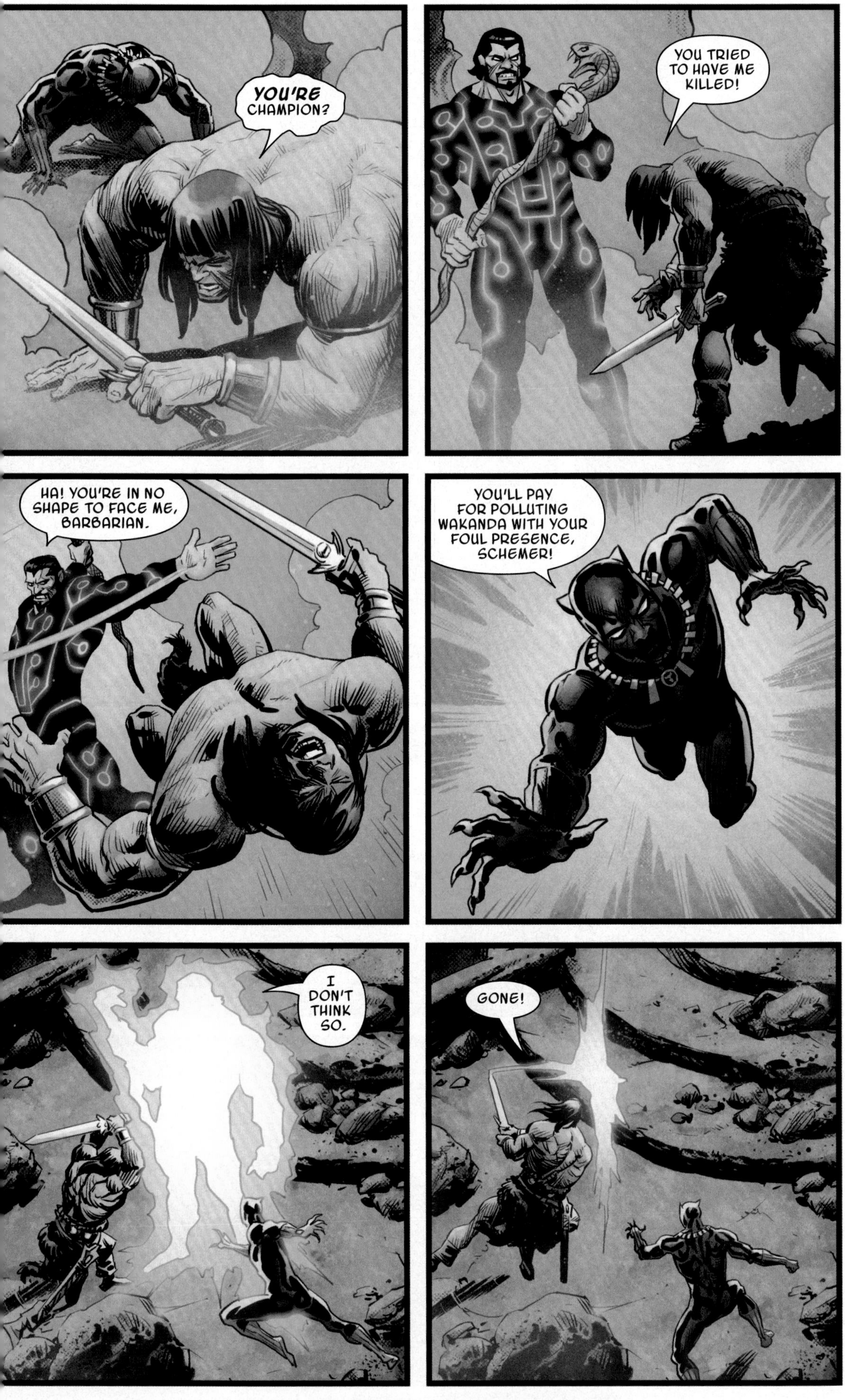
YOU'RE CHAMPION?
YOU TRIED TO HAVE ME KILLED!
HA! YOU'RE IN NO SHAPE TO FACE ME, BARBARIAN.
YOU'LL PAY FOR POLLUTING WAKANDA WITH YOUR FOUL PRESENCE, SCHEMER!
I DON'T THINK SO.
GONE!

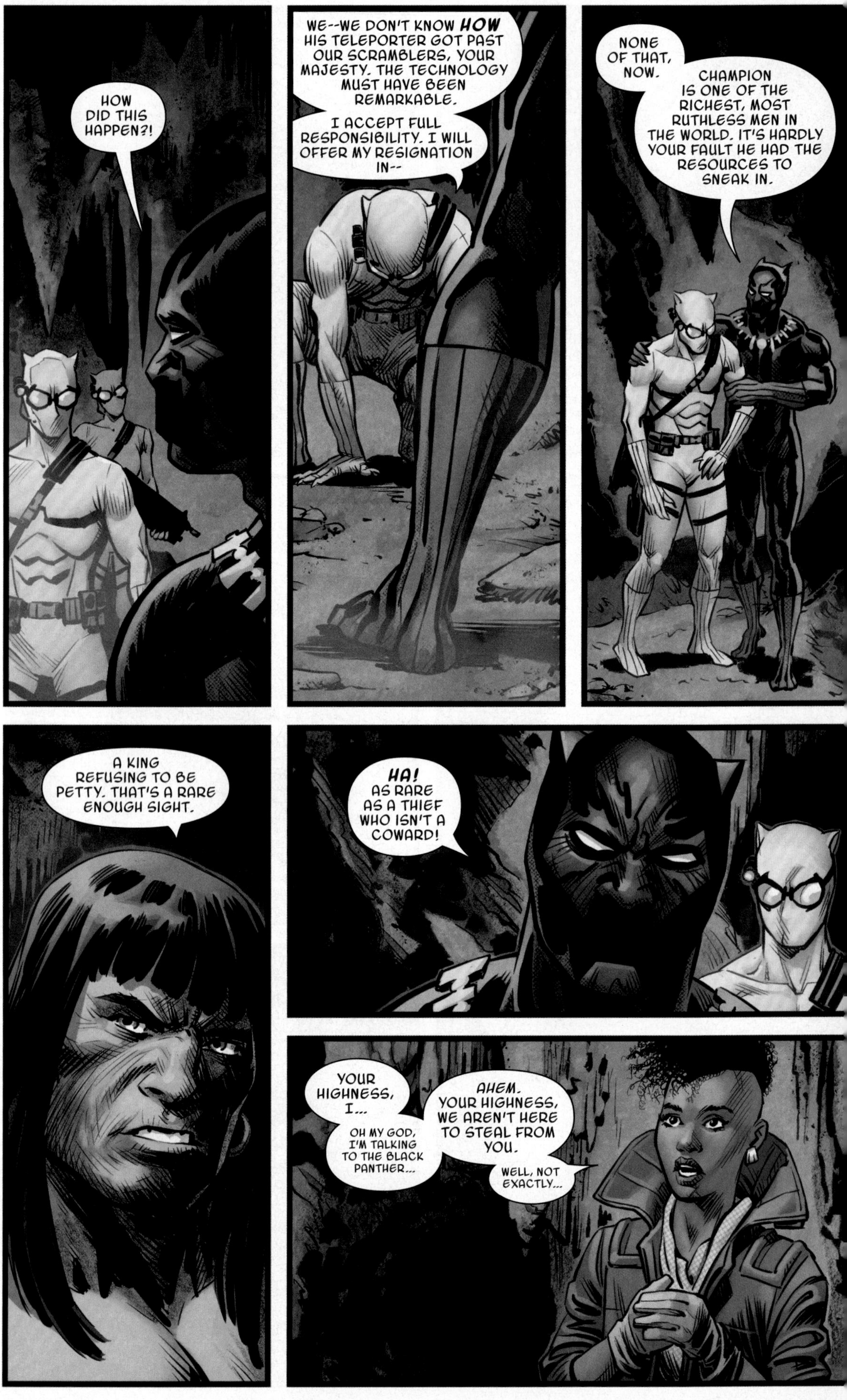
HOW DID THIS HAPPEN?!
WE--WE DON'T KNOW HOW HIS TELEPORTER GOT PAST OUR SCRAMBLERS, YOUR MAJESTY. THE TECHNOLOGY MUST HAVE BEEN REMARKABLE.
I ACCEPT FULL RESPONSIBILITY. I WILL OFFER MY RESIGNATION IN--
NONE OF THAT, NOW.
CHAMPION IS ONE OF THE RICHEST, MOST RUTHLESS MEN IN THE WORLD. IT'S HARDLY YOUR FAULT HE HAD THE RESOURCES TO SNEAK IN.
A KING REFUSING TO BE PETTY. THAT'S A RARE ENOUGH SIGHT.
HA! AS RARE AS A THIEF WHO ISN'T A COWARD!
YOUR HIGHNESS, I...
OH MY GOD, I'M TALKING TO THE BLACK PANTHER...
AHEM. YOUR HIGHNESS, WE AREN'T HERE TO STEAL FROM YOU.
WELL, NOT EXACTLY...

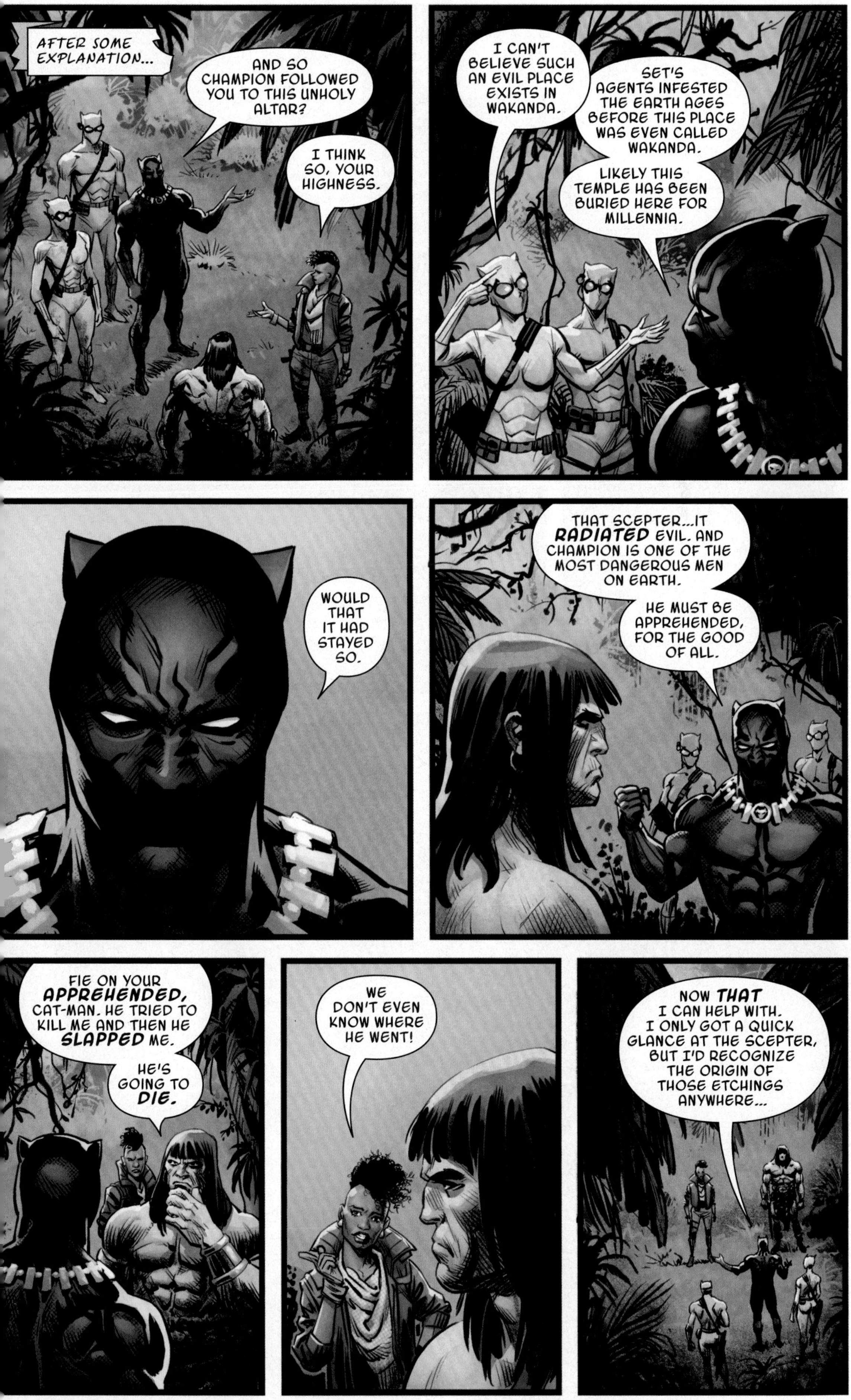

AFTER SOME EXPLANATION...
AND SO CHAMPION FOLLOWED YOU TO THIS UNHOLY ALTAR?
I THINK SO, YOUR HIGHNESS.
I CAN'T BELIEVE SUCH AN EVIL PLACE EXISTS IN WAKANDA.
SET'S AGENTS INFESTED THE EARTH AGES BEFORE THIS PLACE WAS EVEN CALLED WAKANDA.
LIKELY THIS TEMPLE HAS BEEN BURIED HERE FOR MILLENNIA.
WOULD THAT IT HAD STAYED SO.
THAT SCEPTER...IT RADIATED EVIL. AND CHAMPION IS ONE OF THE MOST DANGEROUS MEN ON EARTH.
HE MUST BE APPREHENDED, FOR THE GOOD OF ALL.
FIE ON YOUR APPREHENDED, CAT-MAN. HE TRIED TO KILL ME AND THEN HE SLAPPED ME.
HE'S GOING TO DIE.
WE DON'T EVEN KNOW WHERE HE WENT!
NOW THAT I CAN HELP WITH. I ONLY GOT A QUICK GLANCE AT THE SCEPTER, BUT I'D RECOGNIZE THE ORIGIN OF THOSE ETCHINGS ANYWHERE...

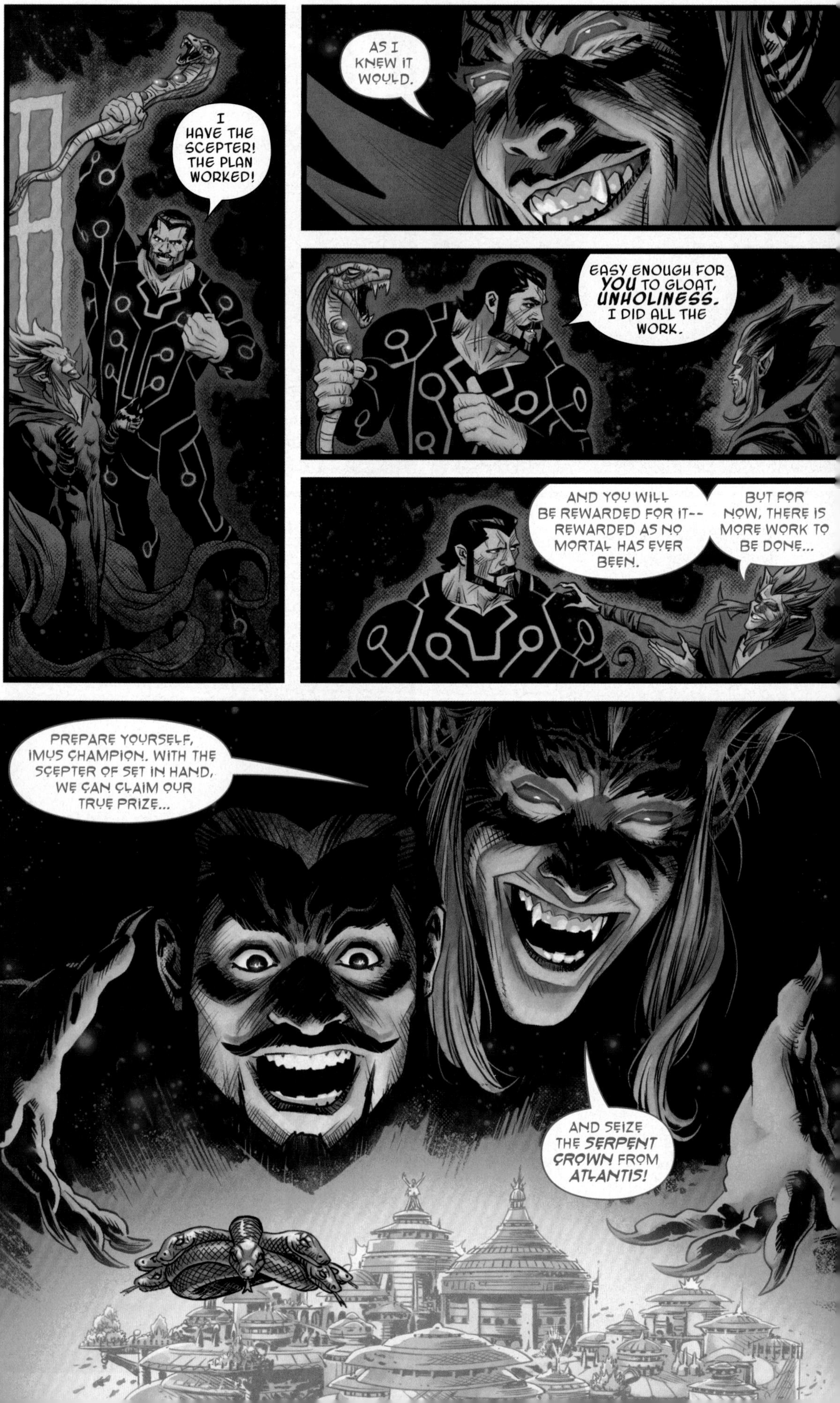
I HAVE THE SCEPTER! THE PLAN WORKED!
AS I KNEW IT WOULD.
EASY ENOUGH FOR **YOU** TO GLOAT, ***UNHOLINESS.*** I DID ALL THE WORK.
AND YOU WILL BE REWARDED FOR IT-- REWARDED AS NO MORTAL HAS EVER BEEN.
BUT FOR NOW, THERE IS MORE WORK TO BE DONE...
PREPARE YOURSELF, IMUS CHAMPION. WITH THE SCEPTER OF SET IN HAND, WE CAN CLAIM OUR TRUE PRIZE...
AND SEIZE THE ***SERPENT CROWN*** FROM ***ATLANTIS!***

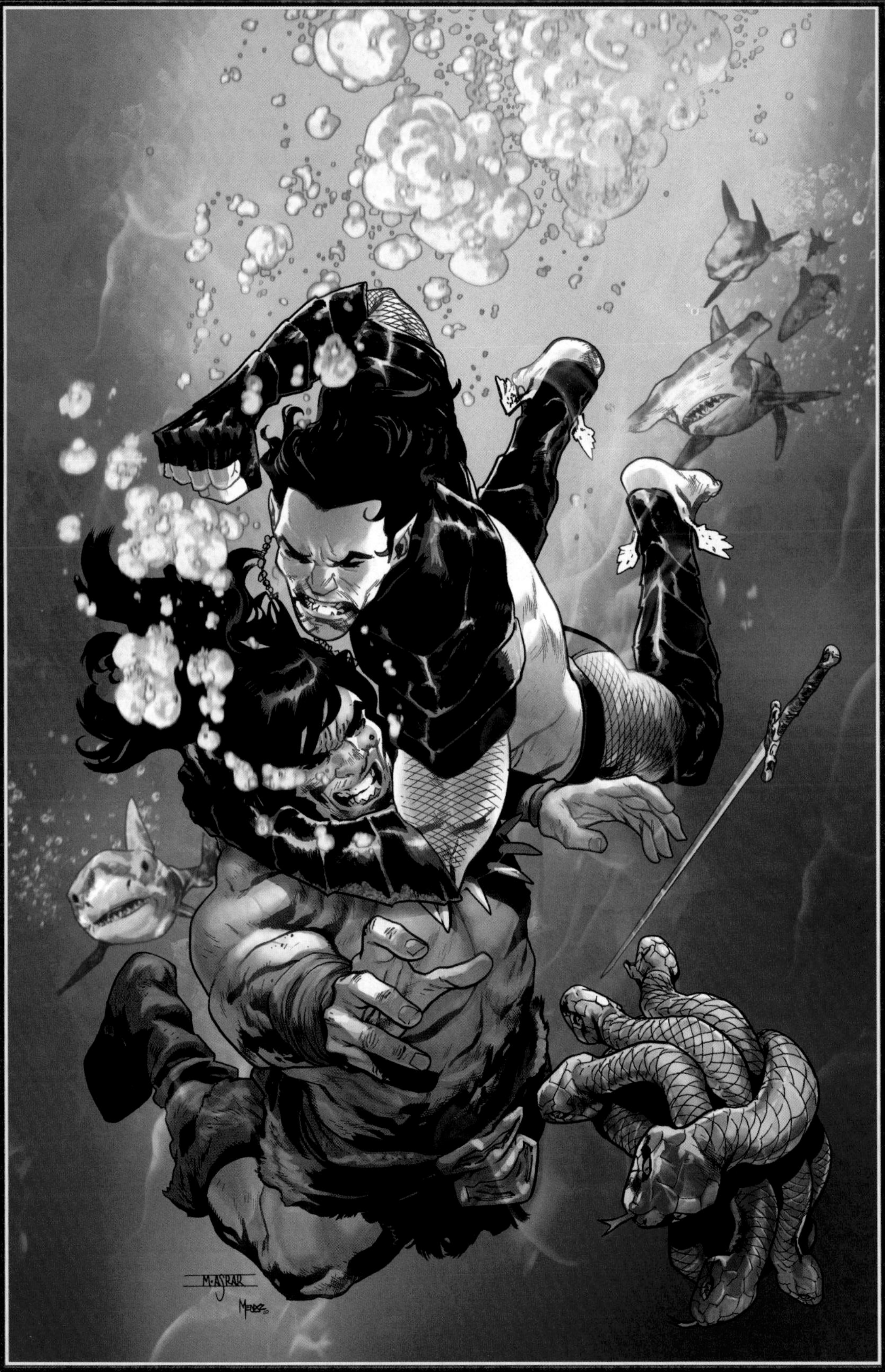
M.ASRAR

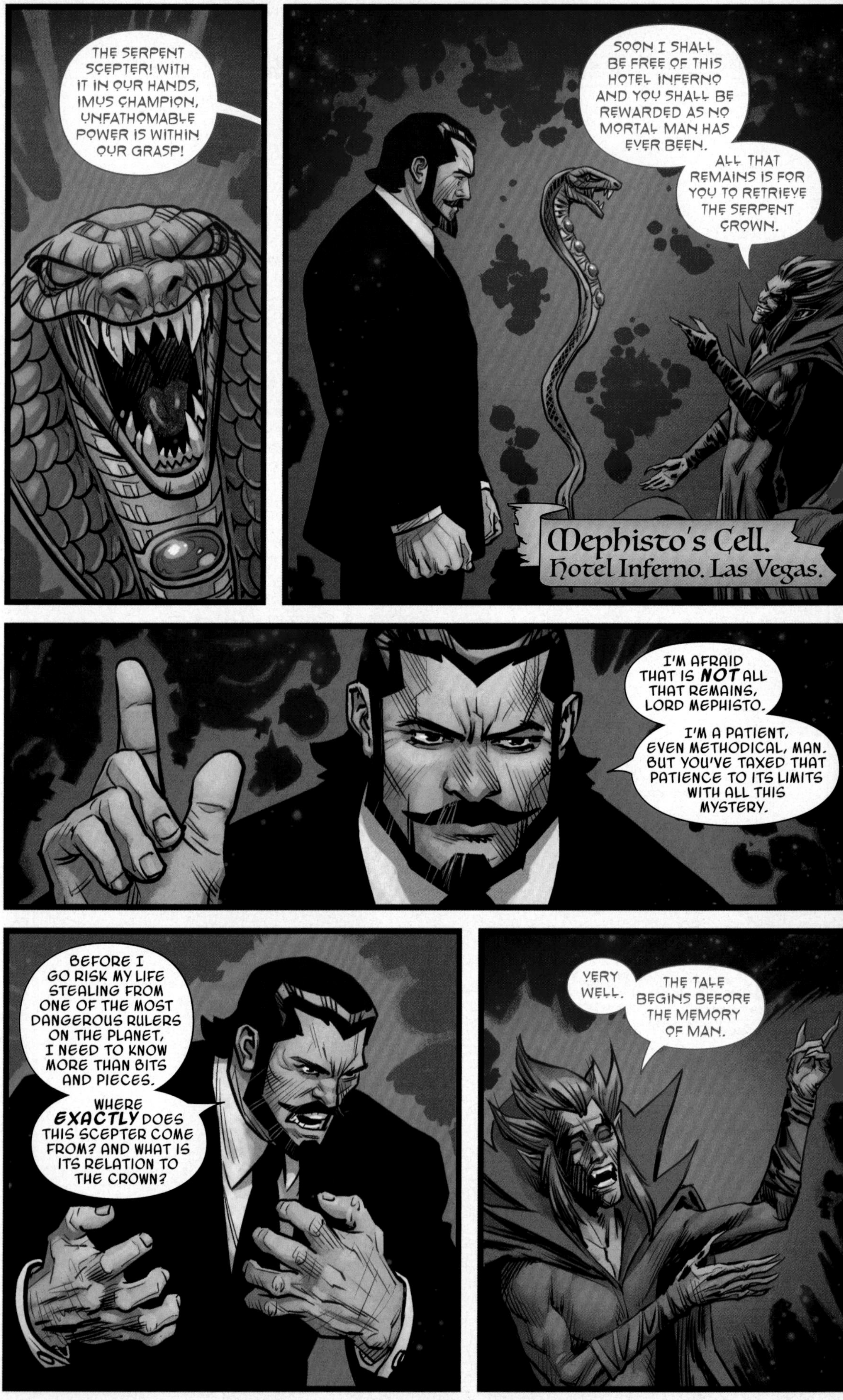
THE SERPENT SCEPTER! WITH IT IN OUR HANDS, IMUS CHAMPION, UNFATHOMABLE POWER IS WITHIN OUR GRASP!
SOON I SHALL BE FREE OF THIS HOTEL INFERNO AND YOU SHALL BE REWARDED AS NO MORTAL MAN HAS EVER BEEN.
ALL THAT REMAINS IS FOR YOU TO RETRIEVE THE SERPENT CROWN.
Mephisto's Cell. Hotel Inferno. Las Vegas.
I'M AFRAID THAT IS NOT ALL THAT REMAINS, LORD MEPHISTO.
I'M A PATIENT, EVEN METHODICAL, MAN. BUT YOU'VE TAXED THAT PATIENCE TO ITS LIMITS WITH ALL THIS MYSTERY.
BEFORE I GO RISK MY LIFE STEALING FROM ONE OF THE MOST DANGEROUS RULERS ON THE PLANET, I NEED TO KNOW MORE THAN BITS AND PIECES.
WHERE EXACTLY DOES THIS SCEPTER COME FROM? AND WHAT IS ITS RELATION TO THE CROWN?
VERY WELL.
THE TALE BEGINS BEFORE THE MEMORY OF MAN.

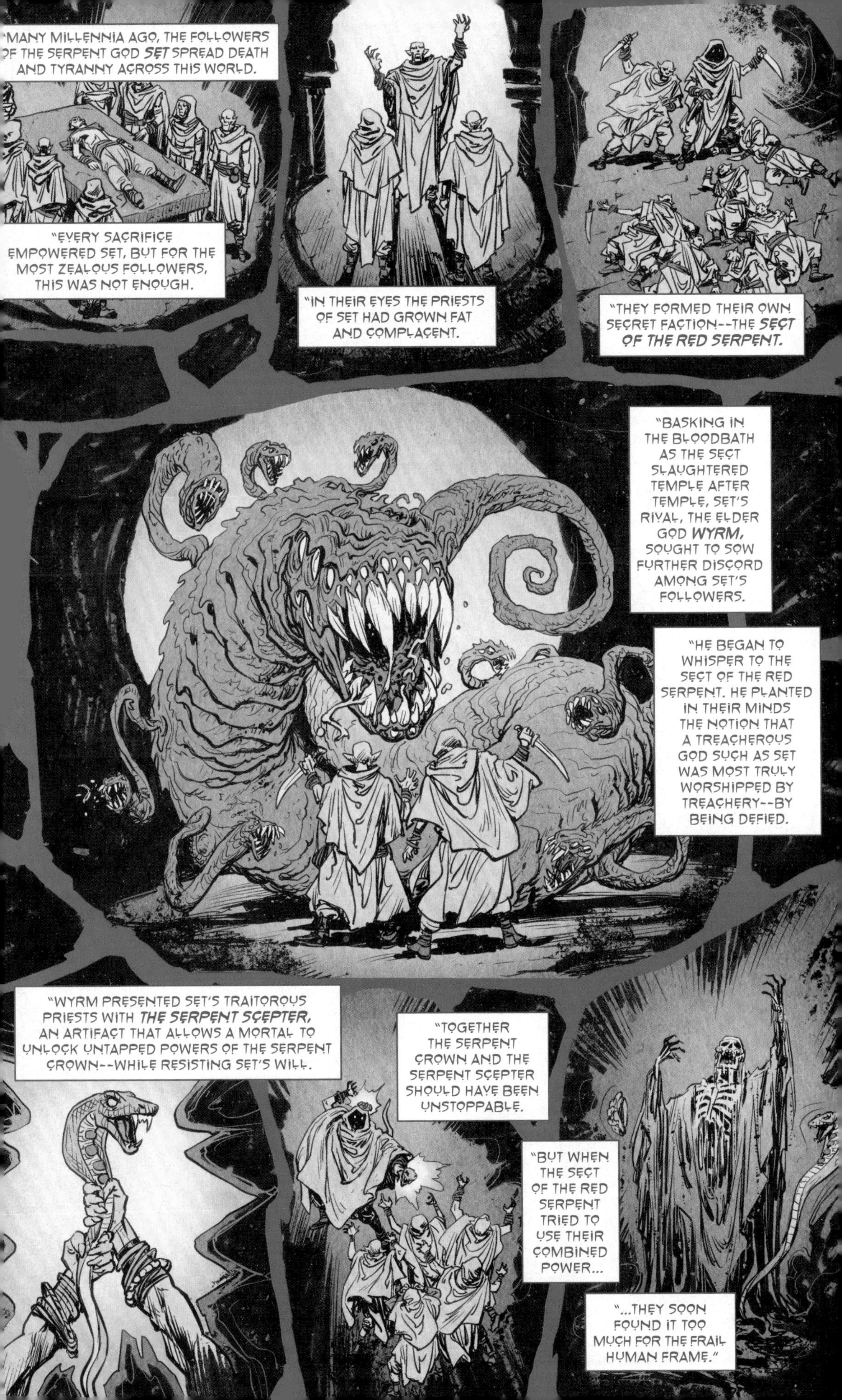
"MANY MILLENNIA AGO, THE FOLLOWERS OF THE SERPENT GOD *SET* SPREAD DEATH AND TYRANNY ACROSS THIS WORLD.
"EVERY SACRIFICE EMPOWERED SET, BUT FOR THE MOST ZEALOUS FOLLOWERS, THIS WAS NOT ENOUGH.
"IN THEIR EYES THE PRIESTS OF SET HAD GROWN FAT AND COMPLACENT.
"THEY FORMED THEIR OWN SECRET FACTION--THE *SECT OF THE RED SERPENT.*
"BASKING IN THE BLOODBATH AS THE SECT SLAUGHTERED TEMPLE AFTER TEMPLE, SET'S RIVAL, THE ELDER GOD *WYRM,* SOUGHT TO SOW FURTHER DISCORD AMONG SET'S FOLLOWERS.
"HE BEGAN TO WHISPER TO THE SECT OF THE RED SERPENT. HE PLANTED IN THEIR MINDS THE NOTION THAT A TREACHEROUS GOD SUCH AS SET WAS MOST TRULY WORSHIPPED BY TREACHERY--BY BEING DEFIED.
"WYRM PRESENTED SET'S TRAITOROUS PRIESTS WITH *THE SERPENT SCEPTER,* AN ARTIFACT THAT ALLOWS A MORTAL TO UNLOCK UNTAPPED POWERS OF THE SERPENT CROWN--WHILE RESISTING SET'S WILL.
"TOGETHER THE SERPENT CROWN AND THE SERPENT SCEPTER SHOULD HAVE BEEN UNSTOPPABLE.
"BUT WHEN THE SECT OF THE RED SERPENT TRIED TO USE THEIR COMBINED POWER...
"...THEY SOON FOUND IT TOO MUCH FOR THE FRAIL HUMAN FRAME."

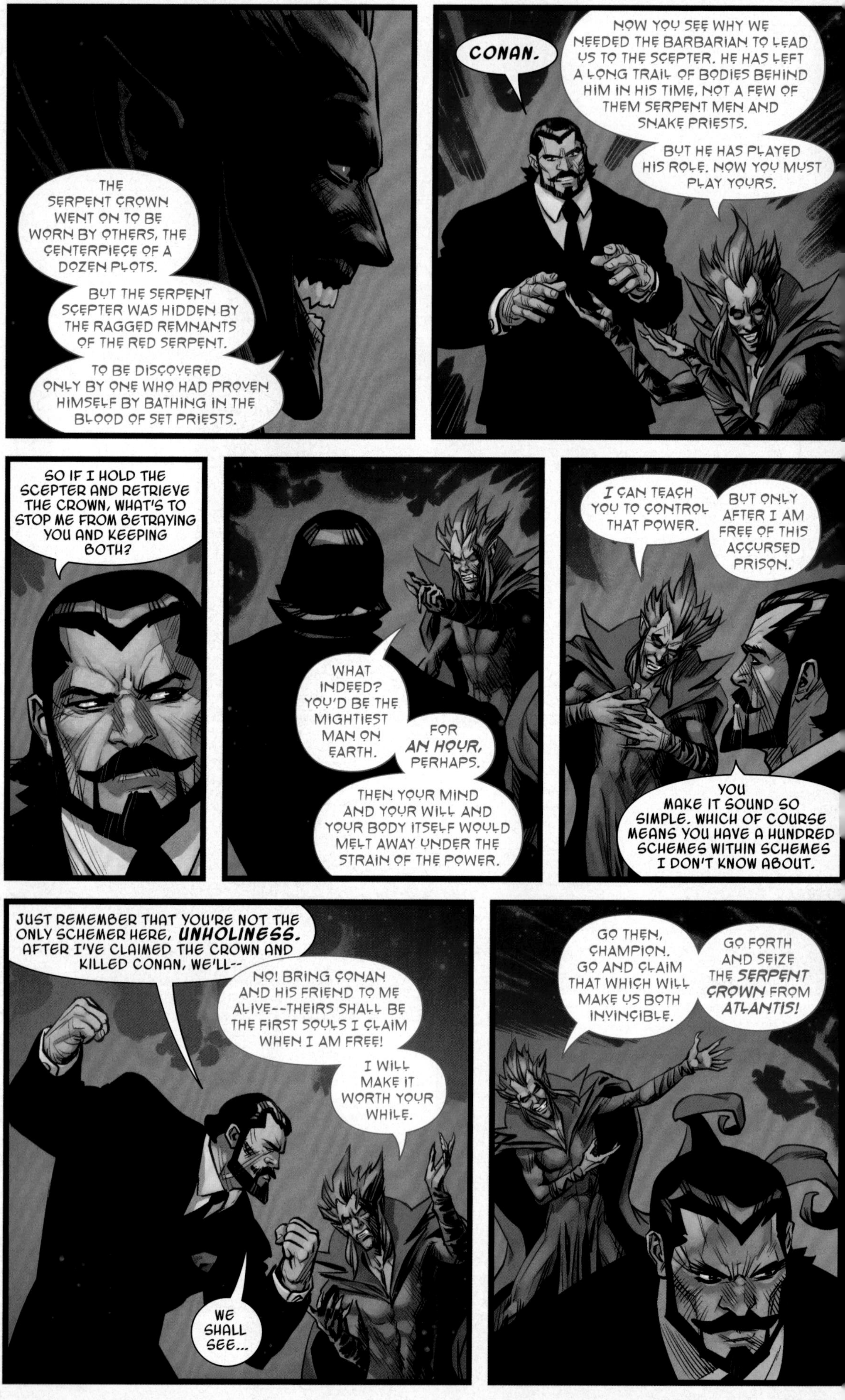
THE SERPENT CROWN WENT ON TO BE WORN BY OTHERS, THE CENTERPIECE OF A DOZEN PLOTS.
BUT THE SERPENT SCEPTER WAS HIDDEN BY THE RAGGED REMNANTS OF THE RED SERPENT.
TO BE DISCOVERED ONLY BY ONE WHO HAD PROVEN HIMSELF BY BATHING IN THE BLOOD OF SET PRIESTS.
CONAN.
NOW YOU SEE WHY WE NEEDED THE BARBARIAN TO LEAD US TO THE SCEPTER. HE HAS LEFT A LONG TRAIL OF BODIES BEHIND HIM IN HIS TIME, NOT A FEW OF THEM SERPENT MEN AND SNAKE PRIESTS.
BUT HE HAS PLAYED HIS ROLE. NOW YOU MUST PLAY YOURS.
SO IF I HOLD THE SCEPTER AND RETRIEVE THE CROWN, WHAT'S TO STOP ME FROM BETRAYING YOU AND KEEPING BOTH?
WHAT INDEED? YOU'D BE THE MIGHTIEST MAN ON EARTH.
FOR AN HOUR, PERHAPS.
THEN YOUR MIND AND YOUR WILL AND YOUR BODY ITSELF WOULD MELT AWAY UNDER THE STRAIN OF THE POWER.
I CAN TEACH YOU TO CONTROL THAT POWER.
BUT ONLY AFTER I AM FREE OF THIS ACCURSED PRISON.
YOU MAKE IT SOUND SO SIMPLE. WHICH OF COURSE MEANS YOU HAVE A HUNDRED SCHEMES WITHIN SCHEMES I DON'T KNOW ABOUT.
JUST REMEMBER THAT YOU'RE NOT THE ONLY SCHEMER HERE, UNHOLINESS. AFTER I'VE CLAIMED THE CROWN AND KILLED CONAN, WE'LL--
NO! BRING CONAN AND HIS FRIEND TO ME ALIVE--THEIRS SHALL BE THE FIRST SOULS I CLAIM WHEN I AM FREE!
I WILL MAKE IT WORTH YOUR WHILE.
WE SHALL SEE...
GO THEN, CHAMPION. GO AND CLAIM THAT WHICH WILL MAKE US BOTH INVINCIBLE.
GO FORTH AND SEIZE THE SERPENT CROWN FROM ATLANTIS!

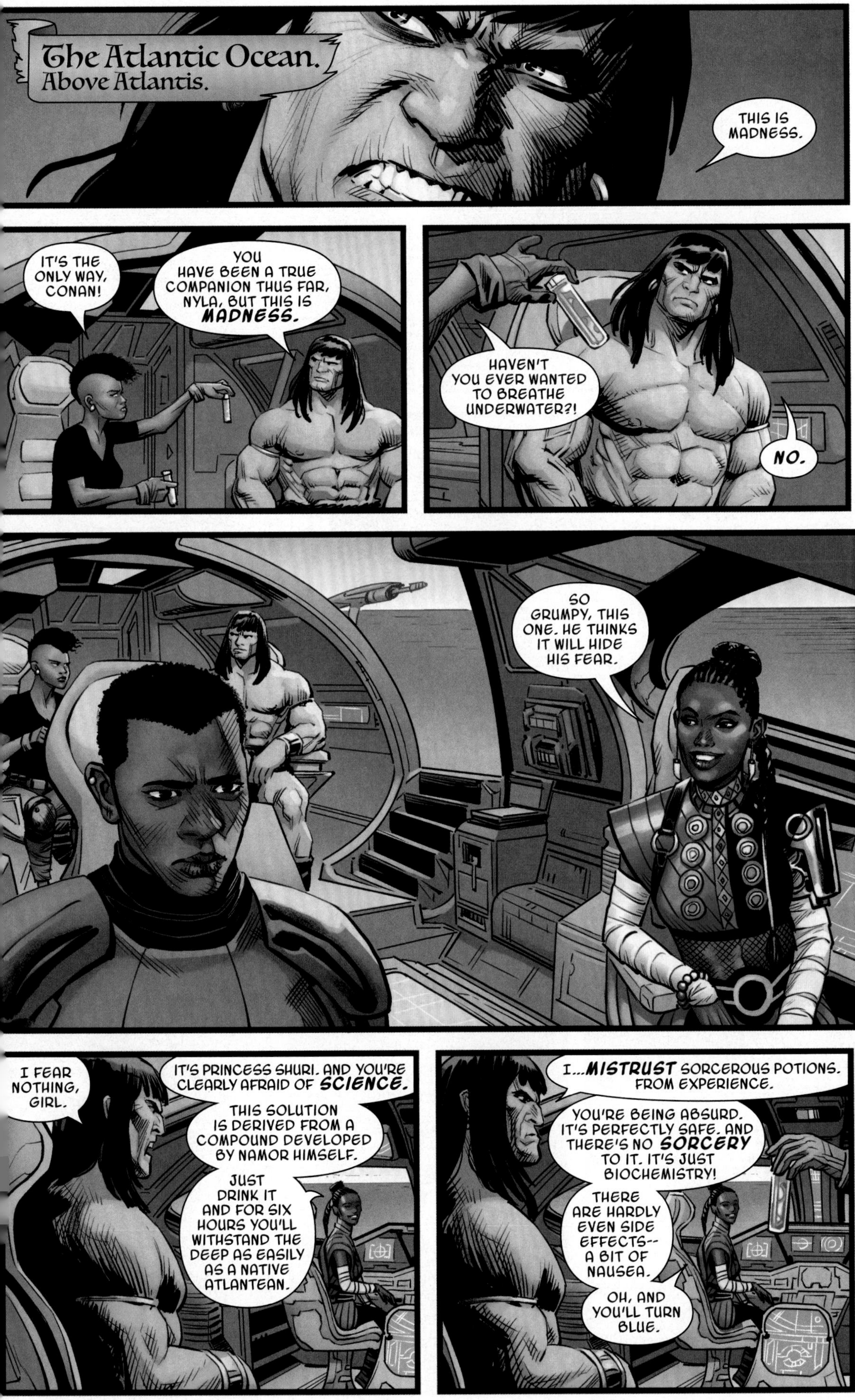
The Atlantic Ocean.
Above Atlantis.
THIS IS MADNESS.
IT'S THE ONLY WAY, CONAN!
YOU HAVE BEEN A TRUE COMPANION THUS FAR, NYLA, BUT THIS IS MADNESS.
HAVEN'T YOU EVER WANTED TO BREATHE UNDERWATER?!
NO.
SO GRUMPY, THIS ONE. HE THINKS IT WILL HIDE HIS FEAR.
I FEAR NOTHING, GIRL.
IT'S PRINCESS SHURI. AND YOU'RE CLEARLY AFRAID OF SCIENCE.
THIS SOLUTION IS DERIVED FROM A COMPOUND DEVELOPED BY NAMOR HIMSELF.
JUST DRINK IT AND FOR SIX HOURS YOU'LL WITHSTAND THE DEEP AS EASILY AS A NATIVE ATLANTEAN.
I...MISTRUST SORCEROUS POTIONS. FROM EXPERIENCE.
YOU'RE BEING ABSURD. IT'S PERFECTLY SAFE. AND THERE'S NO SORCERY TO IT. IT'S JUST BIOCHEMISTRY!
THERE ARE HARDLY EVEN SIDE EFFECTS-- A BIT OF NAUSEA.
OH, AND YOU'LL TURN BLUE.

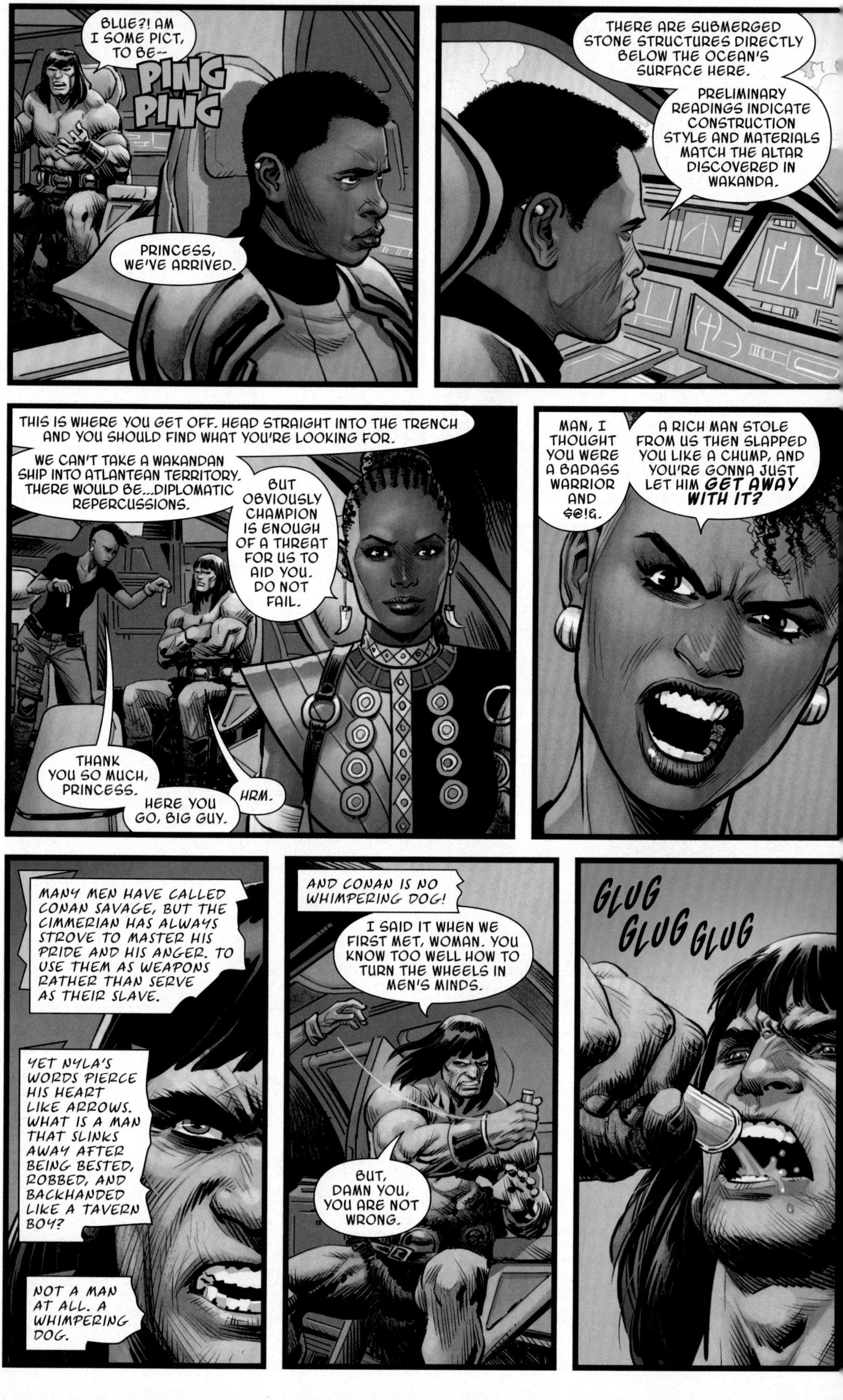
BLUE?! AM I SOME PICT, TO BE--
PING PING
PRINCESS, WE'VE ARRIVED.
THERE ARE SUBMERGED STONE STRUCTURES DIRECTLY BELOW THE OCEAN'S SURFACE HERE.
PRELIMINARY READINGS INDICATE CONSTRUCTION STYLE AND MATERIALS MATCH THE ALTAR DISCOVERED IN WAKANDA.
THIS IS WHERE YOU GET OFF. HEAD STRAIGHT INTO THE TRENCH AND YOU SHOULD FIND WHAT YOU'RE LOOKING FOR.
WE CAN'T TAKE A WAKANDAN SHIP INTO ATLANTEAN TERRITORY. THERE WOULD BE...DIPLOMATIC REPERCUSSIONS.
BUT OBVIOUSLY CHAMPION IS ENOUGH OF A THREAT FOR US TO AID YOU. DO NOT FAIL.
THANK YOU SO MUCH, PRINCESS.
HERE YOU GO, BIG GUY.
HRM.
MAN, I THOUGHT YOU WERE A BADASS WARRIOR AND $@!&.
A RICH MAN STOLE FROM US THEN SLAPPED YOU LIKE A CHUMP, AND YOU'RE GONNA JUST LET HIM GET AWAY WITH IT?
MANY MEN HAVE CALLED CONAN SAVAGE, BUT THE CIMMERIAN HAS ALWAYS STROVE TO MASTER HIS PRIDE AND HIS ANGER. TO USE THEM AS WEAPONS RATHER THAN SERVE AS THEIR SLAVE.
YET NYLA'S WORDS PIERCE HIS HEART LIKE ARROWS. WHAT IS A MAN THAT SLINKS AWAY AFTER BEING BESTED, ROBBED, AND BACKHANDED LIKE A TAVERN BOY?
NOT A MAN AT ALL. A WHIMPERING DOG.
AND CONAN IS NO WHIMPERING DOG!
I SAID IT WHEN WE FIRST MET, WOMAN. YOU KNOW TOO WELL HOW TO TURN THE WHEELS IN MEN'S MINDS.
BUT, DAMN YOU, YOU ARE NOT WRONG.
GLUG GLUG GLUG

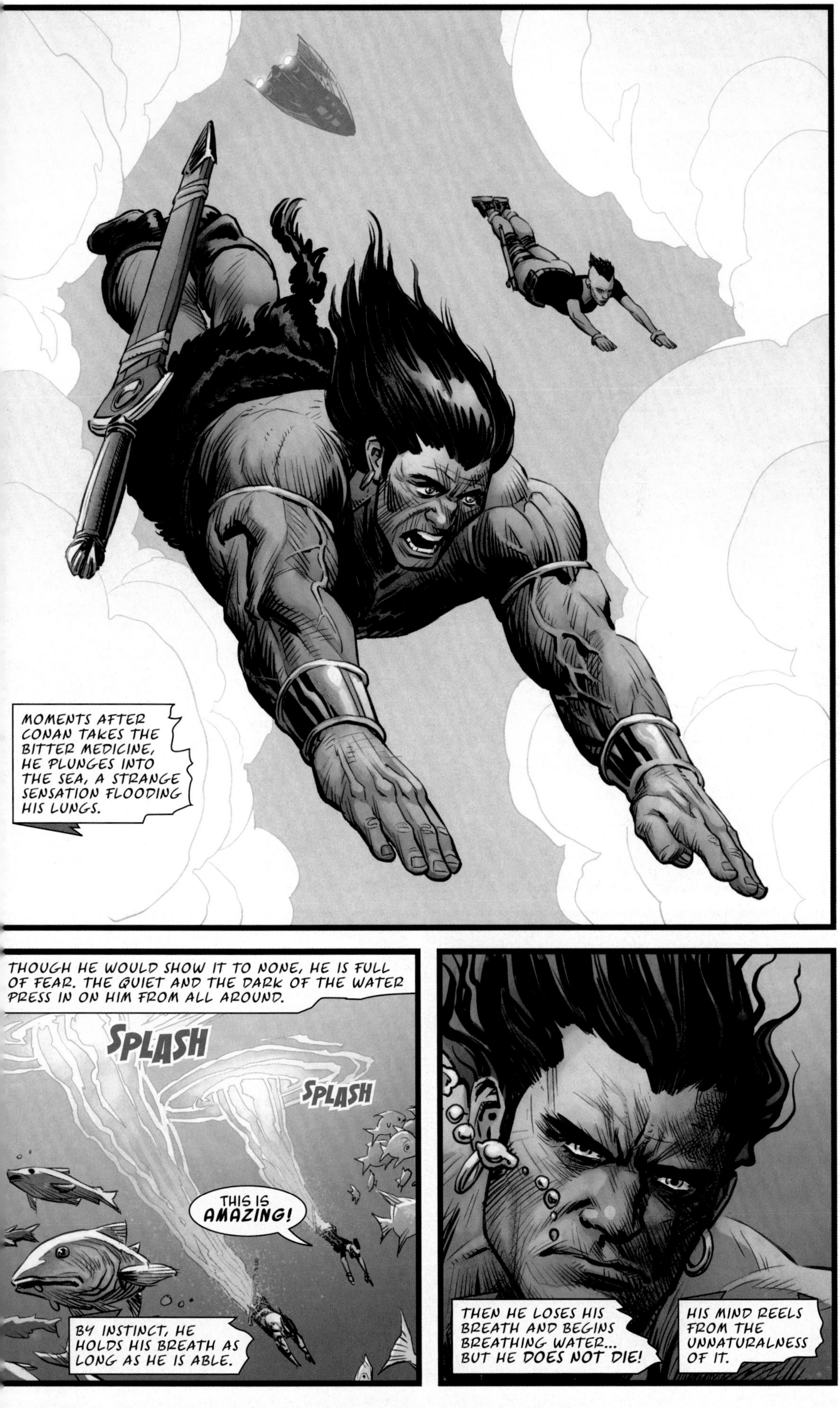
MOMENTS AFTER CONAN TAKES THE BITTER MEDICINE, HE PLUNGES INTO THE SEA, A STRANGE SENSATION FLOODING HIS LUNGS.
THOUGH HE WOULD SHOW IT TO NONE, HE IS FULL OF FEAR. THE QUIET AND THE DARK OF THE WATER PRESS IN ON HIM FROM ALL AROUND.
SPLASH
SPLASH
THIS IS AMAZING!
BY INSTINCT, HE HOLDS HIS BREATH AS LONG AS HE IS ABLE.
THEN HE LOSES HIS BREATH AND BEGINS BREATHING WATER... BUT HE DOES NOT DIE!
HIS MIND REELS FROM THE UNNATURALNESS OF IT.

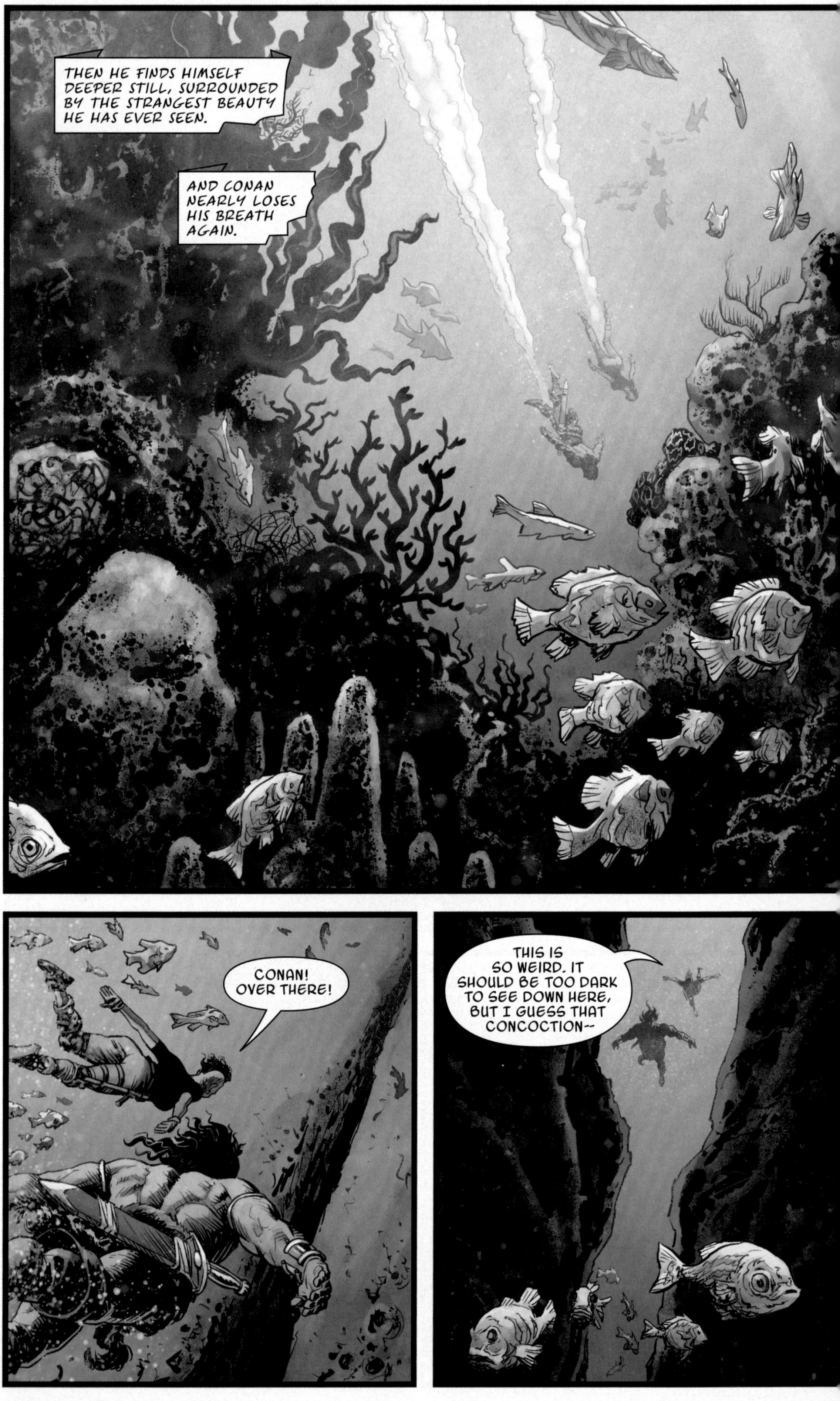
THEN HE FINDS HIMSELF DEEPER STILL, SURROUNDED BY THE STRANGEST BEAUTY HE HAS EVER SEEN.
AND CONAN NEARLY LOSES HIS BREATH AGAIN.
CONAN! OVER THERE!
THIS IS SO WEIRD. IT SHOULD BE TOO DARK TO SEE DOWN HERE, BUT I GUESS THAT CONCOCTION--

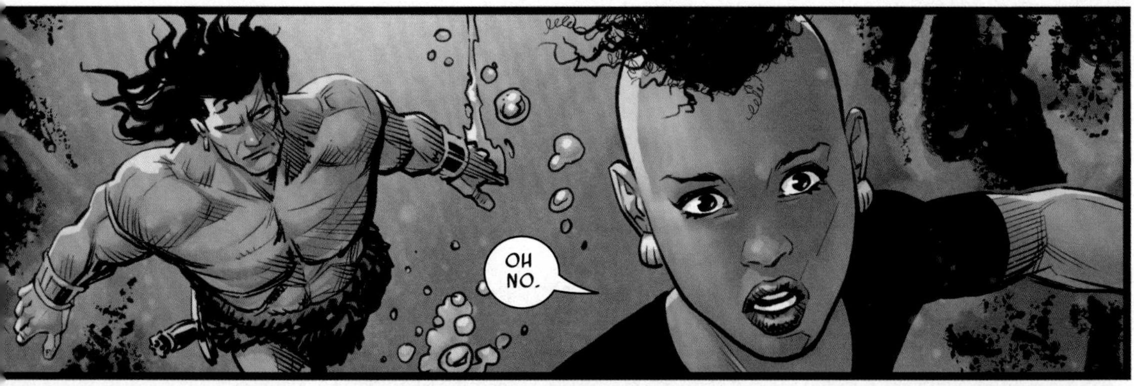
OH NO.

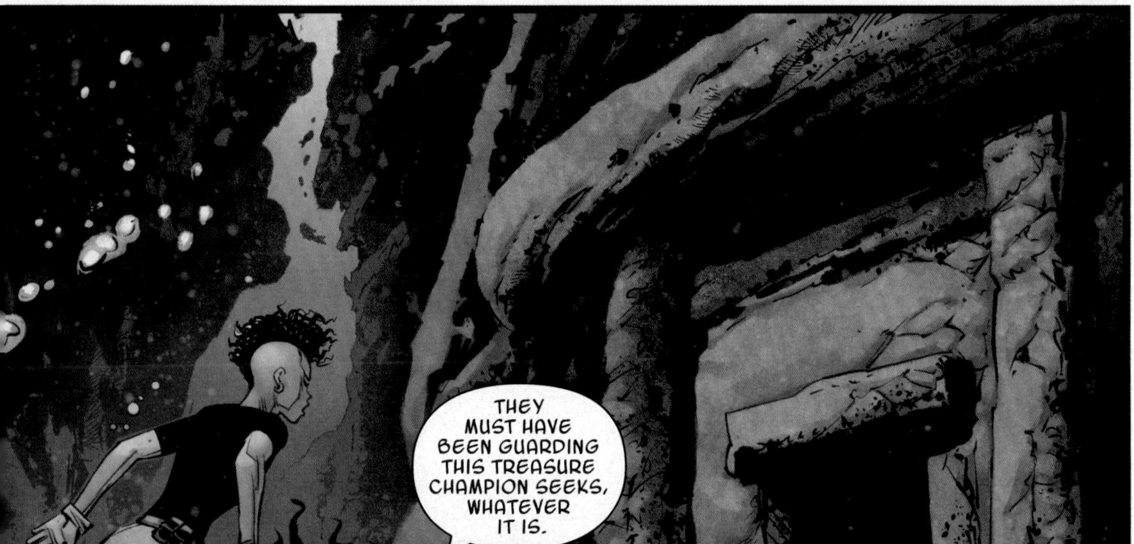
THEY MUST HAVE BEEN GUARDING THIS TREASURE CHAMPION SEEKS, WHATEVER IT IS.

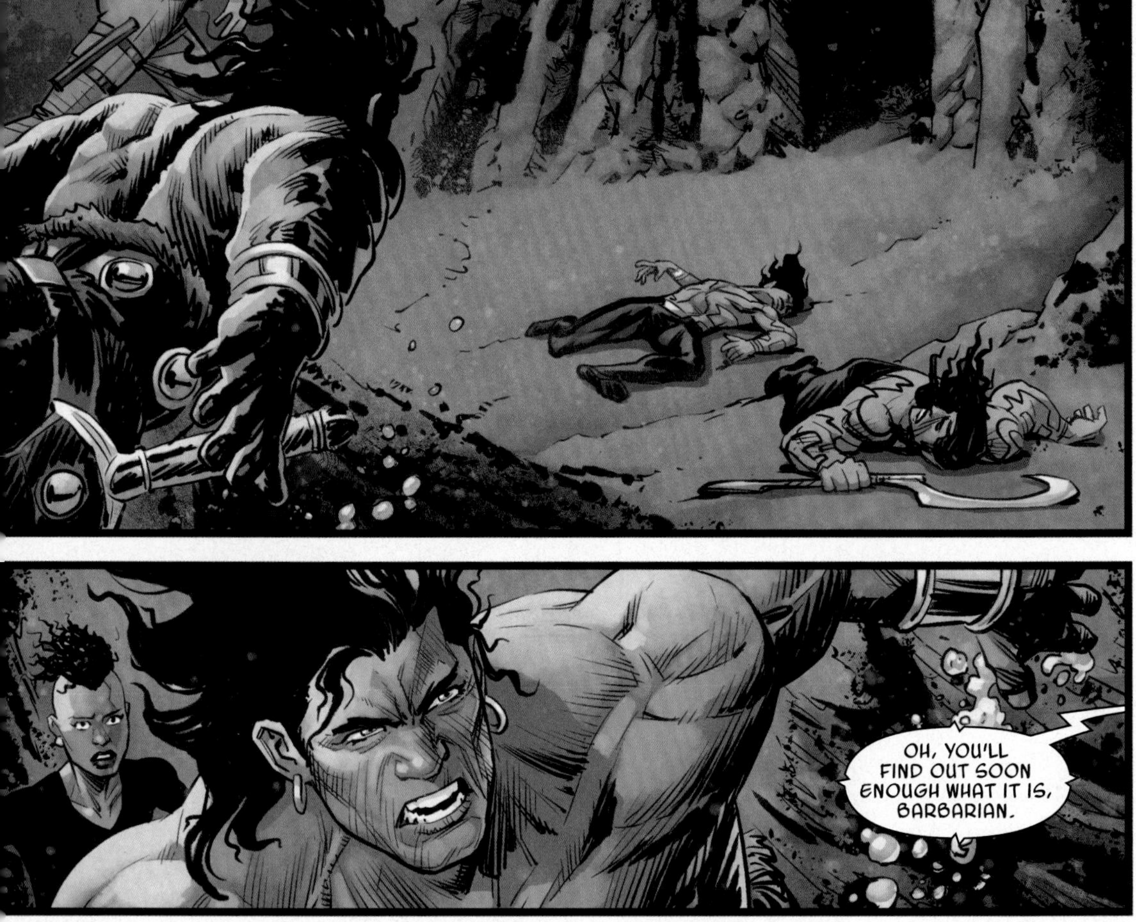
OH, YOU'LL FIND OUT SOON ENOUGH WHAT IT IS, BARBARIAN.

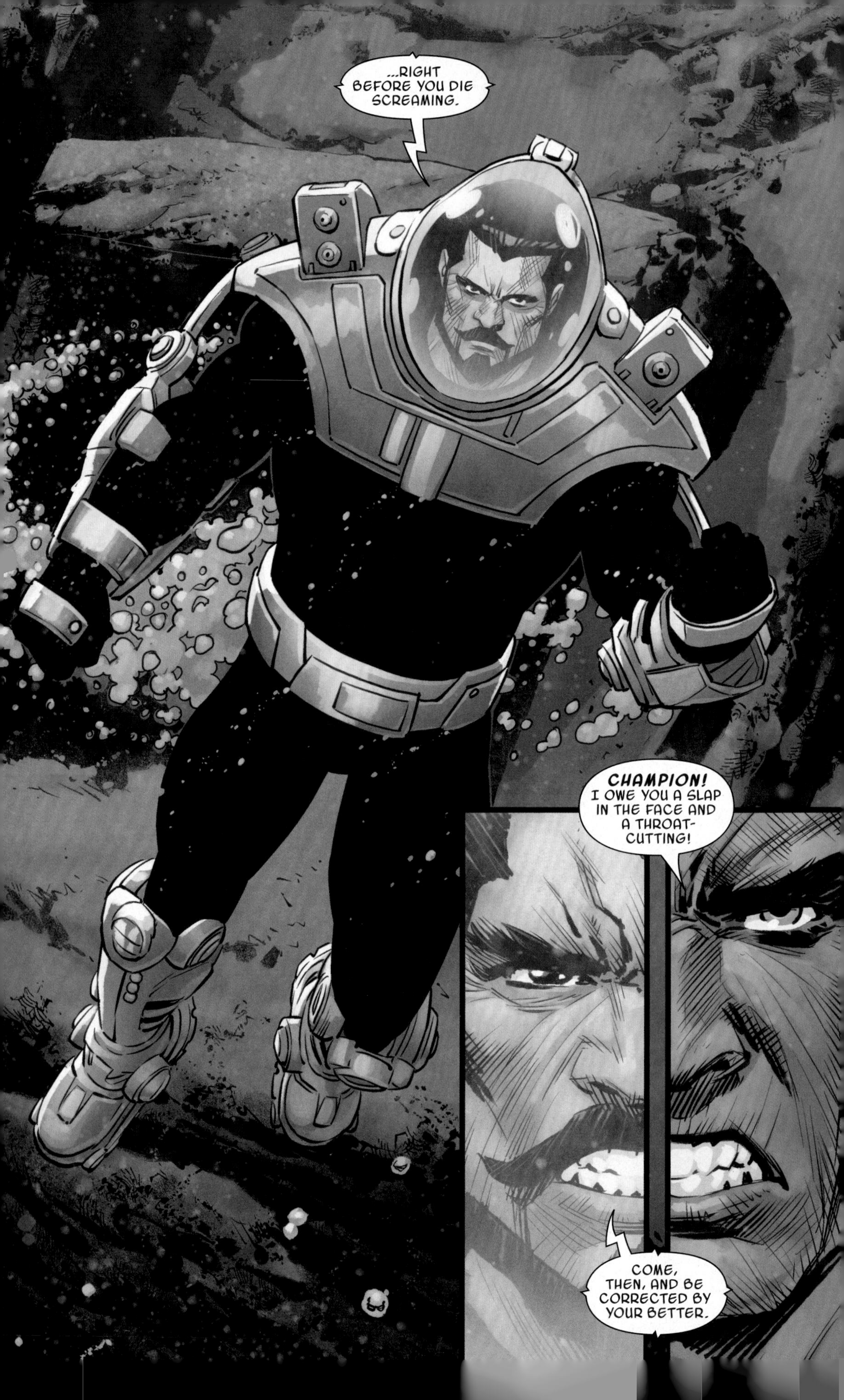
...RIGHT BEFORE YOU DIE SCREAMING.
CHAMPION! I OWE YOU A SLAP IN THE FACE AND A THROAT-CUTTING!
COME, THEN, AND BE CORRECTED BY YOUR BETTER.

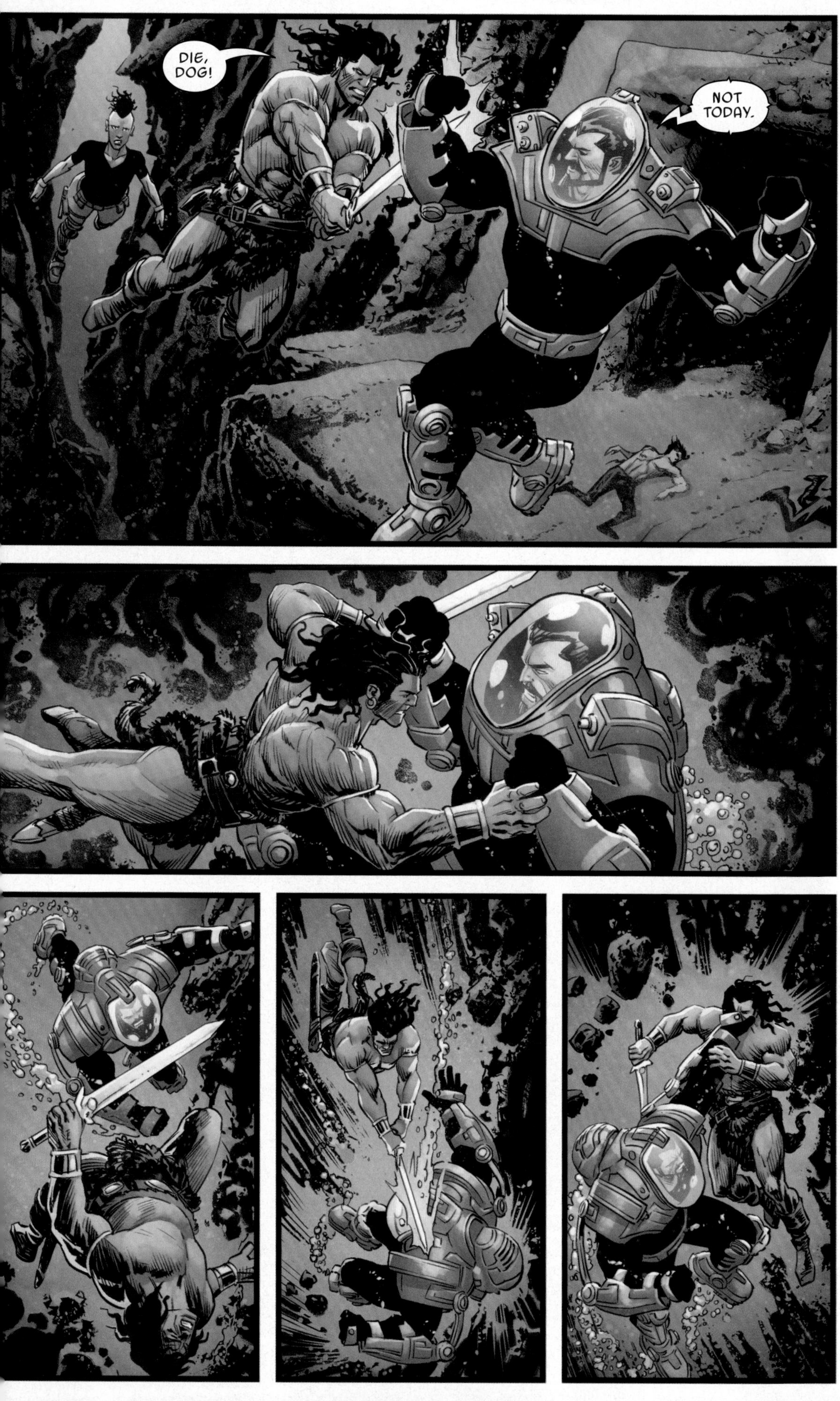
DIE, DOG!
NOT TODAY.

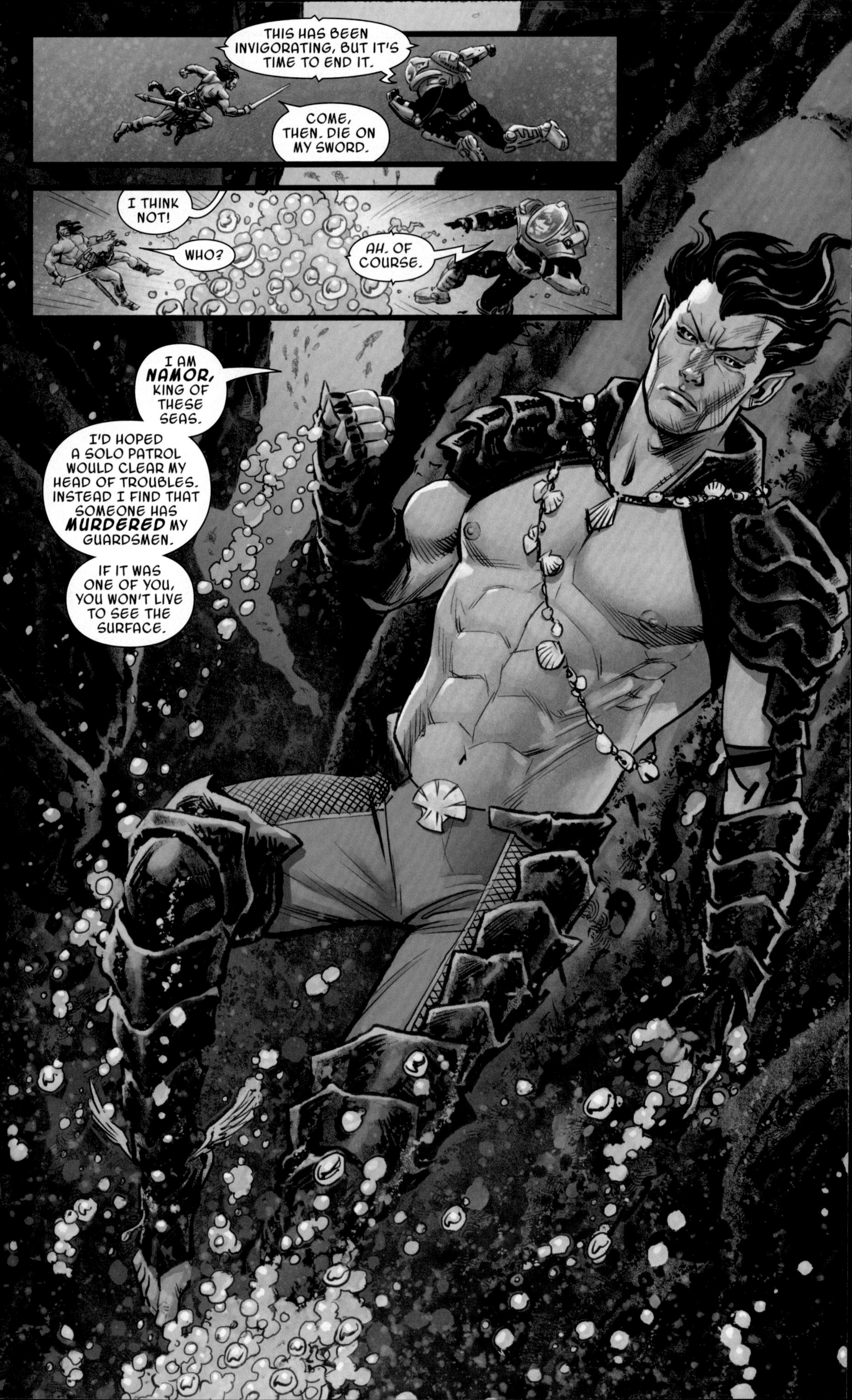
THIS HAS BEEN INVIGORATING, BUT IT'S TIME TO END IT.
COME, THEN. DIE ON MY SWORD.
I THINK NOT!
WHO?
AH. OF COURSE.
I AM **NAMOR,** KING OF THESE SEAS.
I'D HOPED A SOLO PATROL WOULD CLEAR MY HEAD OF TROUBLES. INSTEAD I FIND THAT SOMEONE HAS **MURDERED** MY GUARDSMEN.
IF IT WAS ONE OF YOU, YOU WON'T LIVE TO SEE THE SURFACE.

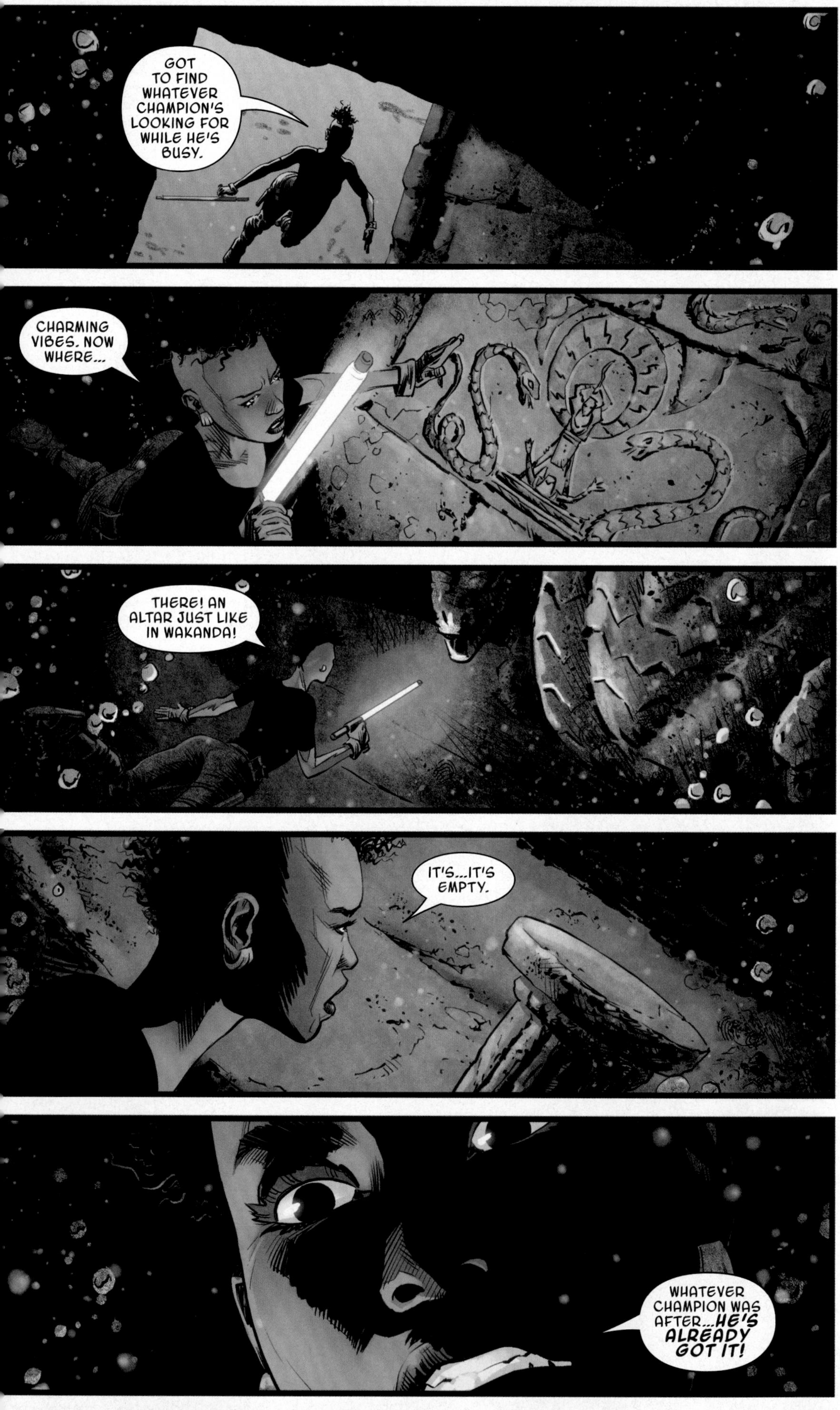
GOT TO FIND WHATEVER CHAMPION'S LOOKING FOR WHILE HE'S BUSY.
CHARMING VIBES. NOW WHERE...
THERE! AN ALTAR JUST LIKE IN WAKANDA!
IT'S...IT'S EMPTY.
WHATEVER CHAMPION WAS AFTER...HE'S ALREADY GOT IT!

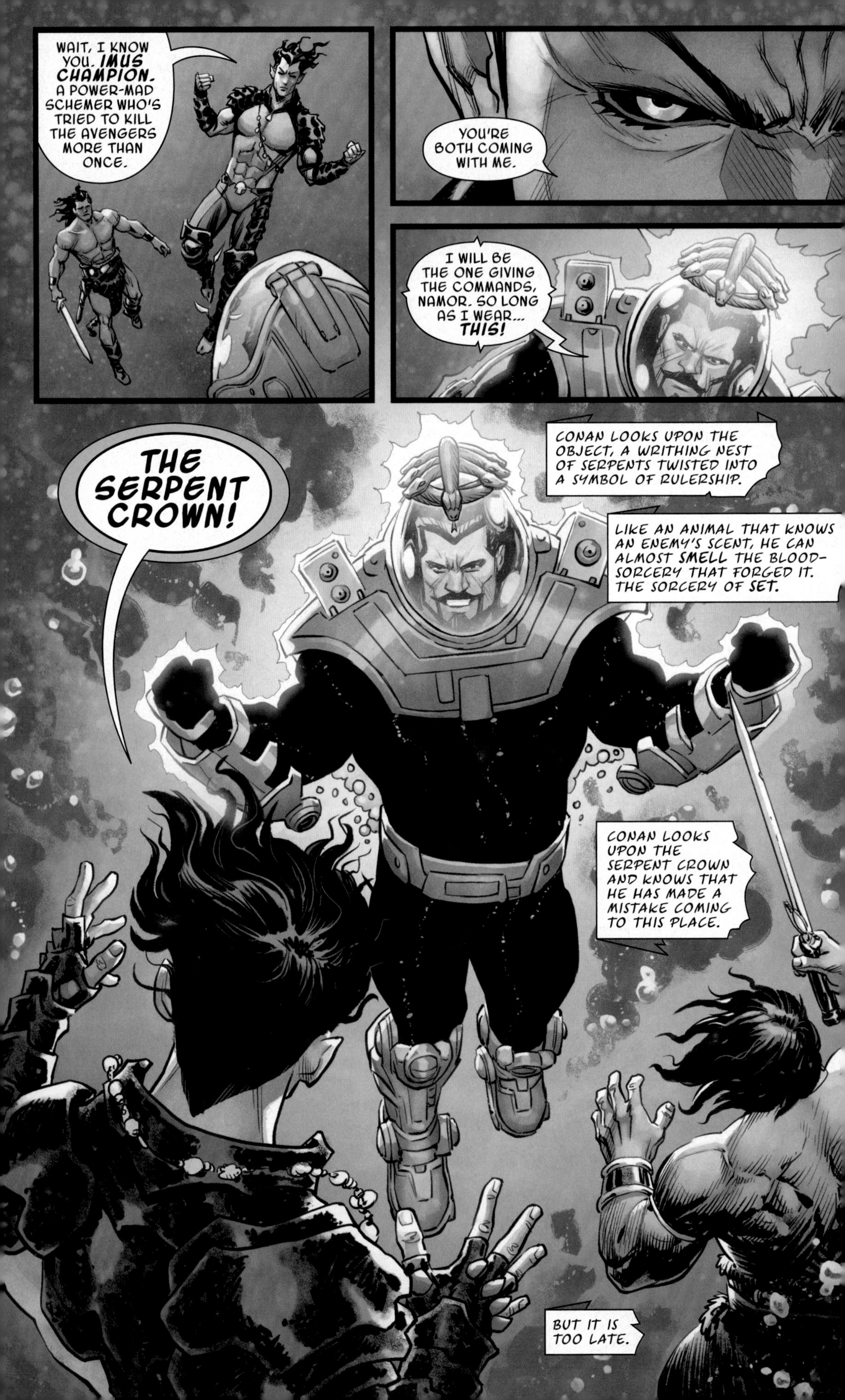
WAIT, I KNOW YOU. IMUS CHAMPION. A POWER-MAD SCHEMER WHO'S TRIED TO KILL THE AVENGERS MORE THAN ONCE.
YOU'RE BOTH COMING WITH ME.
I WILL BE THE ONE GIVING THE COMMANDS, NAMOR. SO LONG AS I WEAR... THIS!
THE SERPENT CROWN!
CONAN LOOKS UPON THE OBJECT, A WRITHING NEST OF SERPENTS TWISTED INTO A SYMBOL OF RULERSHIP.
LIKE AN ANIMAL THAT KNOWS AN ENEMY'S SCENT, HE CAN ALMOST SMELL THE BLOOD-SORCERY THAT FORGED IT. THE SORCERY OF SET.
CONAN LOOKS UPON THE SERPENT CROWN AND KNOWS THAT HE HAS MADE A MISTAKE COMING TO THIS PLACE.
BUT IT IS TOO LATE.

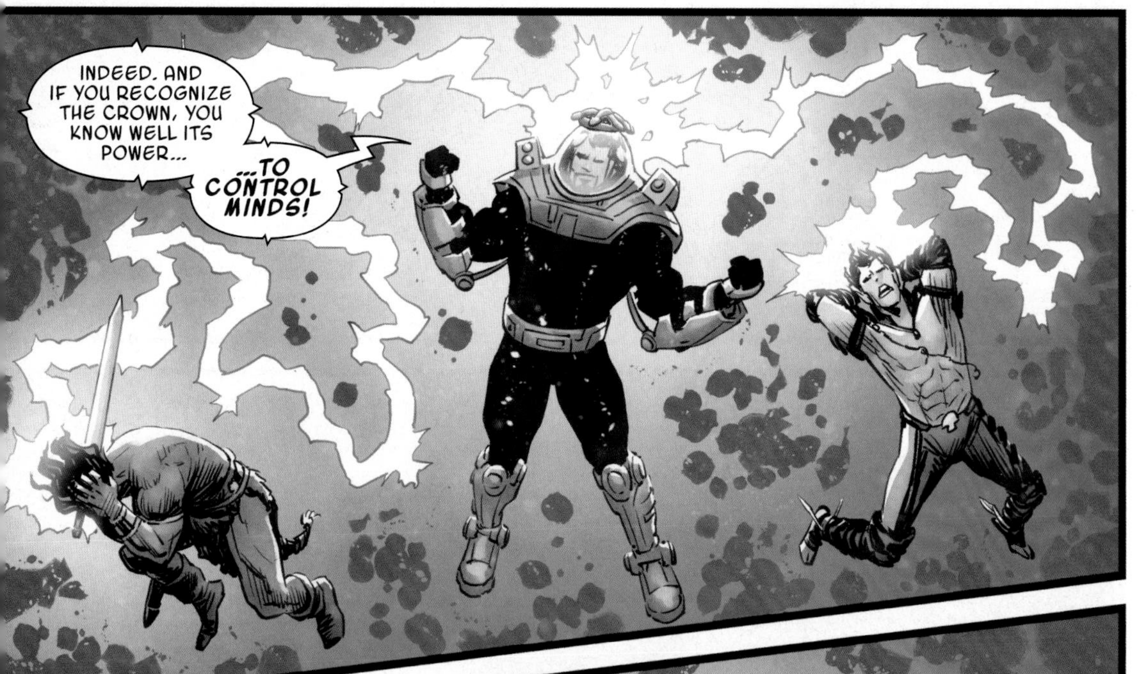
INDEED. AND IF YOU RECOGNIZE THE CROWN, YOU KNOW WELL ITS POWER...
...TO CONTROL MINDS!

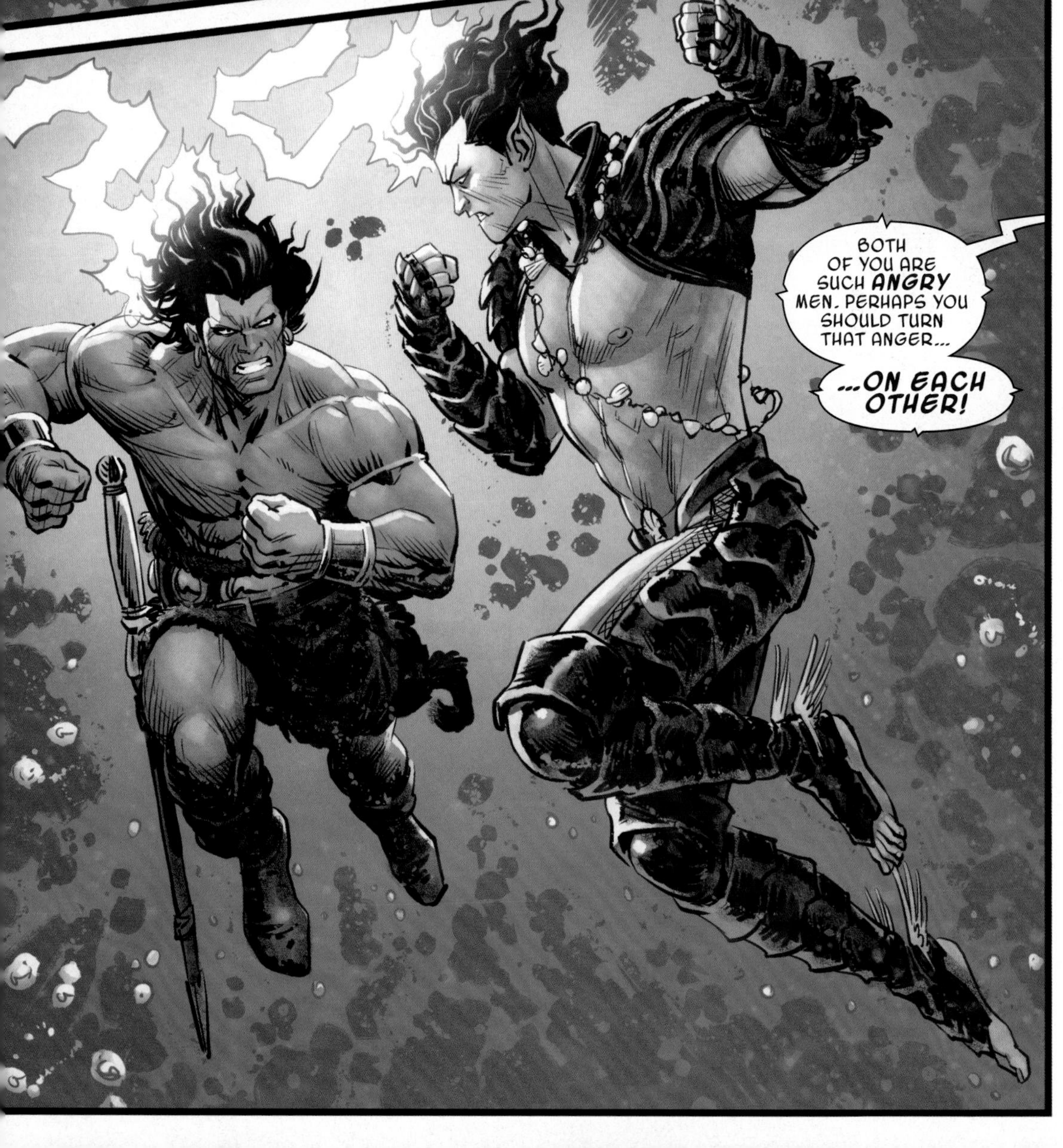
BOTH OF YOU ARE SUCH ANGRY MEN. PERHAPS YOU SHOULD TURN THAT ANGER...
...ON EACH OTHER!

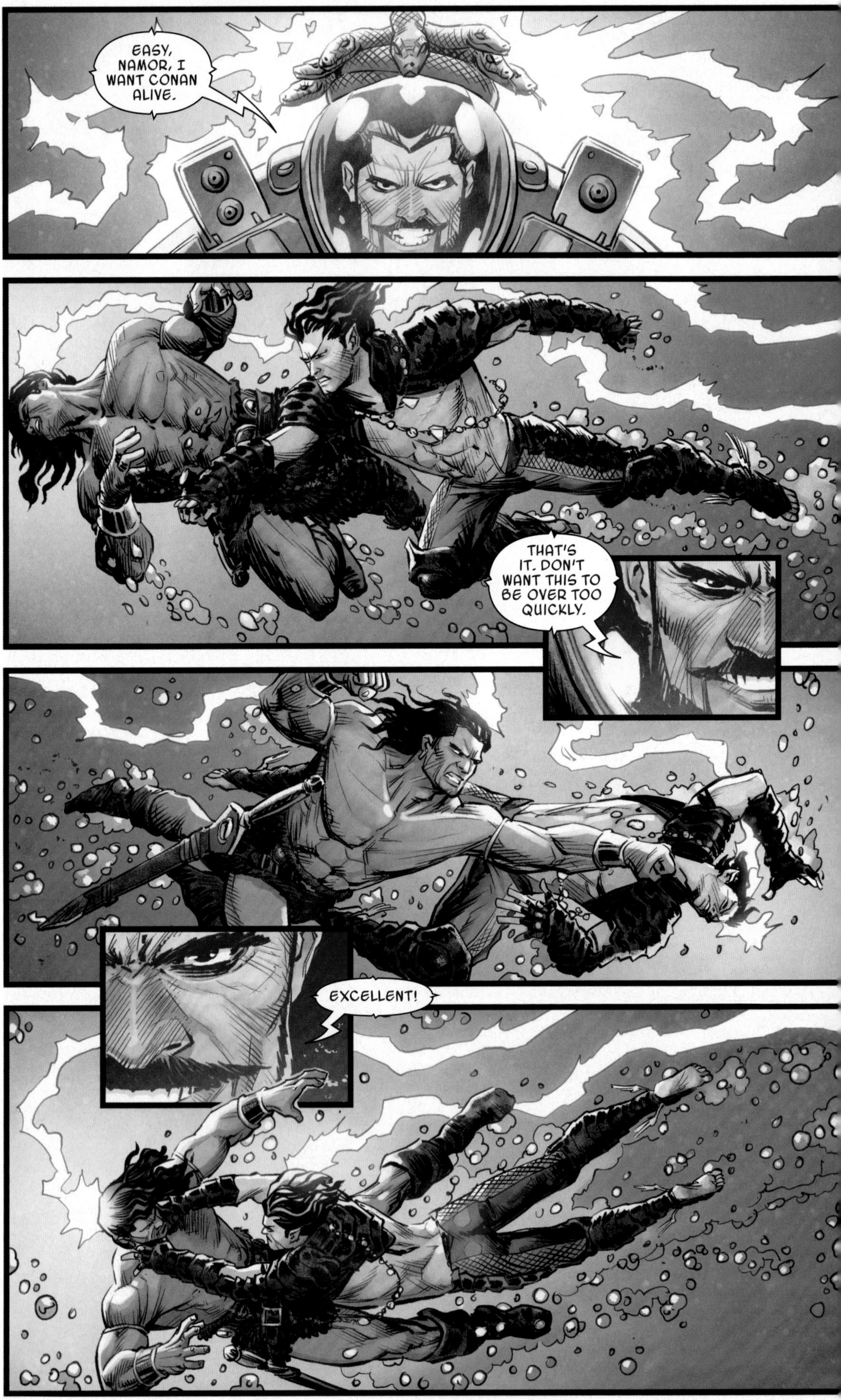
EASY, NAMOR, I WANT CONAN ALIVE.
THAT'S IT. DON'T WANT THIS TO BE OVER TOO QUICKLY.
EXCELLENT!

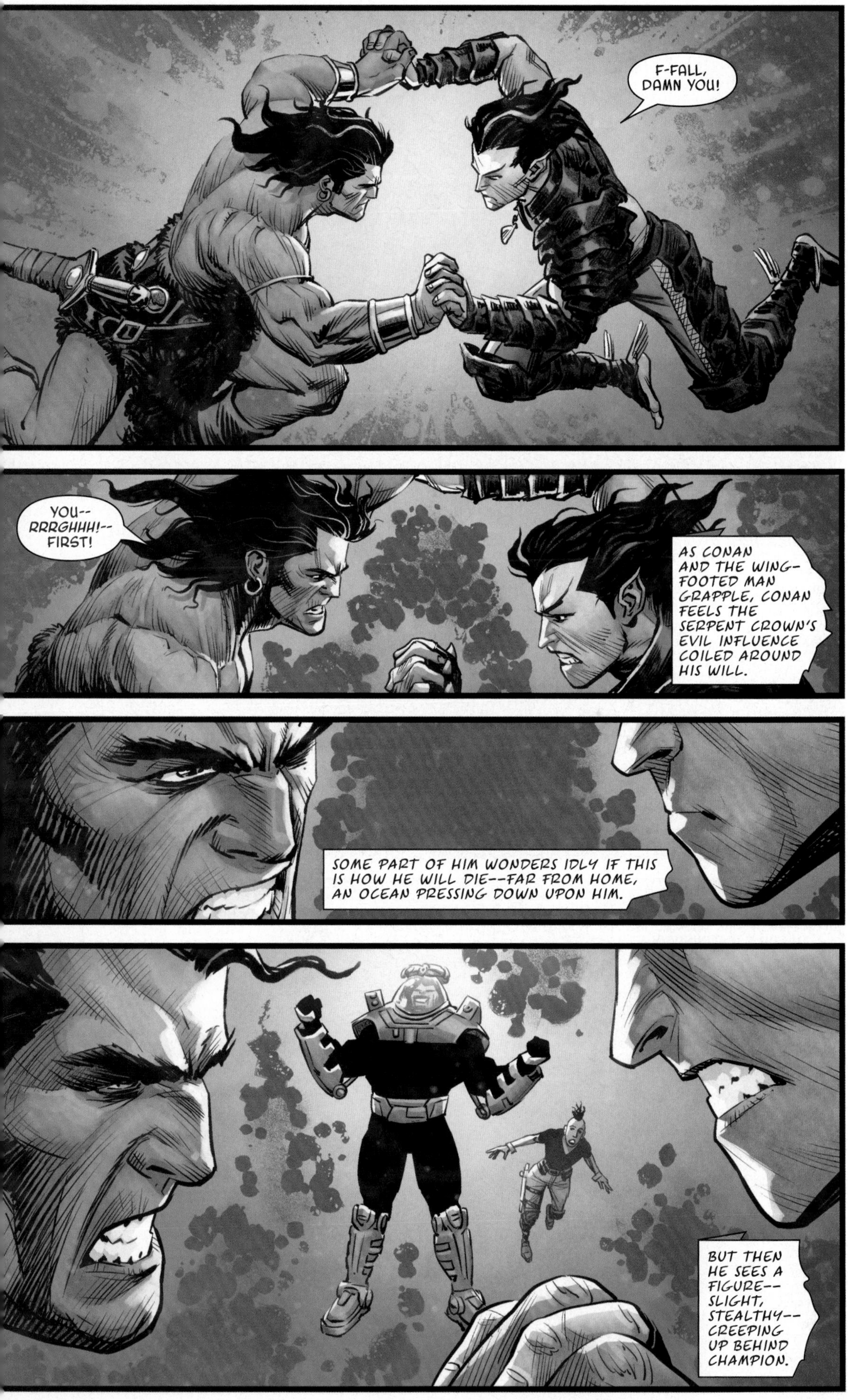
F-FALL, DAMN YOU!
YOU-- RRRGHHH!-- FIRST!
AS CONAN AND THE WING-FOOTED MAN GRAPPLE, CONAN FEELS THE SERPENT CROWN'S EVIL INFLUENCE COILED AROUND HIS WILL.
SOME PART OF HIM WONDERS IDLY IF THIS IS HOW HE WILL DIE--FAR FROM HOME, AN OCEAN PRESSING DOWN UPON HIM.
BUT THEN HE SEES A FIGURE-- SLIGHT, STEALTHY-- CREEPING UP BEHIND CHAMPION.

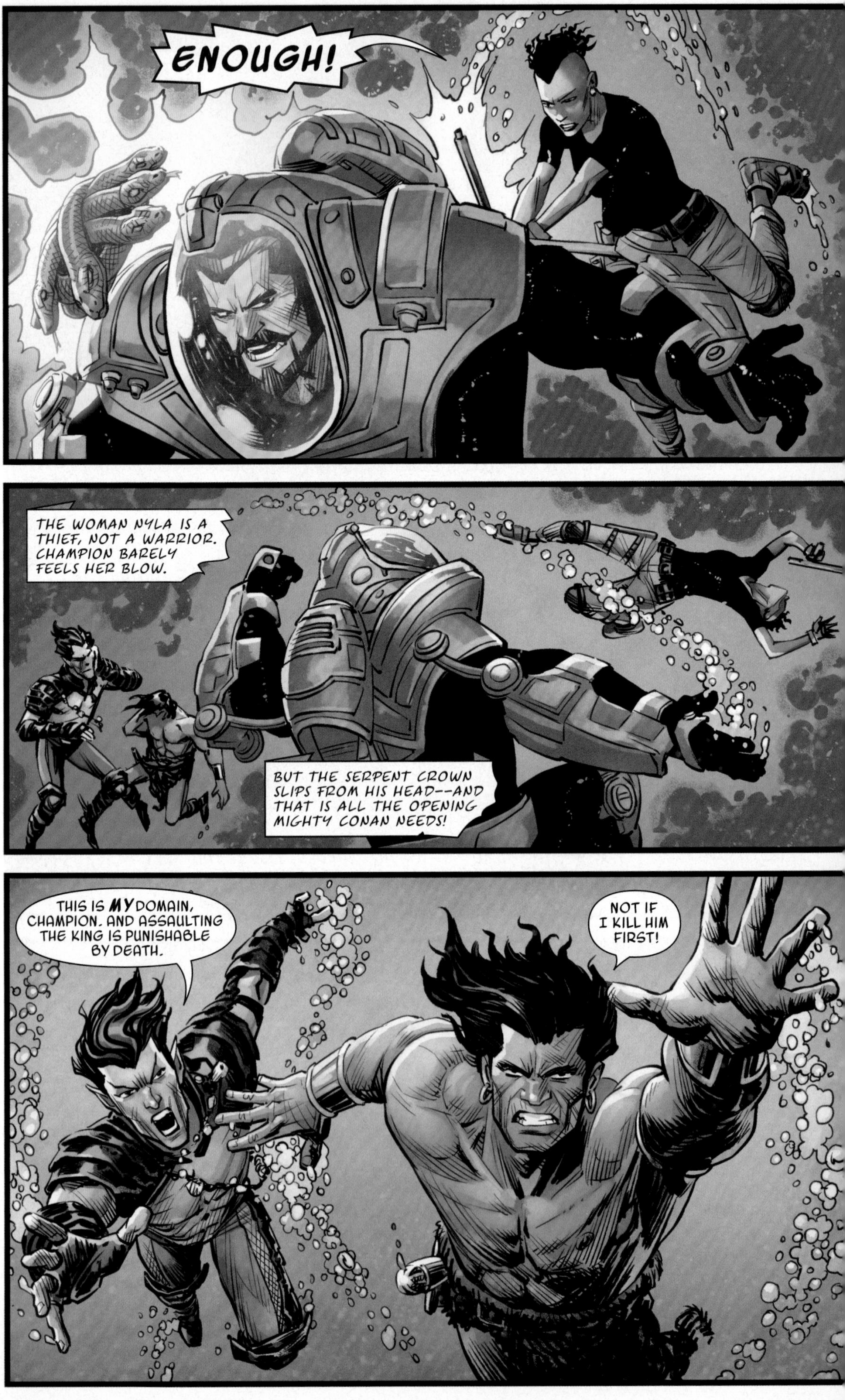
ENOUGH!
THE WOMAN NYLA IS A THIEF, NOT A WARRIOR. CHAMPION BARELY FEELS HER BLOW.
BUT THE SERPENT CROWN SLIPS FROM HIS HEAD--AND THAT IS ALL THE OPENING MIGHTY CONAN NEEDS!
THIS IS MY DOMAIN, CHAMPION. AND ASSAULTING THE KING IS PUNISHABLE BY DEATH.
NOT IF I KILL HIM FIRST!

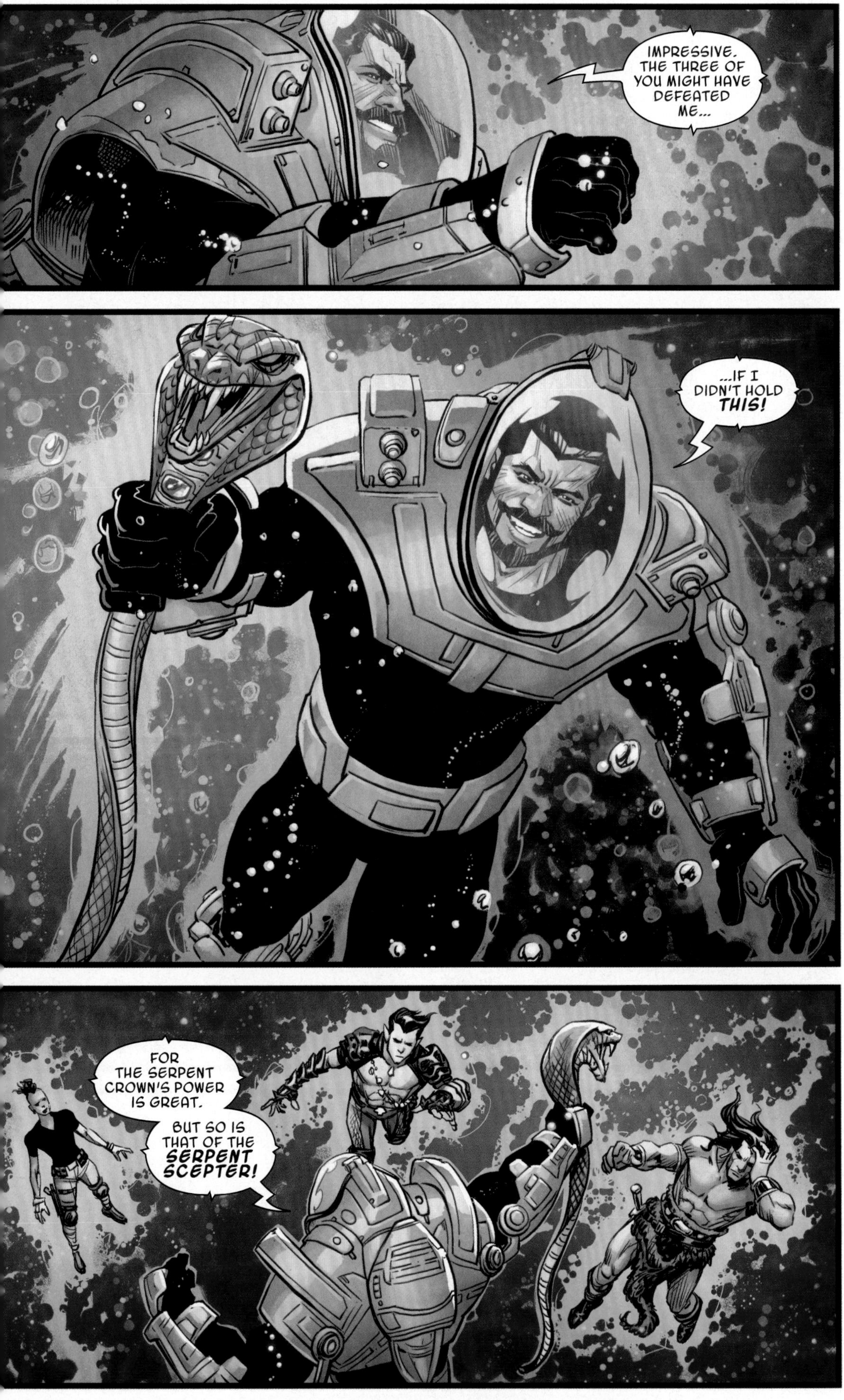
IMPRESSIVE. THE THREE OF YOU MIGHT HAVE DEFEATED ME...
...IF I DIDN'T HOLD THIS!
FOR THE SERPENT CROWN'S POWER IS GREAT.
BUT SO IS THAT OF THE SERPENT SCEPTER!

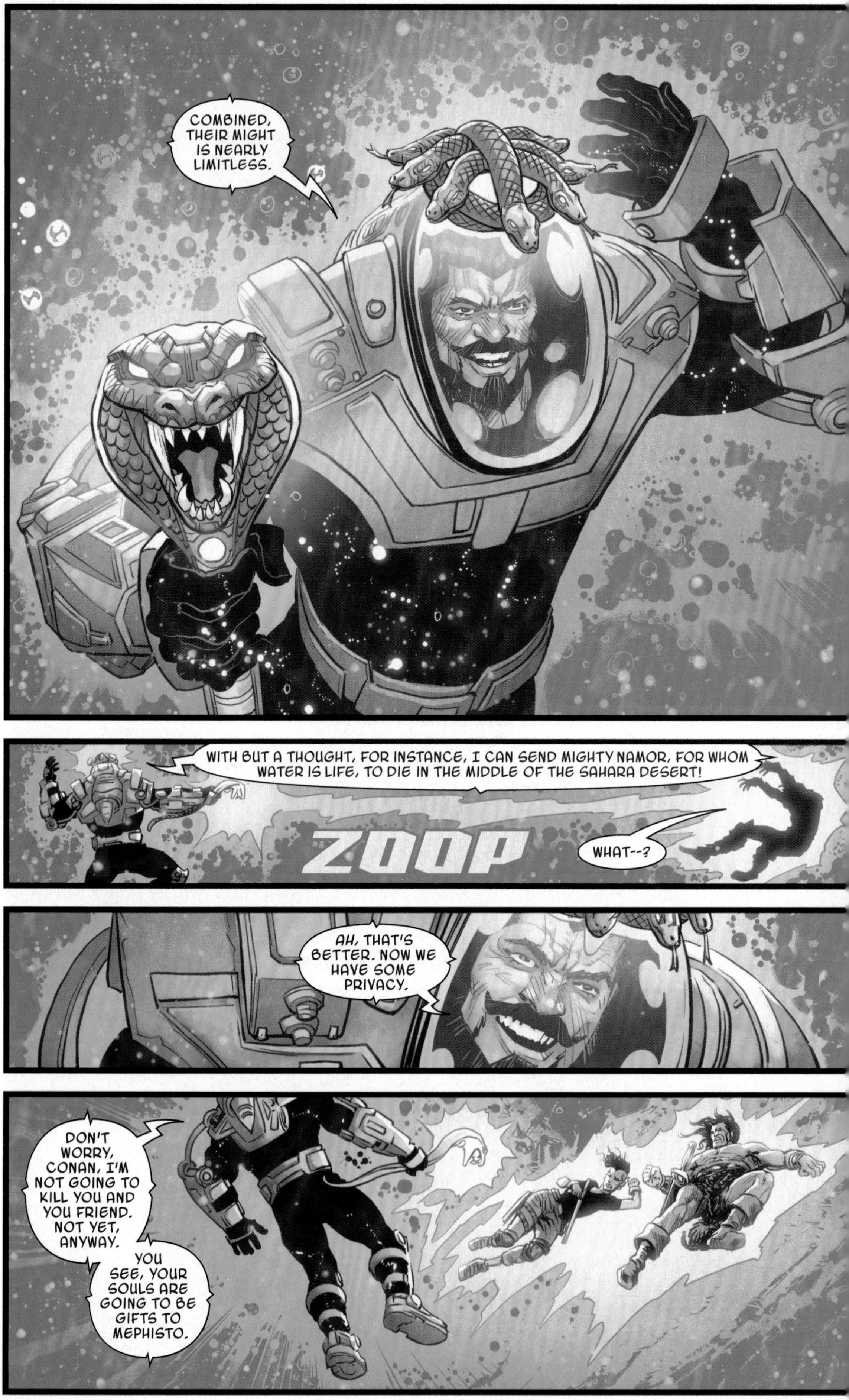
COMBINED, THEIR MIGHT IS NEARLY LIMITLESS.
WITH BUT A THOUGHT, FOR INSTANCE, I CAN SEND MIGHTY NAMOR, FOR WHOM WATER IS LIFE, TO DIE IN THE MIDDLE OF THE SAHARA DESERT!
ZOOP
WHAT--?
AH, THAT'S BETTER. NOW WE HAVE SOME PRIVACY.
DON'T WORRY, CONAN, I'M NOT GOING TO KILL YOU AND YOU FRIEND. NOT YET, ANYWAY.
YOU SEE, YOUR SOULS ARE GOING TO BE GIFTS TO MEPHISTO.

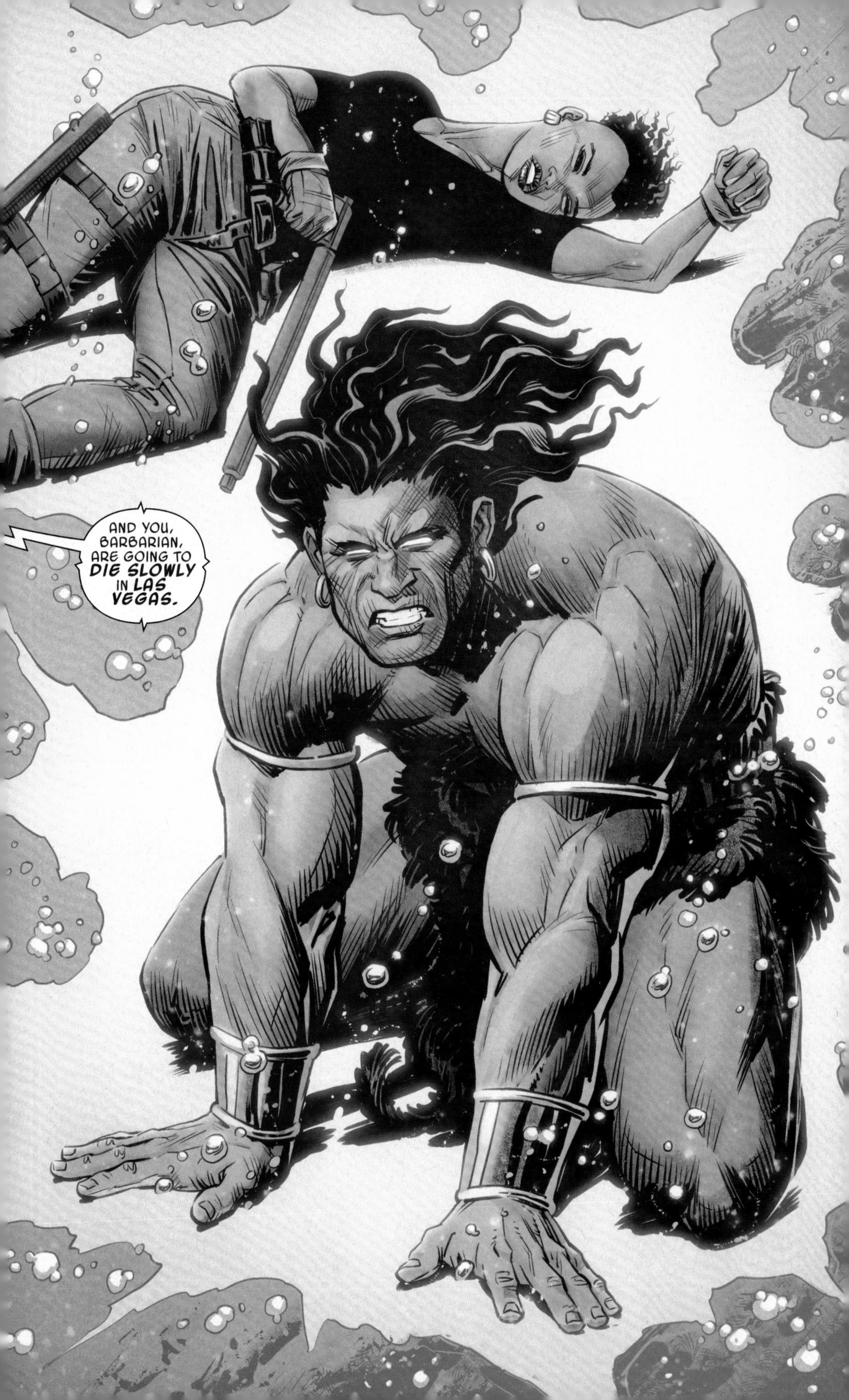
AND YOU, BARBARIAN, ARE GOING TO DIE SLOWLY IN LAS VEGAS.

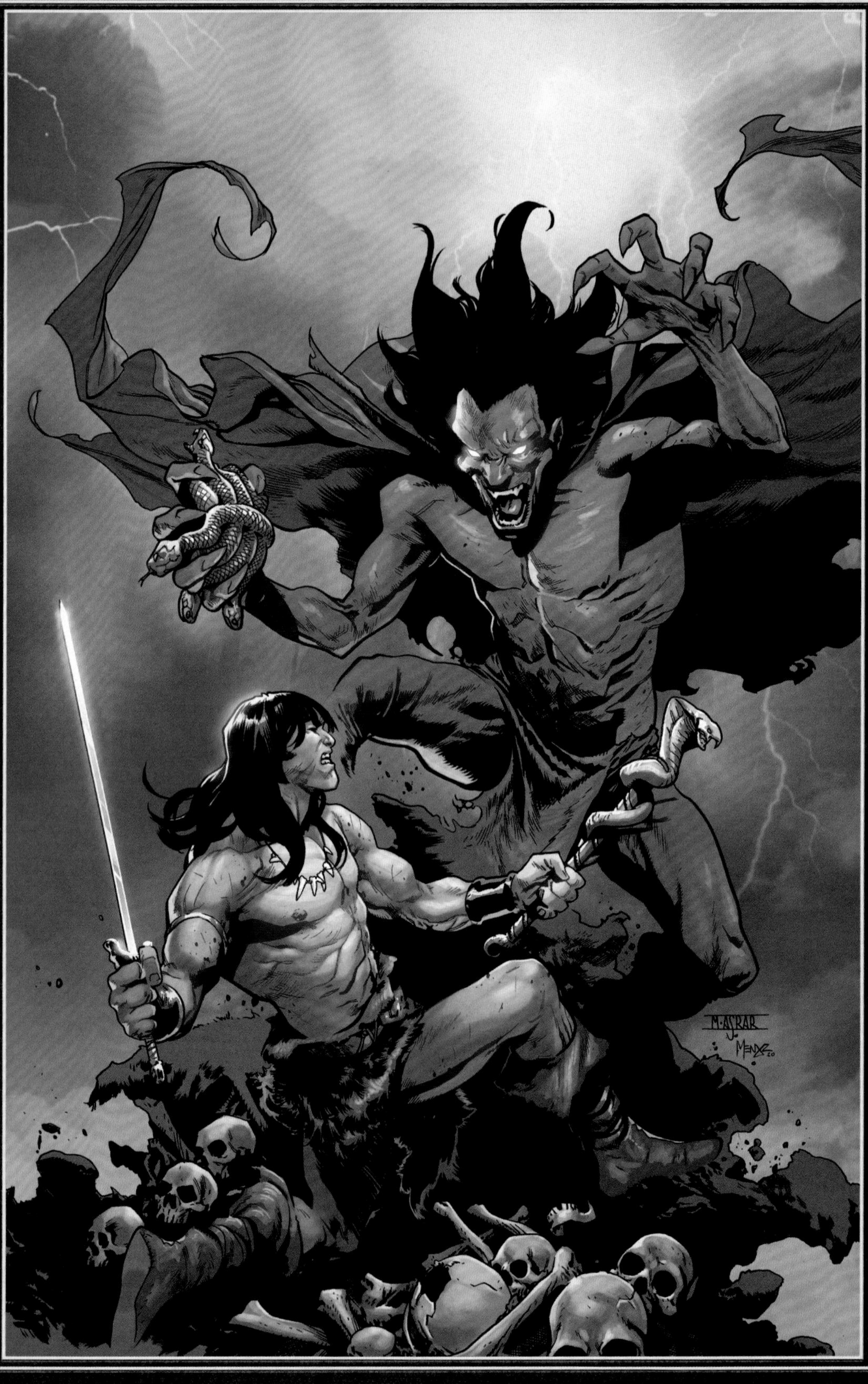
M.ASRAR

5

CONAN OF CIMMERIA STANDS IN A HYBORIAN HALL OF CHANCE, NEWLY RICH AND SURROUNDED BY WINE AND WOMEN.

YET SOMETHING IS WRONG.

THE MEAT HAS NO SCENT. THE WINE NO BITE. THE DANCER IN HIS ARMS FEELS LIKE A GHOST.

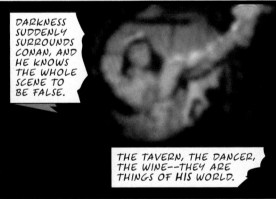

DARKNESS SUDDENLY SURROUNDS CONAN, AND HE KNOWS THE WHOLE SCENE TO BE FALSE.

THE TAVERN, THE DANCER, THE WINE--THEY ARE THINGS OF HIS WORLD.

AND AS CONAN SLOWLY ROUSES HIMSELF FROM THE BLACKNESS INTO NIGHT AIR FULL OF STRANGE SMELLS AND SOUNDS...

...HE RECALLS, AS IF WAKING INTO A DREAM...

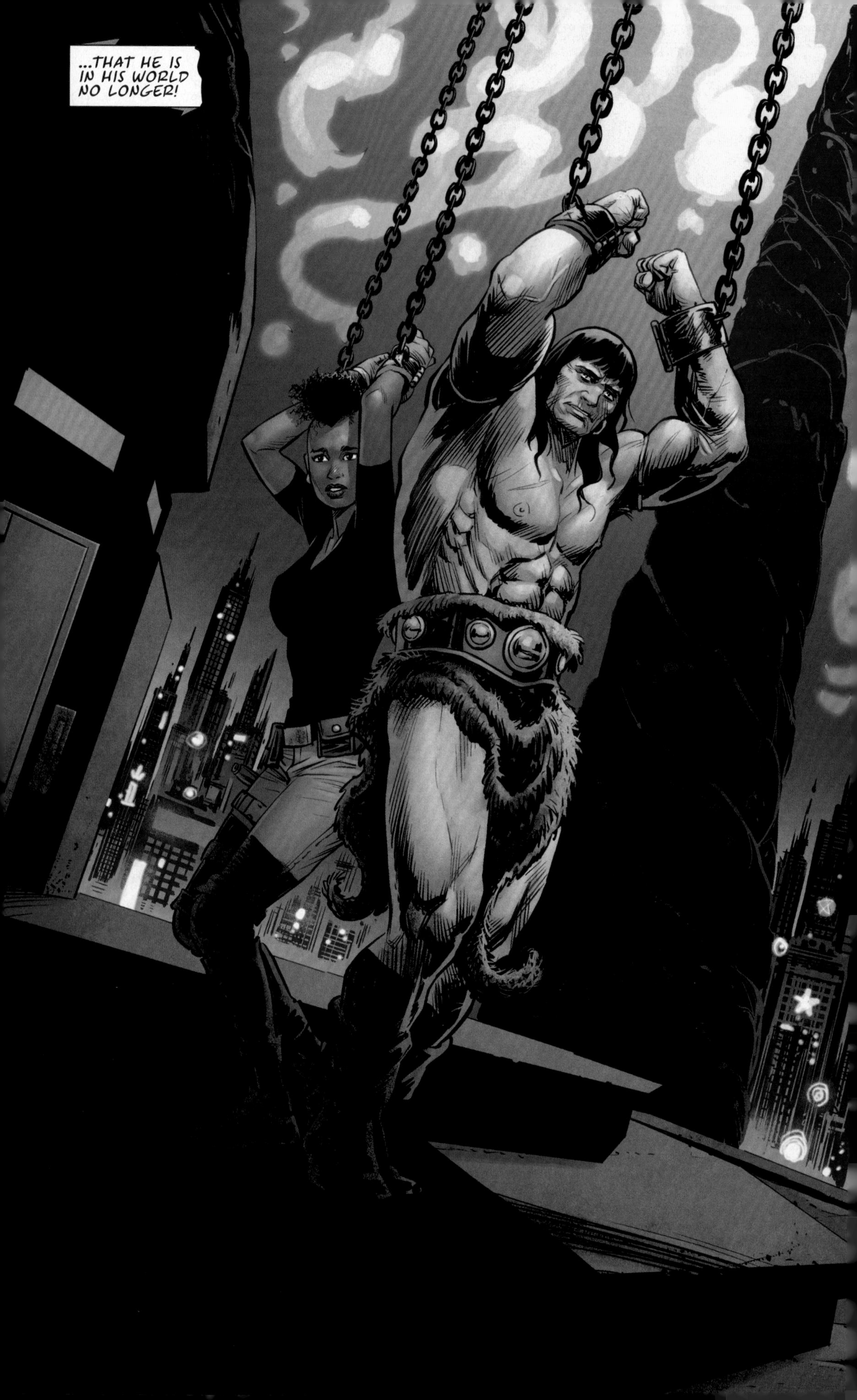
...THAT HE IS IN HIS WORLD NO LONGER!

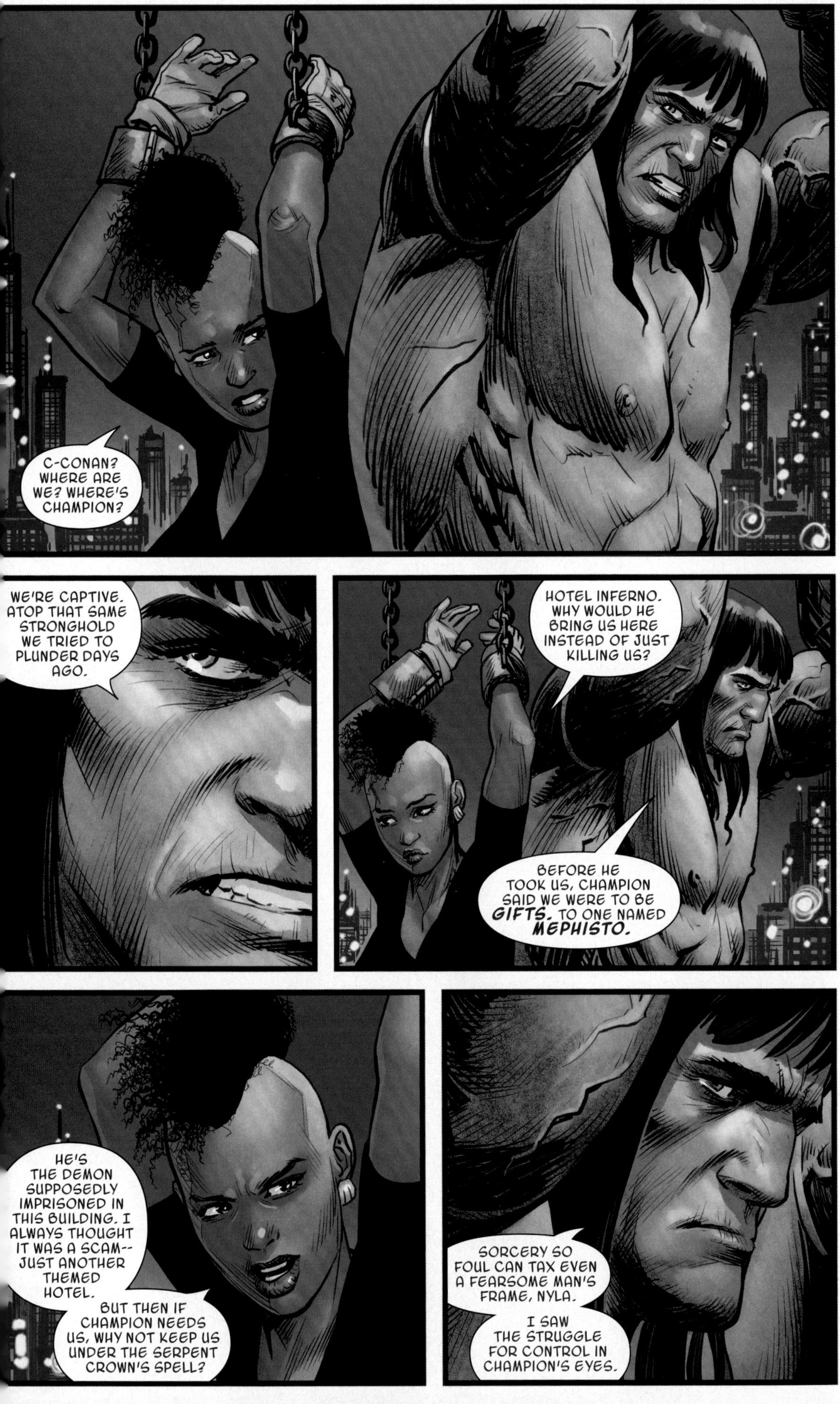
C-CONAN? WHERE ARE WE? WHERE'S CHAMPION?
WE'RE CAPTIVE. ATOP THAT SAME STRONGHOLD WE TRIED TO PLUNDER DAYS AGO.
HOTEL INFERNO. WHY WOULD HE BRING US HERE INSTEAD OF JUST KILLING US?
BEFORE HE TOOK US, CHAMPION SAID WE WERE TO BE GIFTS. TO ONE NAMED MEPHISTO.
HE'S THE DEMON SUPPOSEDLY IMPRISONED IN THIS BUILDING. I ALWAYS THOUGHT IT WAS A SCAM-- JUST ANOTHER THEMED HOTEL.
BUT THEN IF CHAMPION NEEDS US, WHY NOT KEEP US UNDER THE SERPENT CROWN'S SPELL?
SORCERY SO FOUL CAN TAX EVEN A FEARSOME MAN'S FRAME, NYLA.
I SAW THE STRUGGLE FOR CONTROL IN CHAMPION'S EYES.

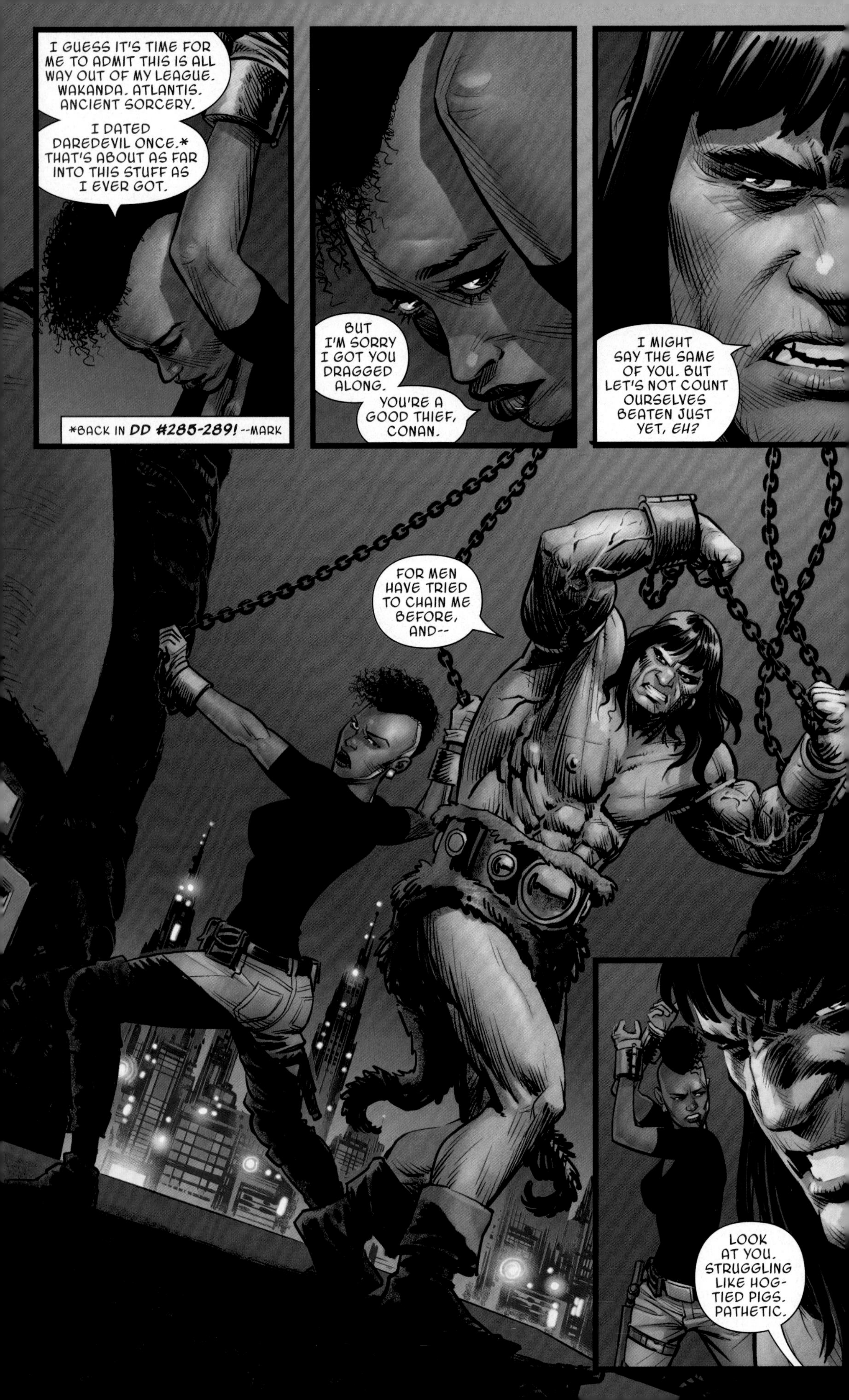
I GUESS IT'S TIME FOR ME TO ADMIT THIS IS ALL WAY OUT OF MY LEAGUE. WAKANDA. ATLANTIS. ANCIENT SORCERY.
I DATED DAREDEVIL ONCE.* THAT'S ABOUT AS FAR INTO THIS STUFF AS I EVER GOT.
*BACK IN DD #285-289! --MARK
BUT I'M SORRY I GOT YOU DRAGGED ALONG.
YOU'RE A GOOD THIEF, CONAN.
I MIGHT SAY THE SAME OF YOU. BUT LET'S NOT COUNT OURSELVES BEATEN JUST YET, EH?
FOR MEN HAVE TRIED TO CHAIN ME BEFORE, AND--
LOOK AT YOU. STRUGGLING LIKE HOG-TIED PIGS. PATHETIC.

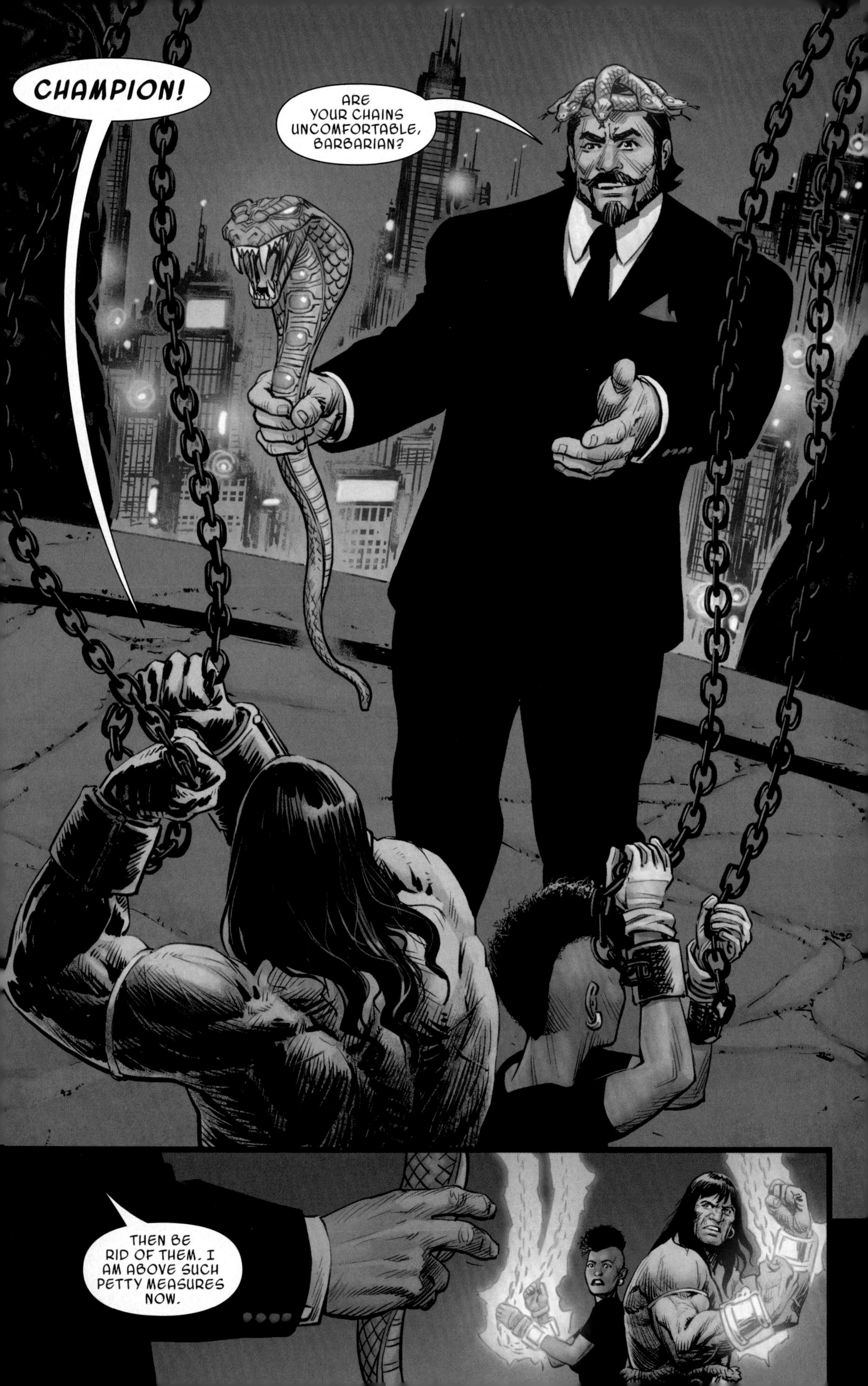
CHAMPION!
ARE YOUR CHAINS UNCOMFORTABLE, BARBARIAN?
THEN BE RID OF THEM. I AM ABOVE SUCH PETTY MEASURES NOW.

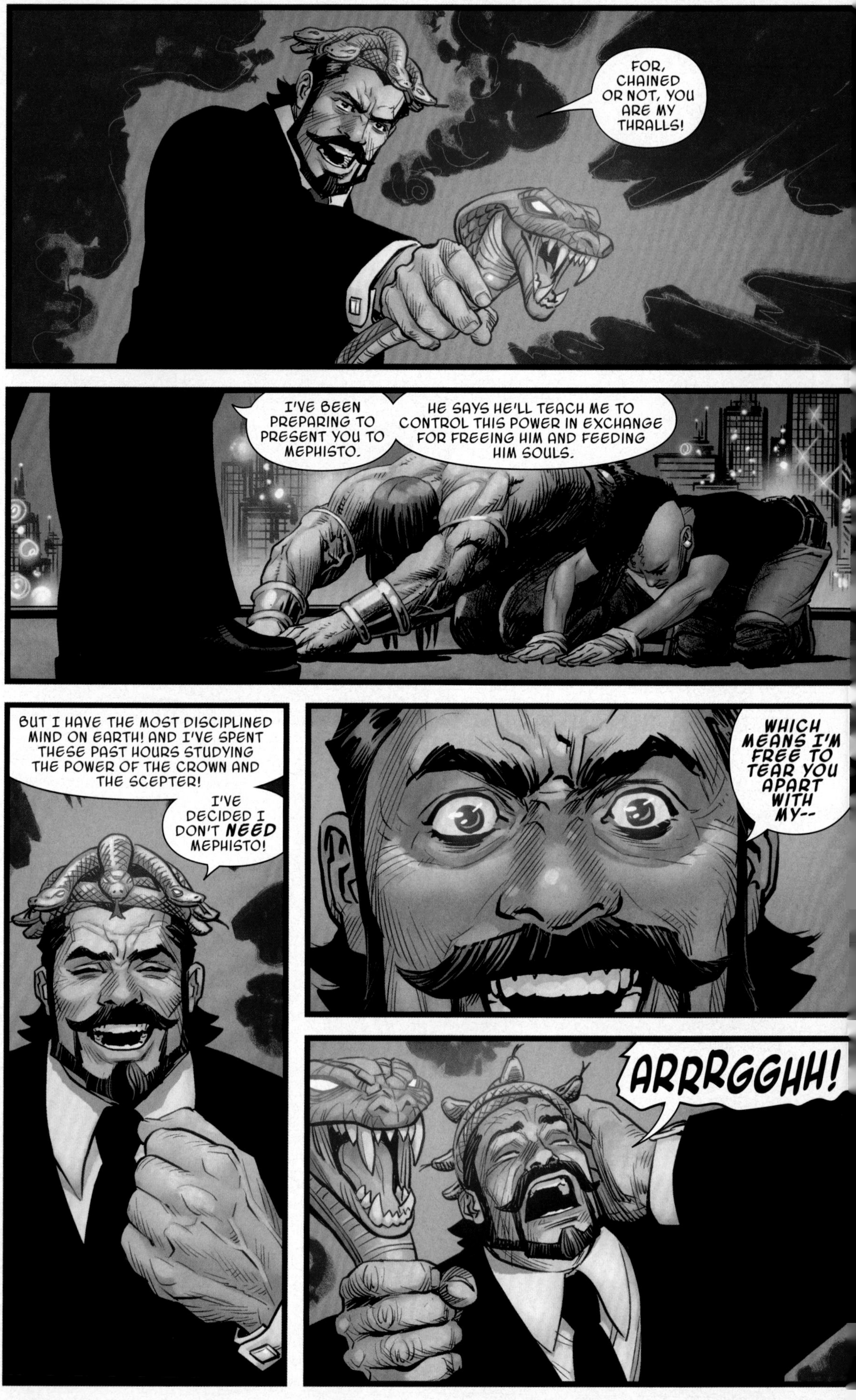
FOR, CHAINED OR NOT, YOU ARE MY THRALLS!
I'VE BEEN PREPARING TO PRESENT YOU TO MEPHISTO.
HE SAYS HE'LL TEACH ME TO CONTROL THIS POWER IN EXCHANGE FOR FREEING HIM AND FEEDING HIM SOULS.
BUT I HAVE THE MOST DISCIPLINED MIND ON EARTH! AND I'VE SPENT THESE PAST HOURS STUDYING THE POWER OF THE CROWN AND THE SCEPTER!
I'VE DECIDED I DON'T NEED MEPHISTO!
WHICH MEANS I'M FREE TO TEAR YOU APART WITH MY--
ARRRGGHH!

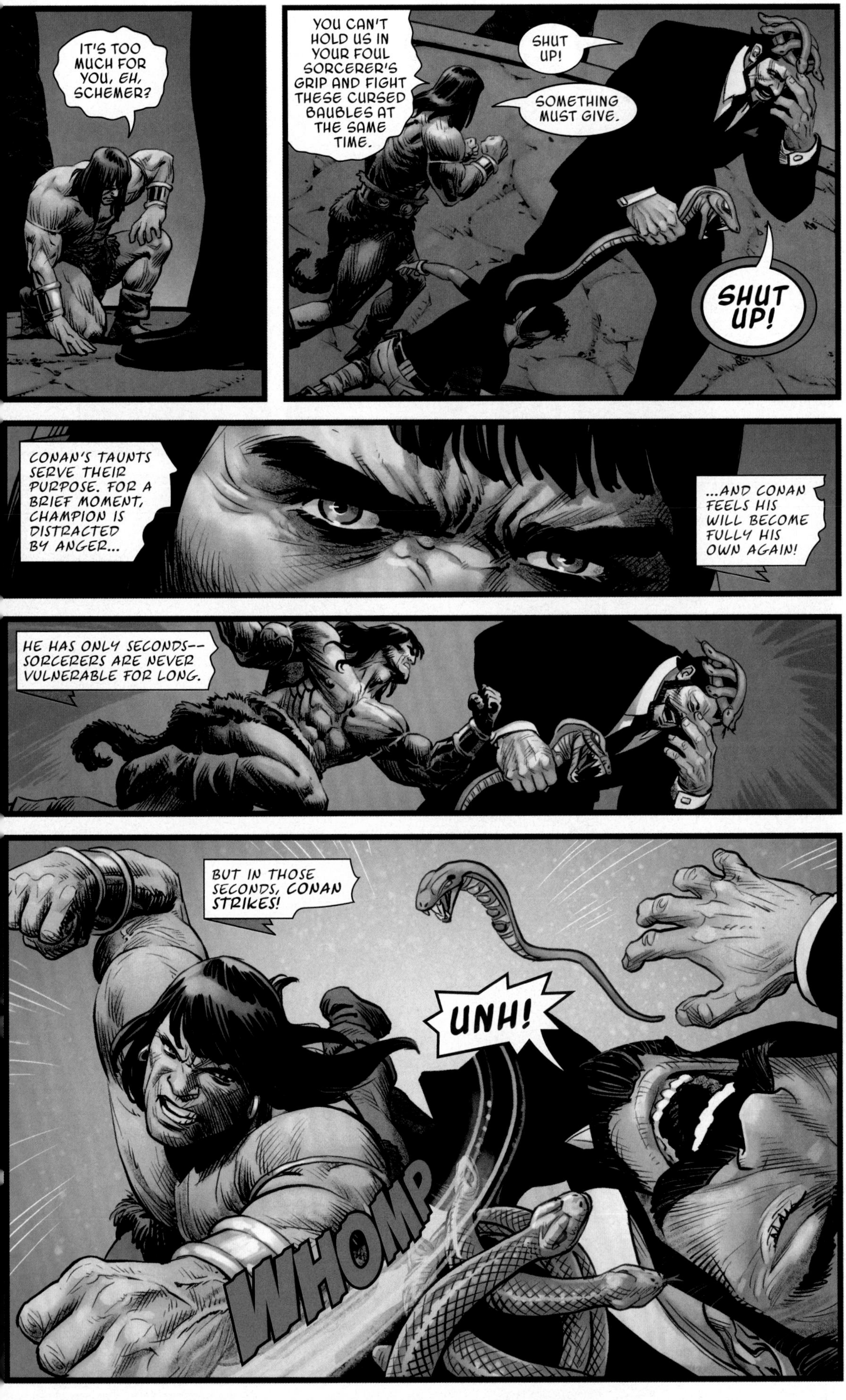
IT'S TOO MUCH FOR YOU, EH, SCHEMER?
YOU CAN'T HOLD US IN YOUR FOUL SORCERER'S GRIP AND FIGHT THESE CURSED BAUBLES AT THE SAME TIME.
SHUT UP!
SOMETHING MUST GIVE.
SHUT UP!
CONAN'S TAUNTS SERVE THEIR PURPOSE. FOR A BRIEF MOMENT, CHAMPION IS DISTRACTED BY ANGER...
...AND CONAN FEELS HIS WILL BECOME FULLY HIS OWN AGAIN!
HE HAS ONLY SECONDS-- SORCERERS ARE NEVER VULNERABLE FOR LONG.
BUT IN THOSE SECONDS, CONAN STRIKES!
UNH!
WHOMP

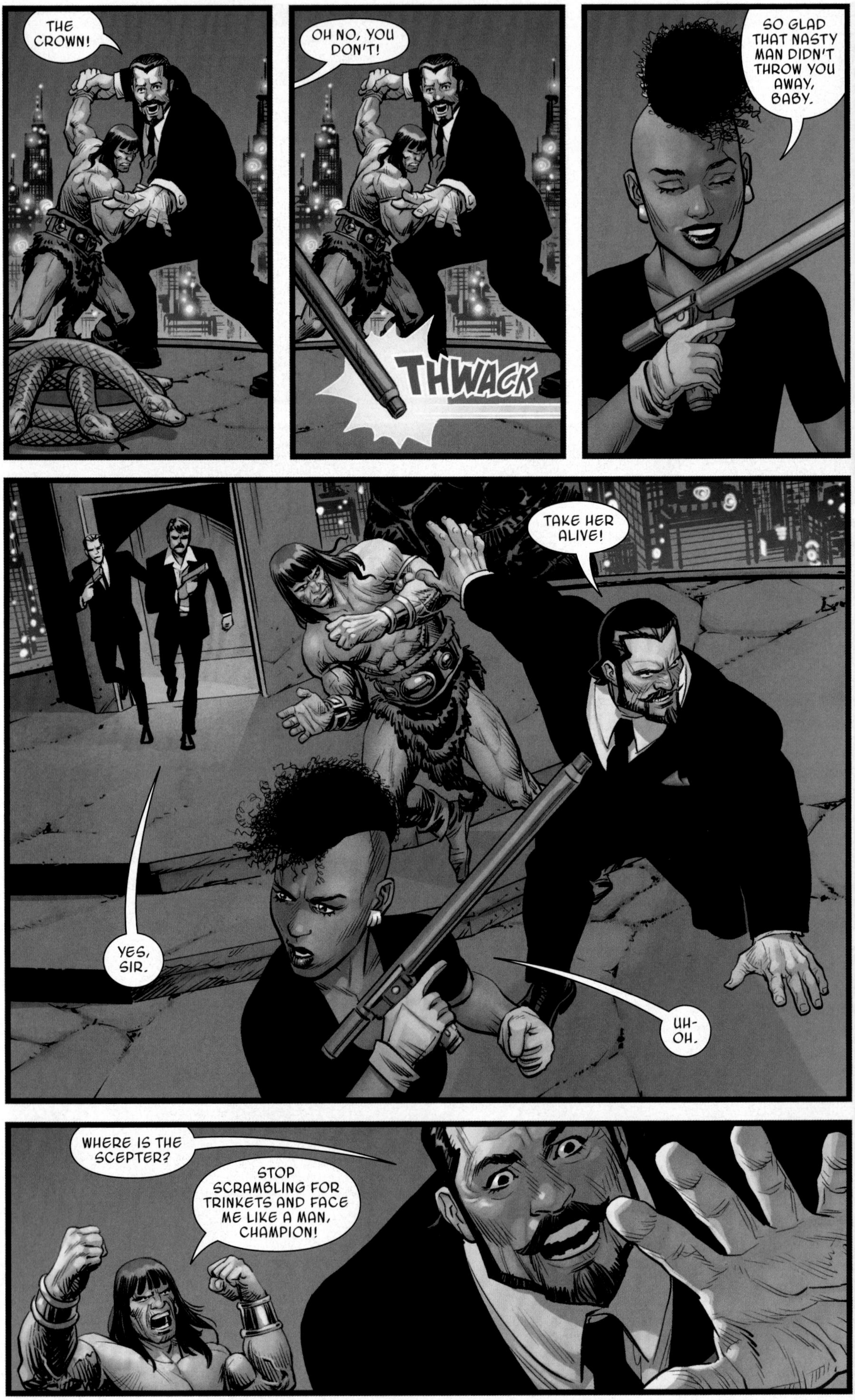
THE CROWN!
OH NO, YOU DON'T!
THWACK
SO GLAD THAT NASTY MAN DIDN'T THROW YOU AWAY, BABY.
TAKE HER ALIVE!
YES, SIR.
UH-OH.
WHERE IS THE SCEPTER?
STOP SCRAMBLING FOR TRINKETS AND FACE ME LIKE A MAN, CHAMPION!

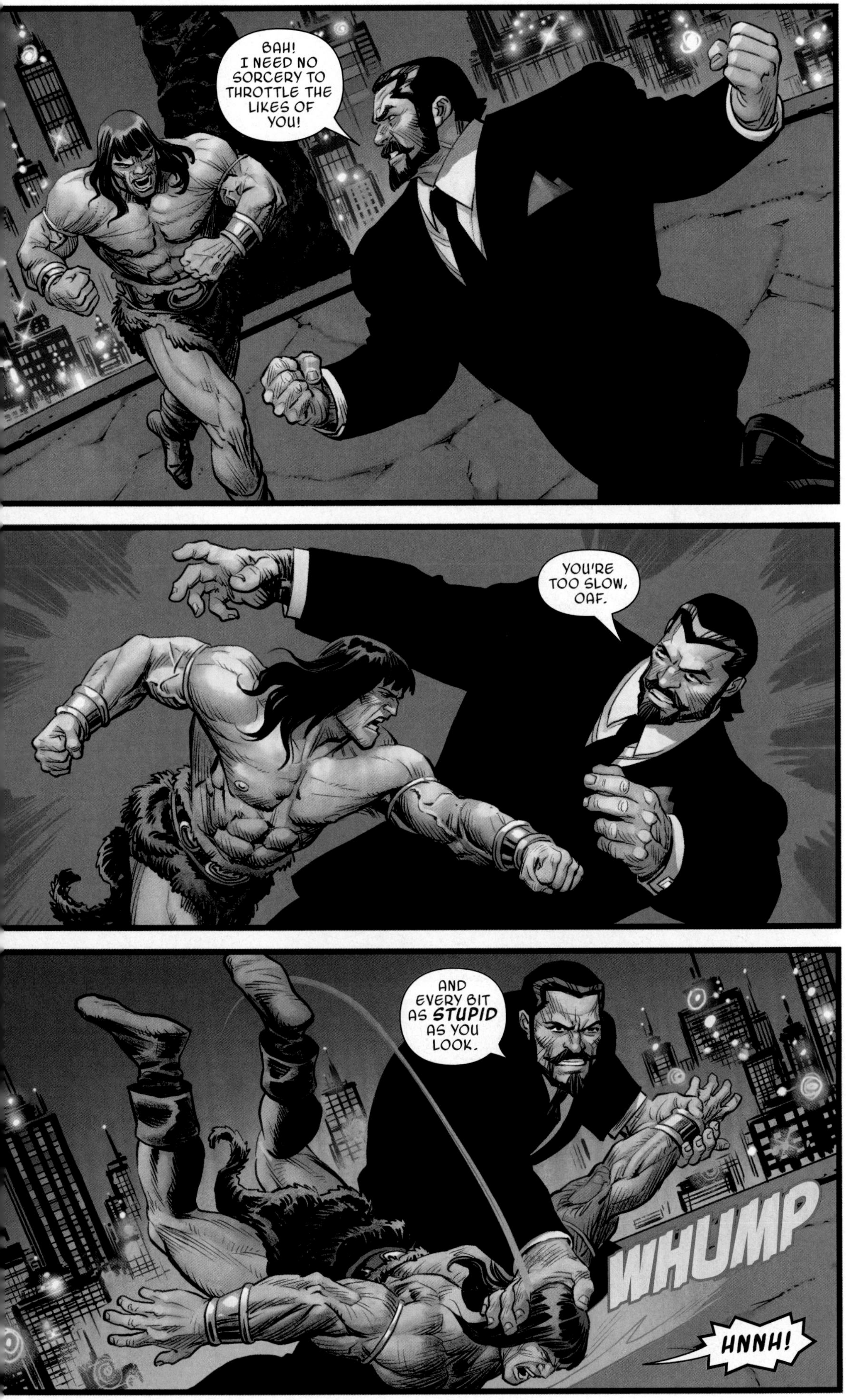

BAH! I NEED NO SORCERY TO THROTTLE THE LIKES OF YOU!
YOU'RE TOO SLOW, OAF.
AND EVERY BIT AS STUPID AS YOU LOOK.
WHUMP
HNNH!

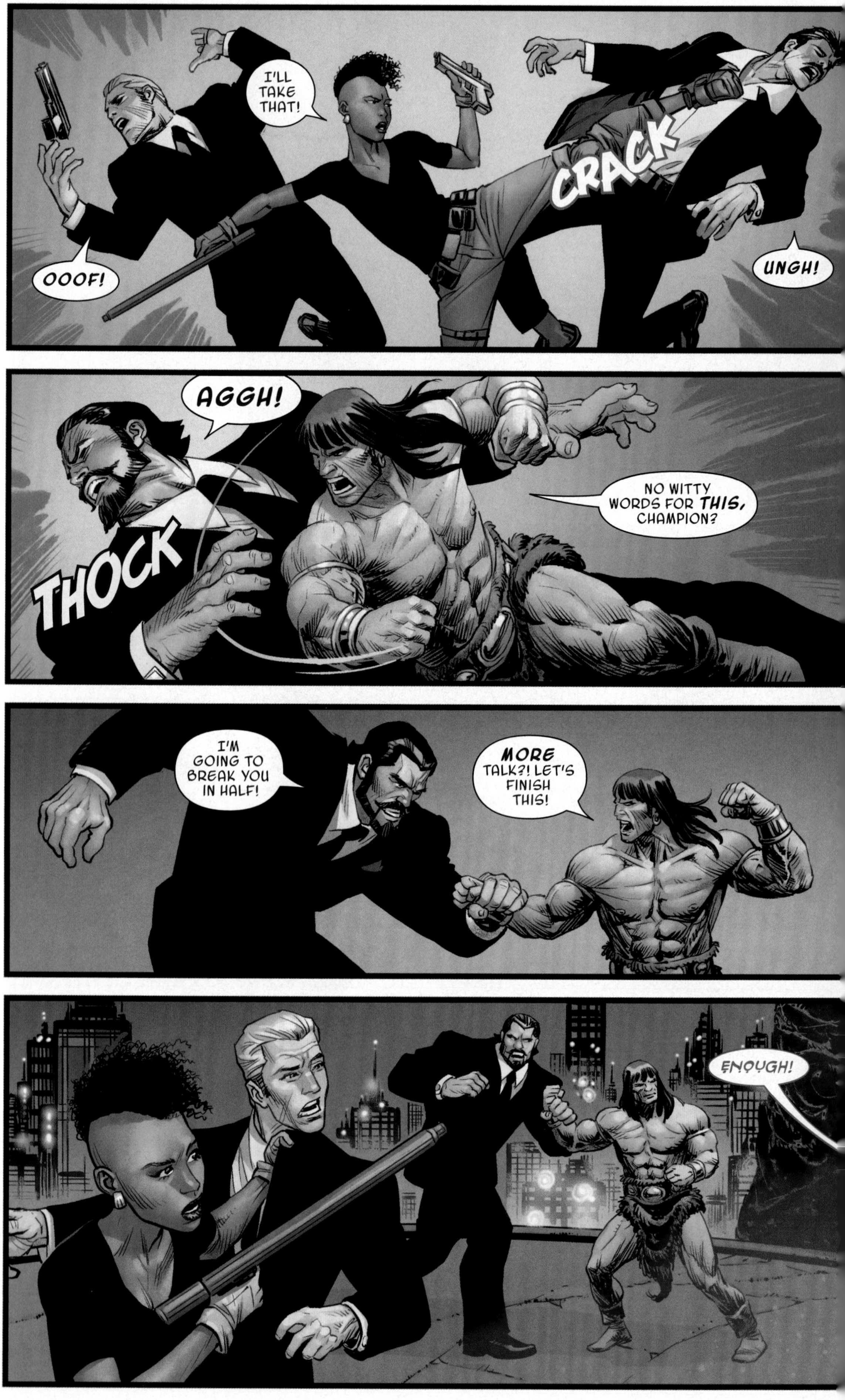
I'LL TAKE THAT!
OOOF!
CRACK
UNGH!
AGGH!
NO WITTY WORDS FOR THIS, CHAMPION?
THOCK
I'M GOING TO BREAK YOU IN HALF!
MORE TALK?! LET'S FINISH THIS!
ENOUGH!

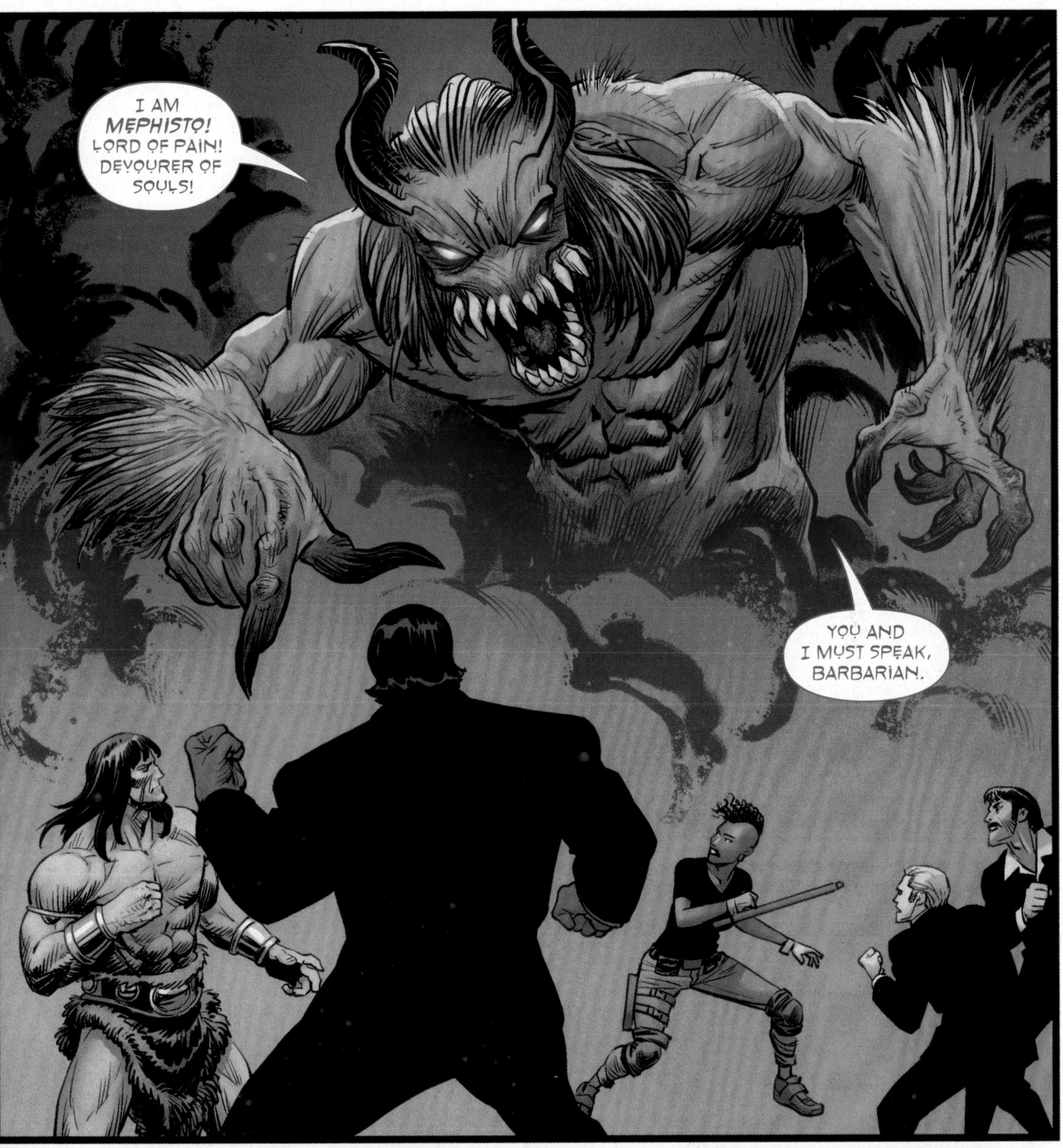
I AM MEPHISTO! LORD OF PAIN! DEVOURER OF SOULS!
YOU AND I MUST SPEAK, BARBARIAN.

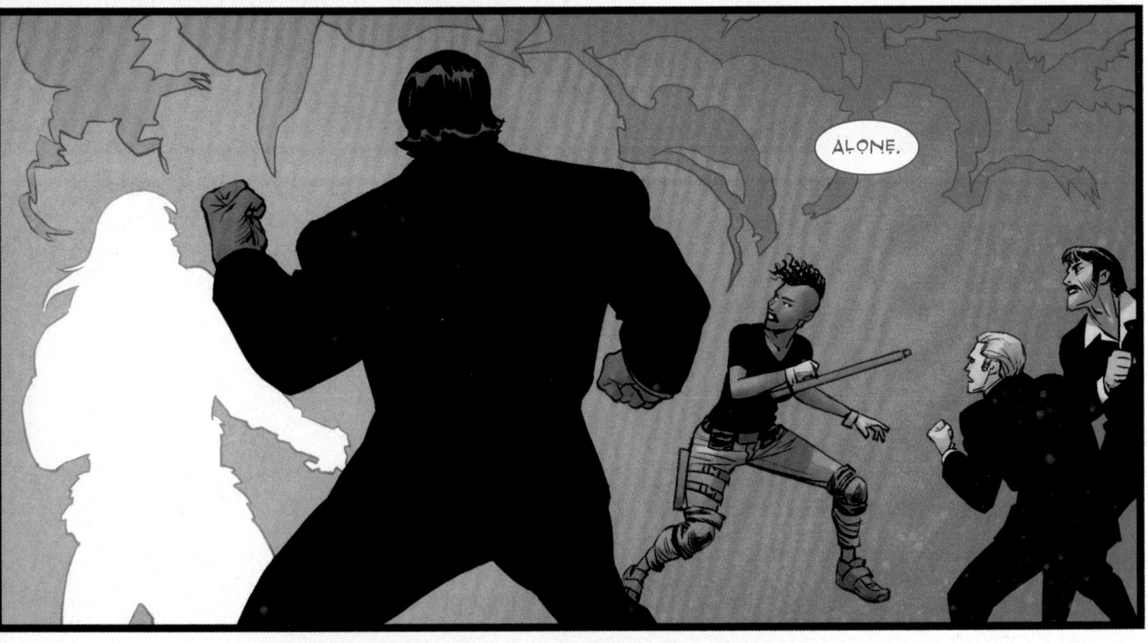
ALONE.

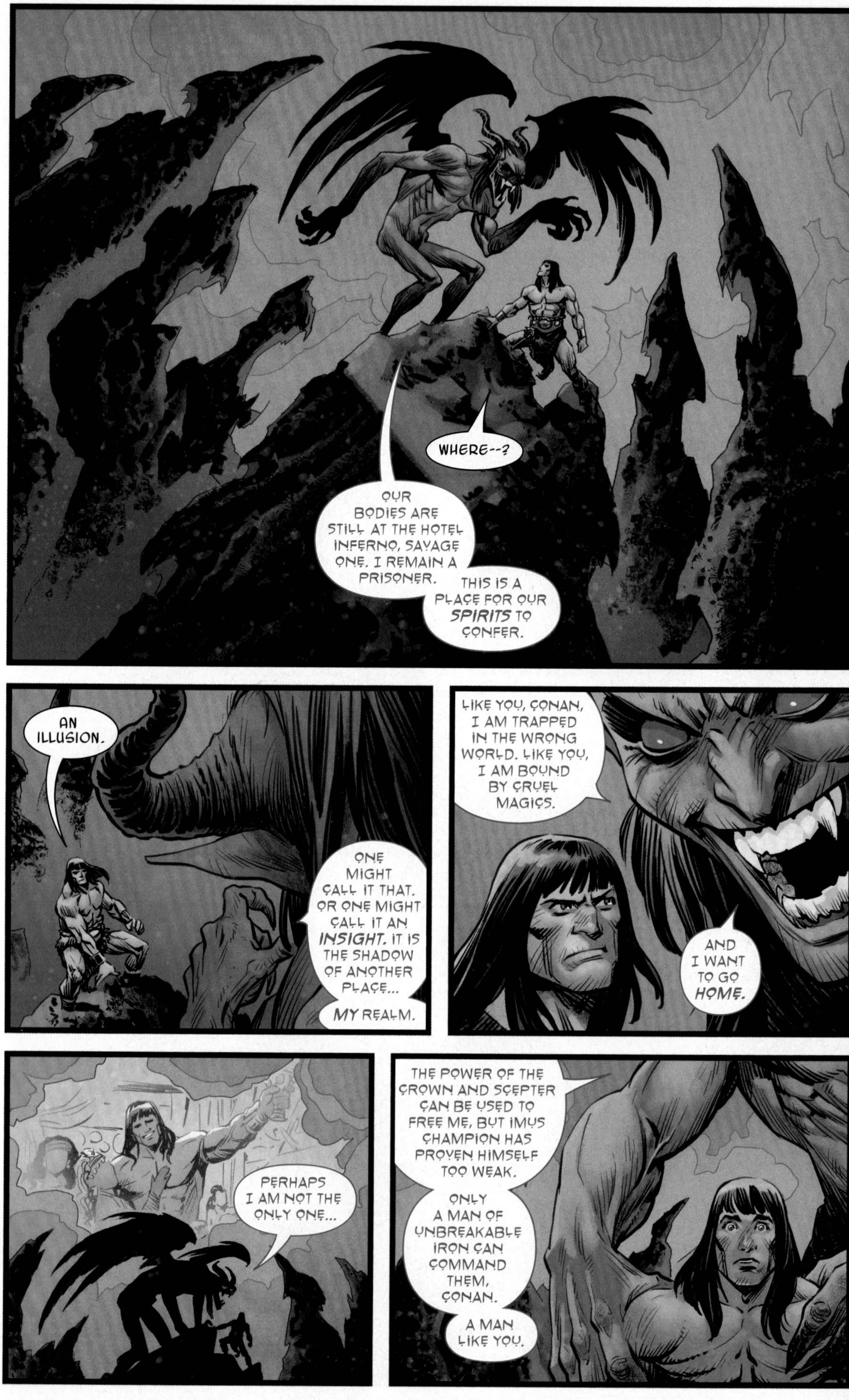
WHERE--?
OUR BODIES ARE STILL AT THE HOTEL INFERNO, SAVAGE ONE. I REMAIN A PRISONER.
THIS IS A PLACE FOR OUR SPIRITS TO CONFER.
AN ILLUSION.
ONE MIGHT CALL IT THAT. OR ONE MIGHT CALL IT AN INSIGHT. IT IS THE SHADOW OF ANOTHER PLACE...
MY REALM.
LIKE YOU, CONAN, I AM TRAPPED IN THE WRONG WORLD. LIKE YOU, I AM BOUND BY CRUEL MAGICS.
AND I WANT TO GO HOME.
PERHAPS I AM NOT THE ONLY ONE...
THE POWER OF THE CROWN AND SCEPTER CAN BE USED TO FREE ME, BUT IMUS CHAMPION HAS PROVEN HIMSELF TOO WEAK.
ONLY A MAN OF UNBREAKABLE IRON CAN COMMAND THEM, CONAN.
A MAN LIKE YOU.

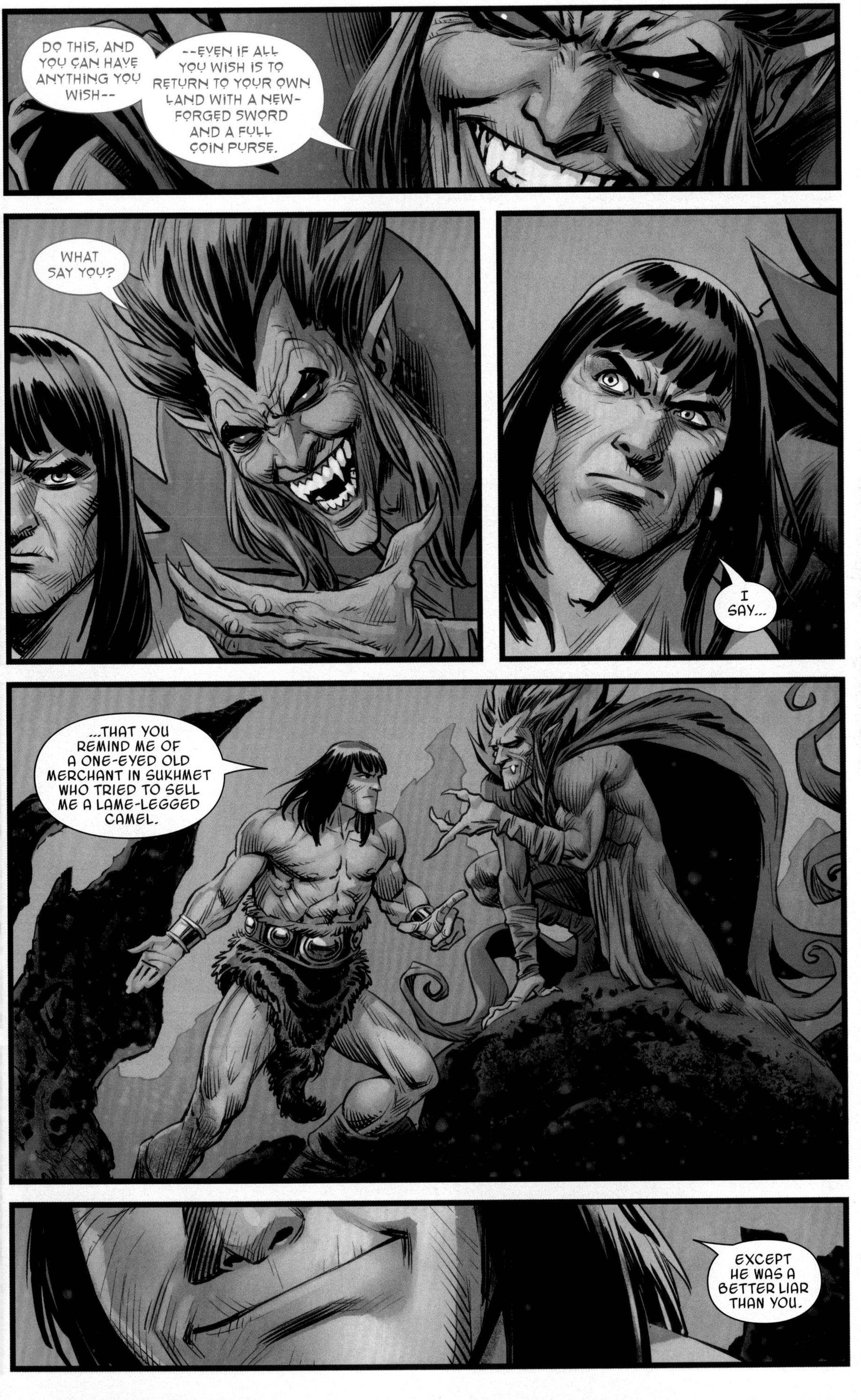
DO THIS, AND YOU CAN HAVE ANYTHING YOU WISH--
--EVEN IF ALL YOU WISH IS TO RETURN TO YOUR OWN LAND WITH A NEW-FORGED SWORD AND A FULL COIN PURSE.
WHAT SAY YOU?
I SAY...
...THAT YOU REMIND ME OF A ONE-EYED OLD MERCHANT IN SUKHMET WHO TRIED TO SELL ME A LAME-LEGGED CAMEL.
EXCEPT HE WAS A BETTER LIAR THAN YOU.

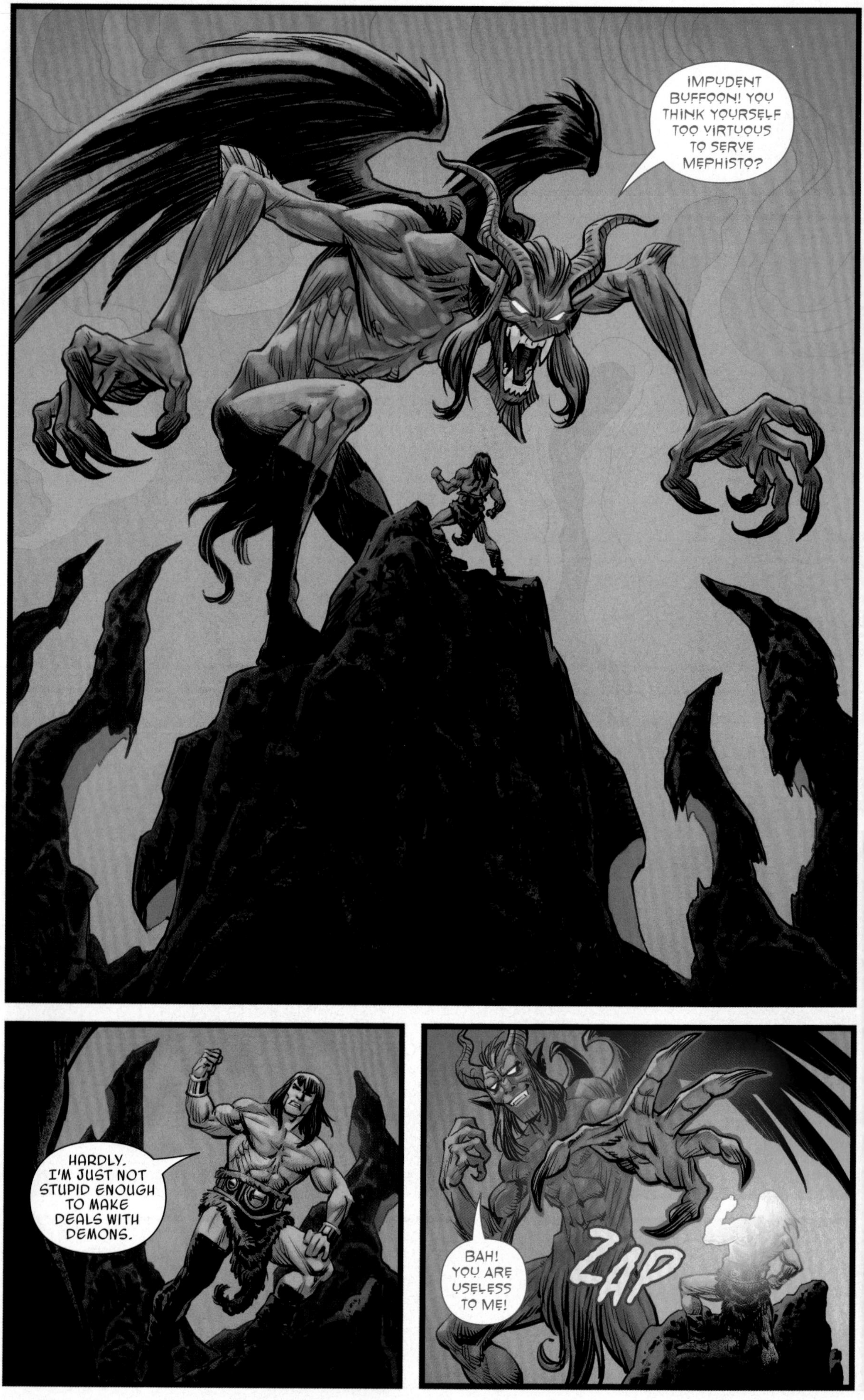
IMPUDENT BUFFOON! YOU THINK YOURSELF TOO VIRTUOUS TO SERVE MEPHISTO?
HARDLY. I'M JUST NOT STUPID ENOUGH TO MAKE DEALS WITH DEMONS.
BAH! YOU ARE USELESS TO ME!
ZAP

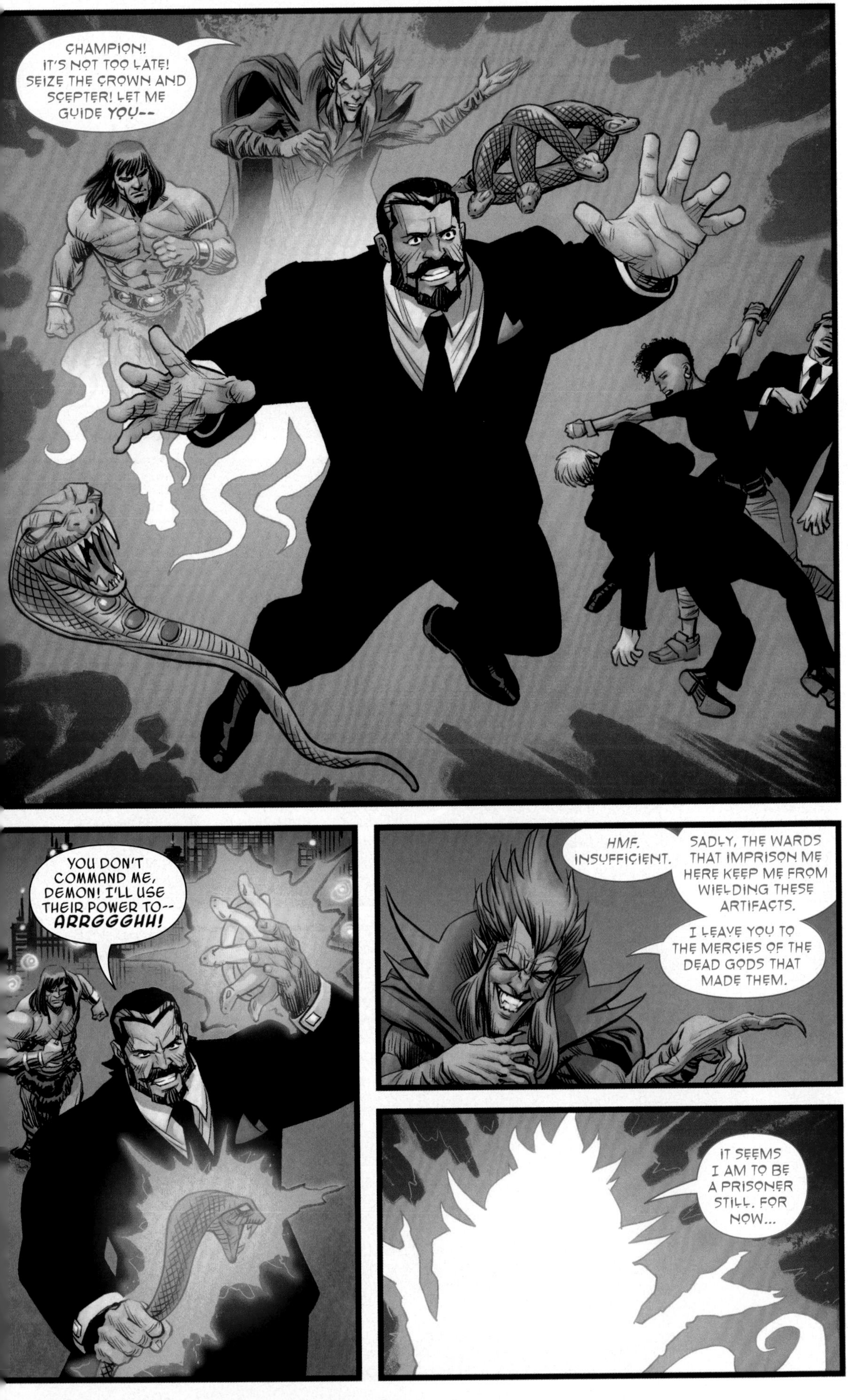
CHAMPION! IT'S NOT TOO LATE! SEIZE THE CROWN AND SCEPTER! LET ME GUIDE *YOU*--
YOU DON'T COMMAND ME, DEMON! I'LL USE THEIR POWER TO-- **ARRGGGHH!**
HMF. INSUFFICIENT.
SADLY, THE WARDS THAT IMPRISON ME HERE KEEP ME FROM WIELDING THESE ARTIFACTS.
I LEAVE YOU TO THE MERCIES OF THE DEAD GODS THAT MADE THEM.
IT SEEMS I AM TO BE A PRISONER STILL. FOR NOW...

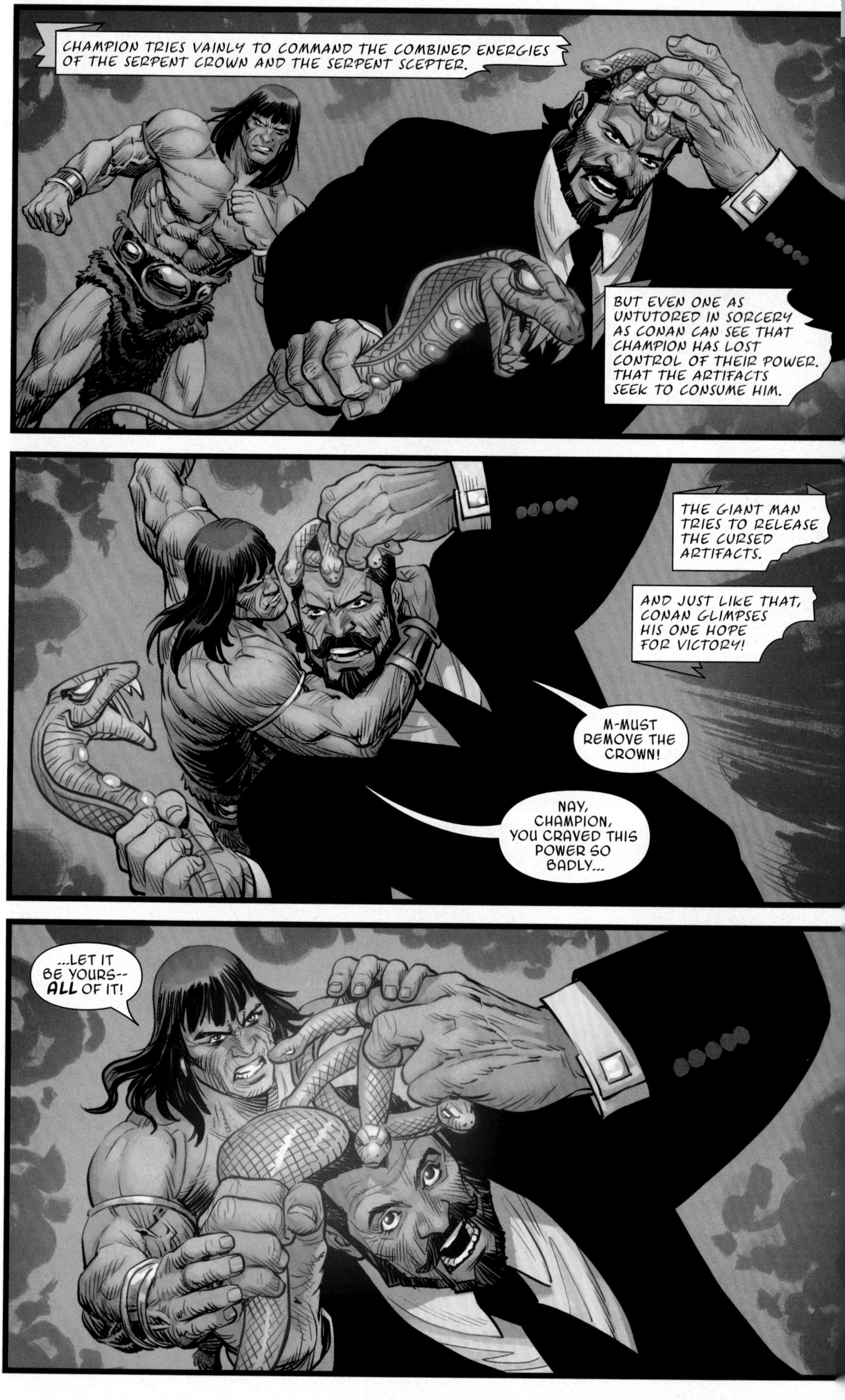
CHAMPION TRIES VAINLY TO COMMAND THE COMBINED ENERGIES OF THE SERPENT CROWN AND THE SERPENT SCEPTER.
BUT EVEN ONE AS UNTUTORED IN SORCERY AS CONAN CAN SEE THAT CHAMPION HAS LOST CONTROL OF THEIR POWER. THAT THE ARTIFACTS SEEK TO CONSUME HIM.
THE GIANT MAN TRIES TO RELEASE THE CURSED ARTIFACTS.
AND JUST LIKE THAT, CONAN GLIMPSES HIS ONE HOPE FOR VICTORY!
M-MUST REMOVE THE CROWN!
NAY, CHAMPION, YOU CRAVED THIS POWER SO BADLY...
...LET IT BE YOURS-- **ALL** OF IT!

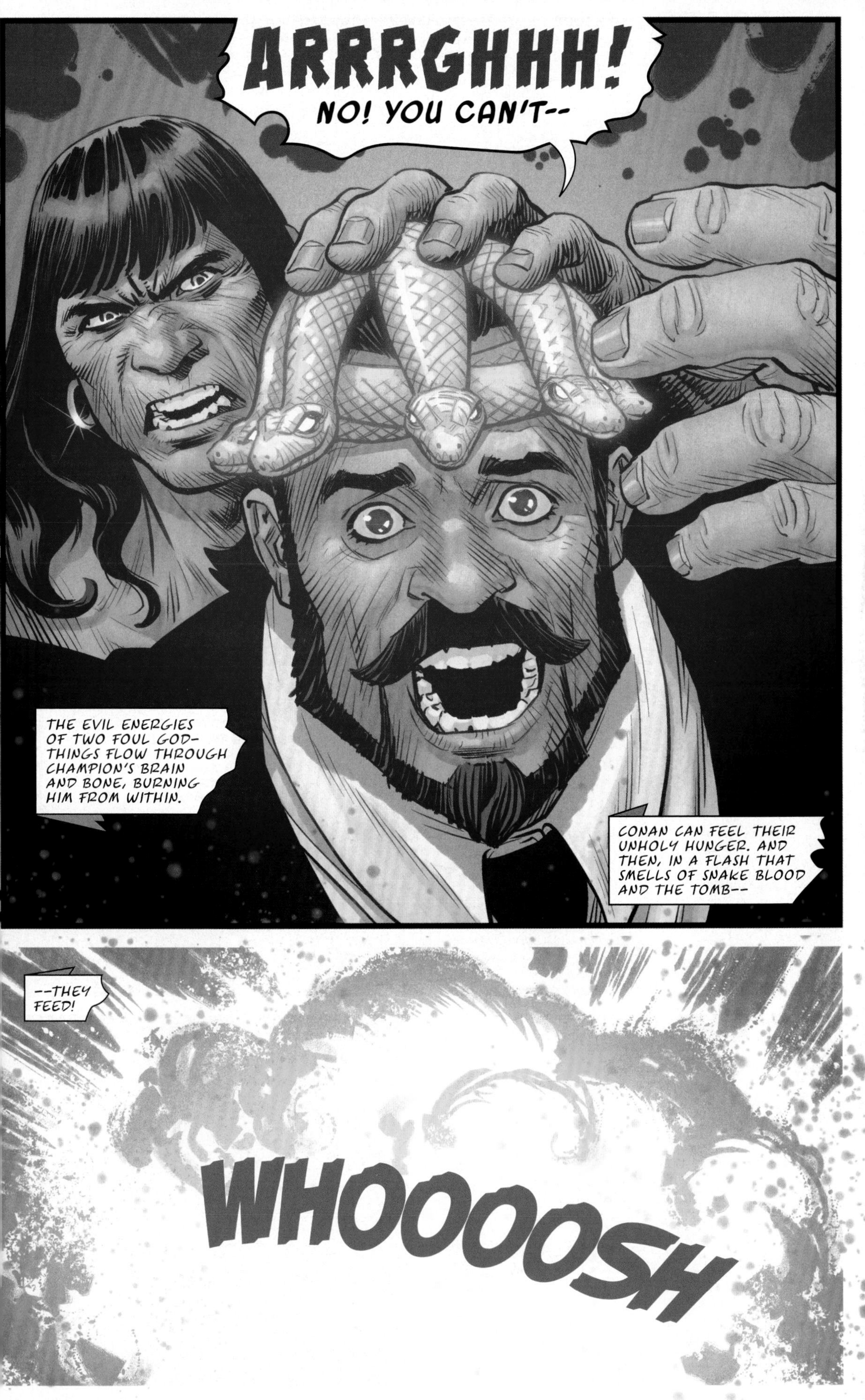
ARRRGHHH!
NO! YOU CAN'T--
THE EVIL ENERGIES OF TWO FOUL GOD-THINGS FLOW THROUGH CHAMPION'S BRAIN AND BONE, BURNING HIM FROM WITHIN.
CONAN CAN FEEL THEIR UNHOLY HUNGER. AND THEN, IN A FLASH THAT SMELLS OF SNAKE BLOOD AND THE TOMB--
--THEY FEED!
WHOOOOOSH

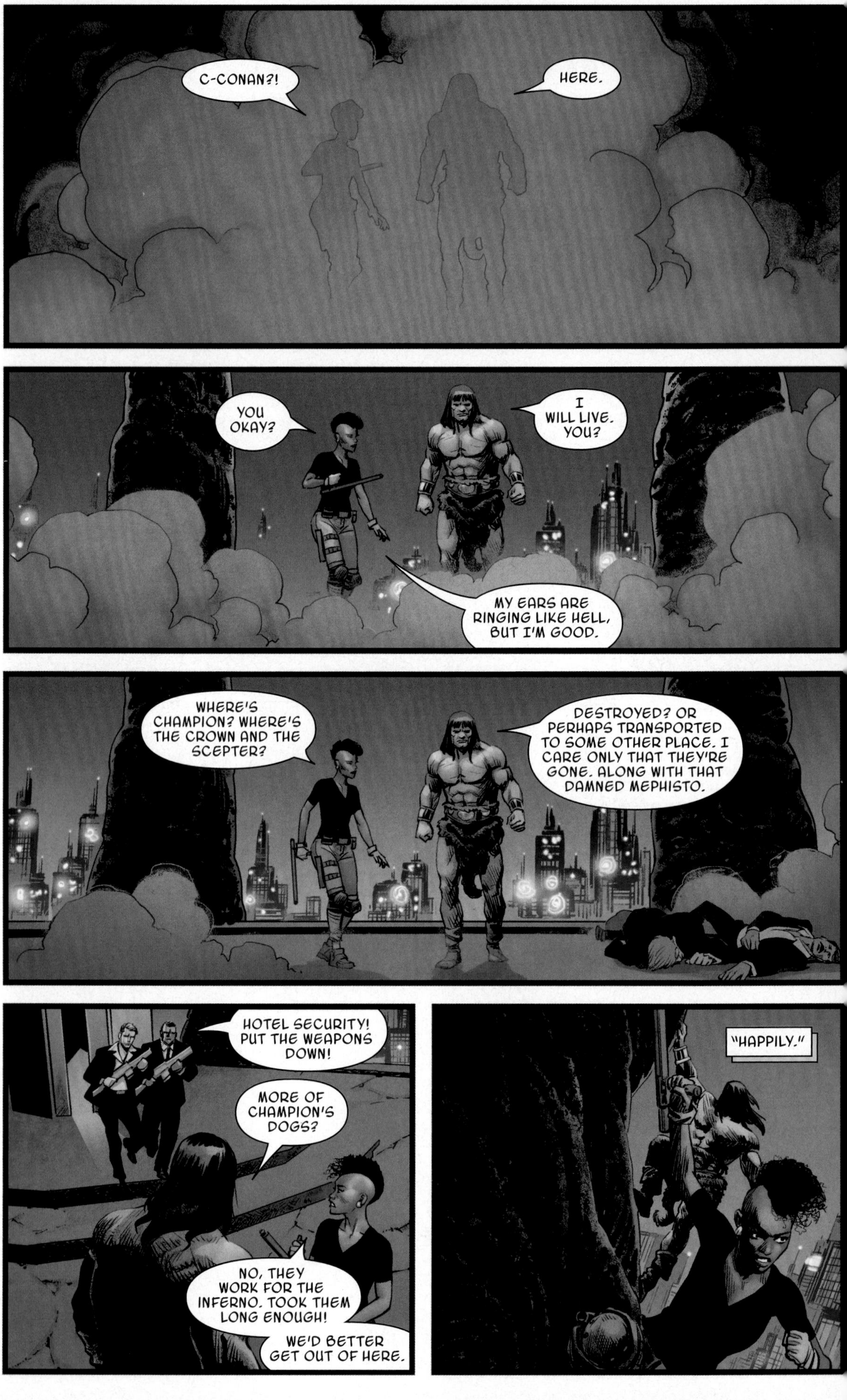
C-CONAN?!
HERE.
YOU OKAY?
I WILL LIVE. YOU?
MY EARS ARE RINGING LIKE HELL, BUT I'M GOOD.
WHERE'S CHAMPION? WHERE'S THE CROWN AND THE SCEPTER?
DESTROYED? OR PERHAPS TRANSPORTED TO SOME OTHER PLACE. I CARE ONLY THAT THEY'RE GONE. ALONG WITH THAT DAMNED MEPHISTO.
HOTEL SECURITY! PUT THE WEAPONS DOWN!
MORE OF CHAMPION'S DOGS?
NO, THEY WORK FOR THE INFERNO. TOOK THEM LONG ENOUGH!
WE'D BETTER GET OUT OF HERE.
"HAPPILY."

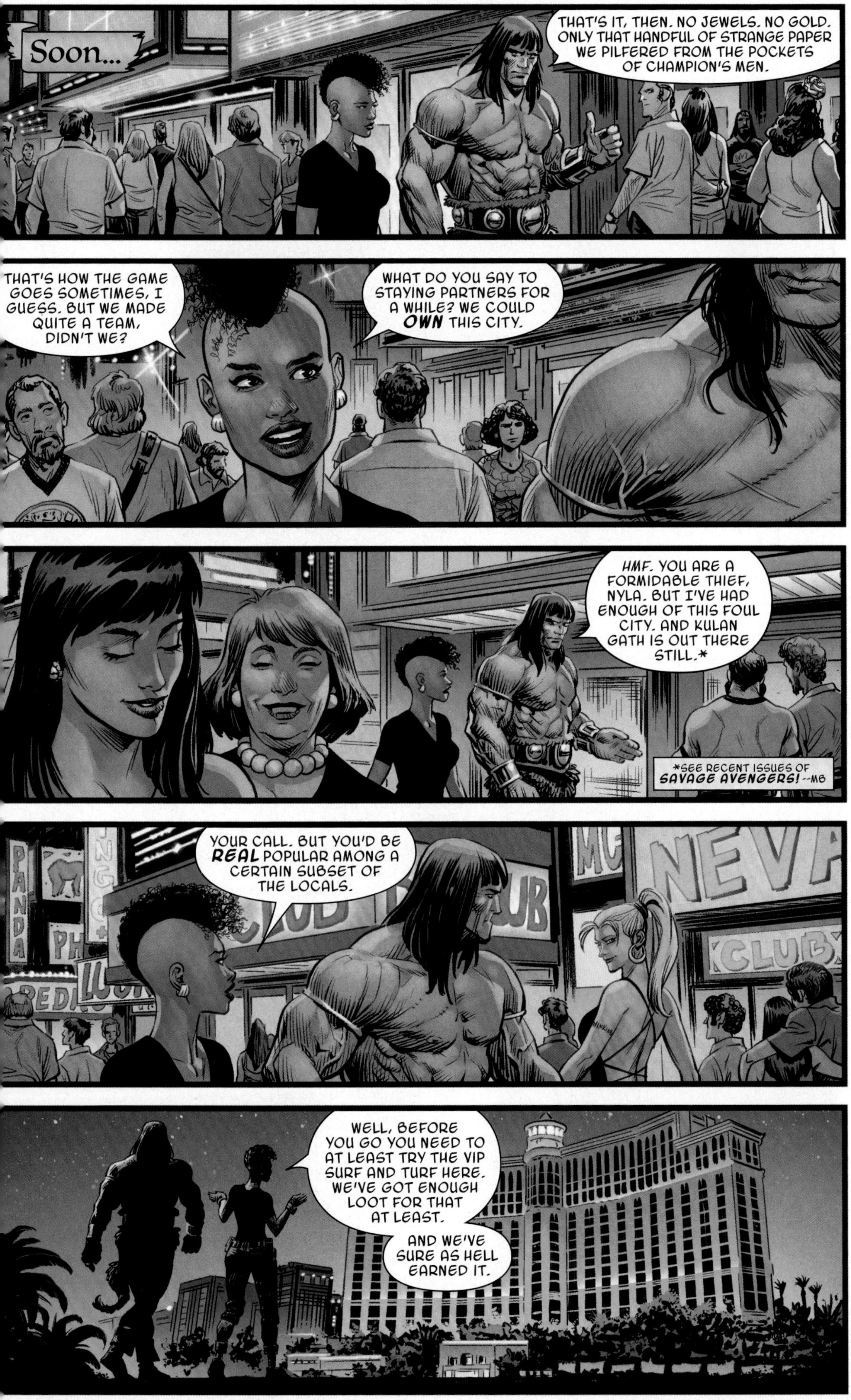
Soon...
THAT'S IT, THEN. NO JEWELS. NO GOLD. ONLY THAT HANDFUL OF STRANGE PAPER WE PILFERED FROM THE POCKETS OF CHAMPION'S MEN.
THAT'S HOW THE GAME GOES SOMETIMES, I GUESS. BUT WE MADE QUITE A TEAM, DIDN'T WE?
WHAT DO YOU SAY TO STAYING PARTNERS FOR A WHILE? WE COULD OWN THIS CITY.
HMF. YOU ARE A FORMIDABLE THIEF, NYLA. BUT I'VE HAD ENOUGH OF THIS FOUL CITY. AND KULAN GATH IS OUT THERE STILL.*
*SEE RECENT ISSUES OF SAVAGE AVENGERS! --MB
YOUR CALL. BUT YOU'D BE REAL POPULAR AMONG A CERTAIN SUBSET OF THE LOCALS.
CLUB
CLUB
WELL, BEFORE YOU GO YOU NEED TO AT LEAST TRY THE VIP SURF AND TURF HERE. WE'VE GOT ENOUGH LOOT FOR THAT AT LEAST.
AND WE'VE SURE AS HELL EARNED IT.

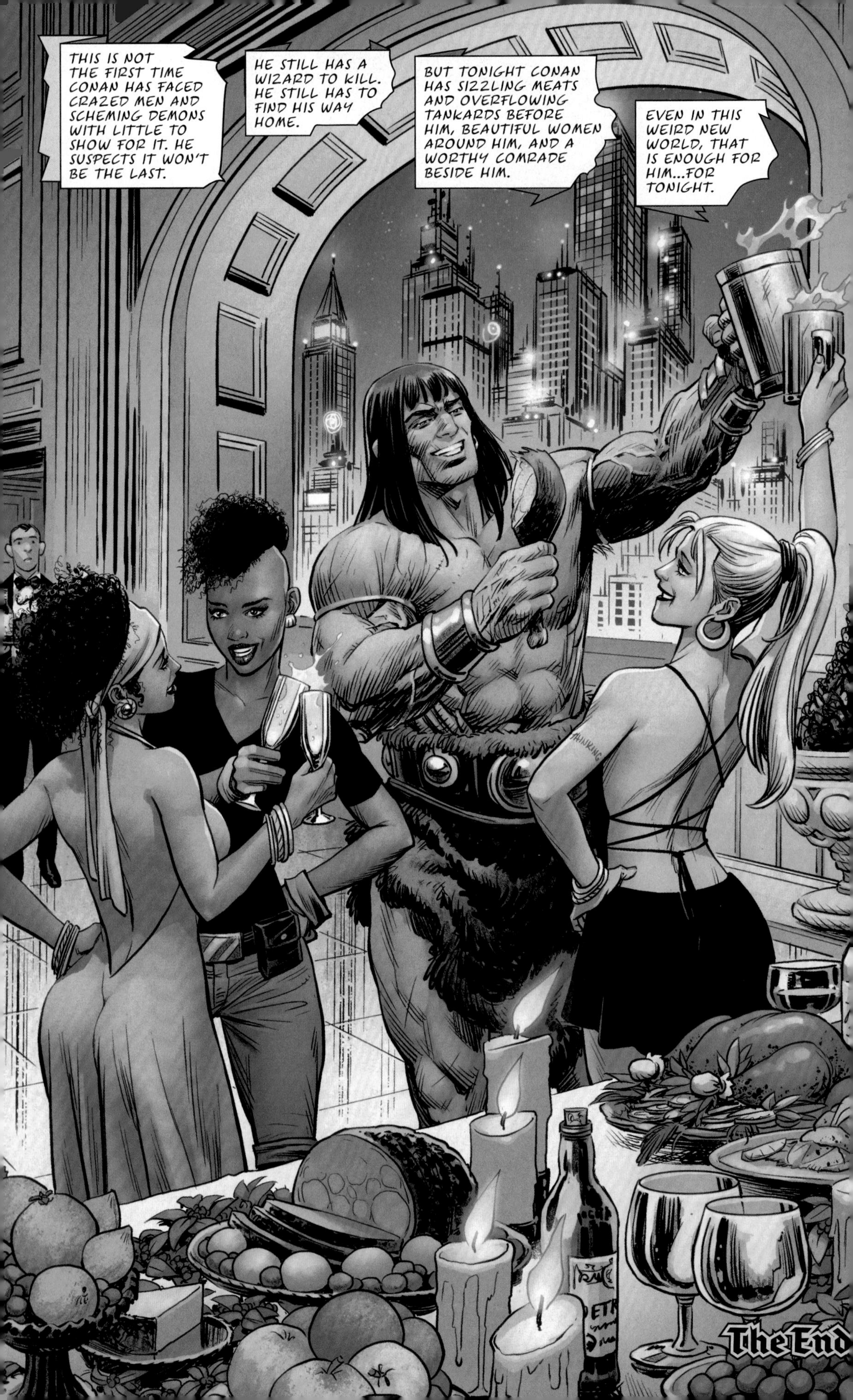
THIS IS NOT THE FIRST TIME CONAN HAS FACED CRAZED MEN AND SCHEMING DEMONS WITH LITTLE TO SHOW FOR IT. HE SUSPECTS IT WON'T BE THE LAST.
HE STILL HAS A WIZARD TO KILL. HE STILL HAS TO FIND HIS WAY HOME.
BUT TONIGHT CONAN HAS SIZZLING MEATS AND OVERFLOWING TANKARDS BEFORE HIM, BEAUTIFUL WOMEN AROUND HIM, AND A WORTHY COMRADE BESIDE HIM.
EVEN IN THIS WEIRD NEW WORLD, THAT IS ENOUGH FOR HIM...FOR TONIGHT.
The End

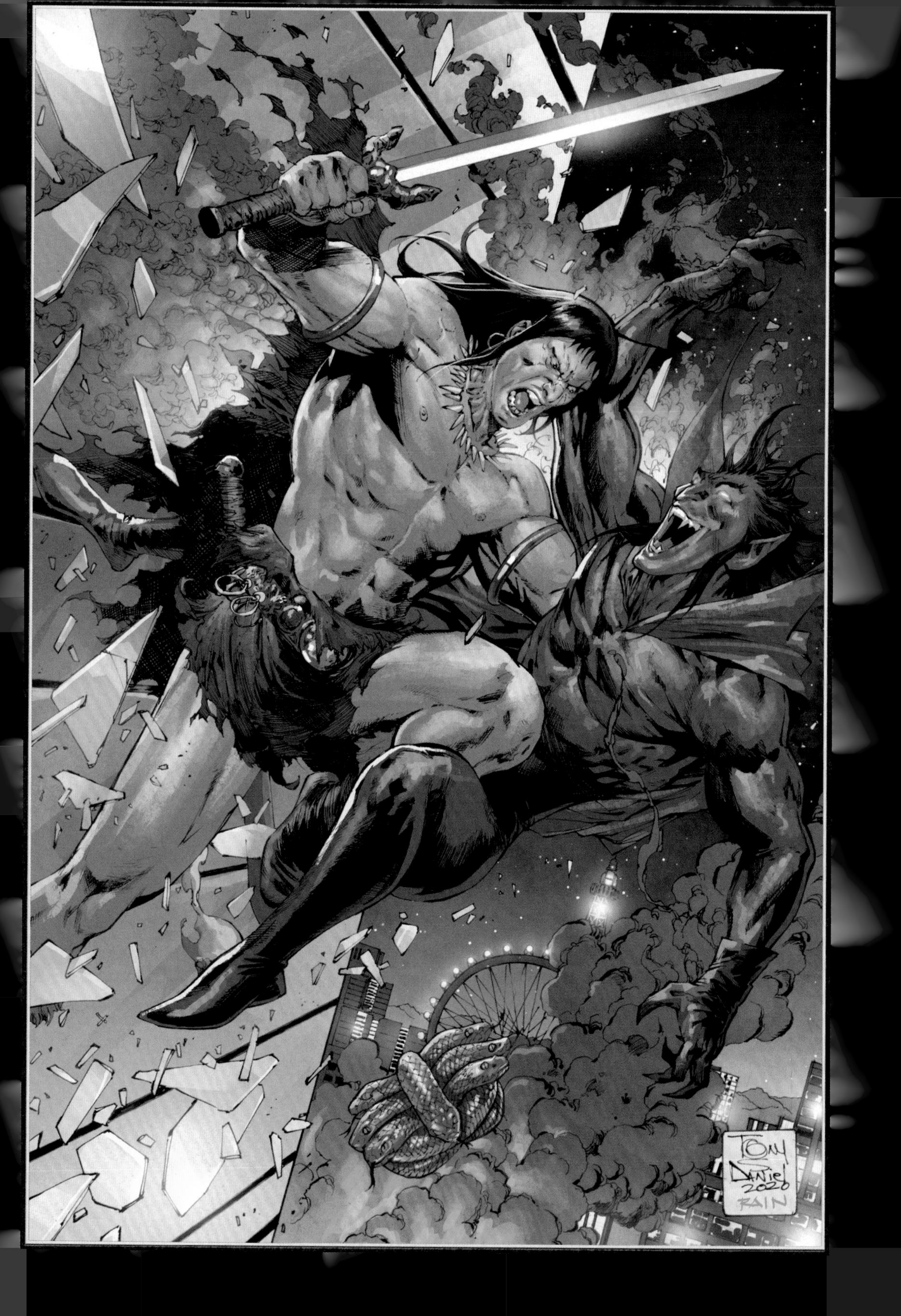
TONY S DANIEL 2020
RAIN

#1 HIDDEN GEM VARIANT BY
JOHN BUSCEMA & MORRY HOLLOWELL

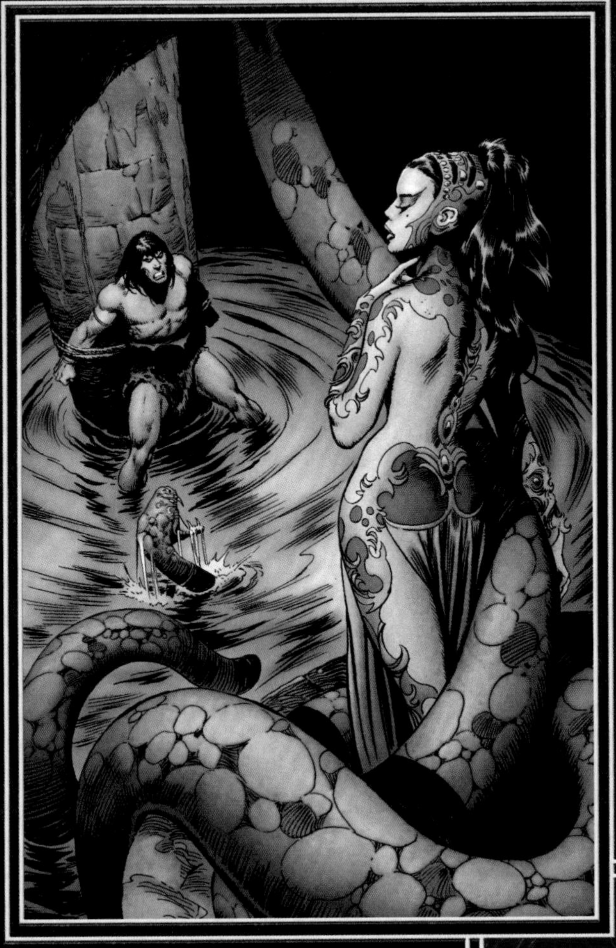

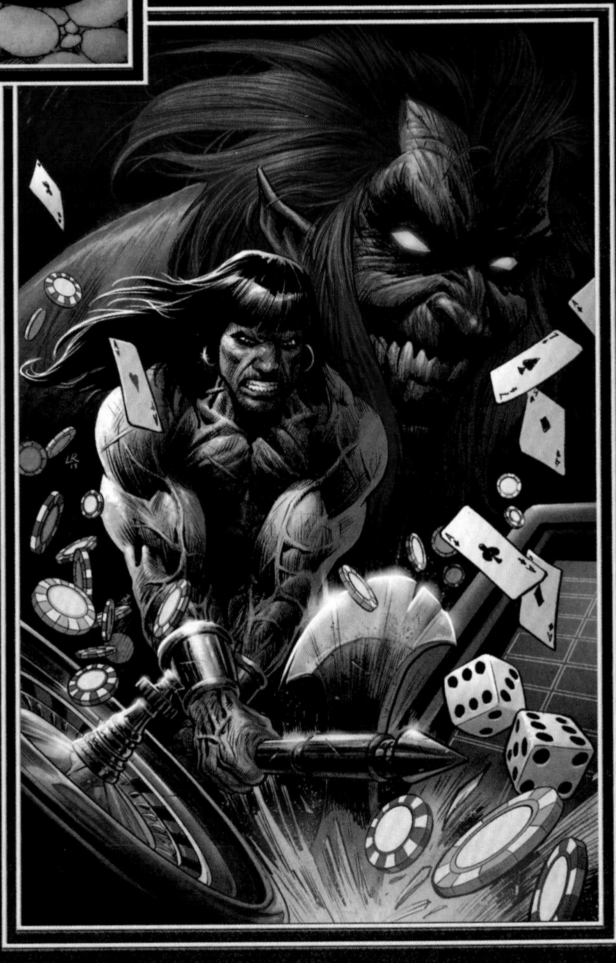

#1 VARIANT BY LUKE ROSS & GURU-eFX

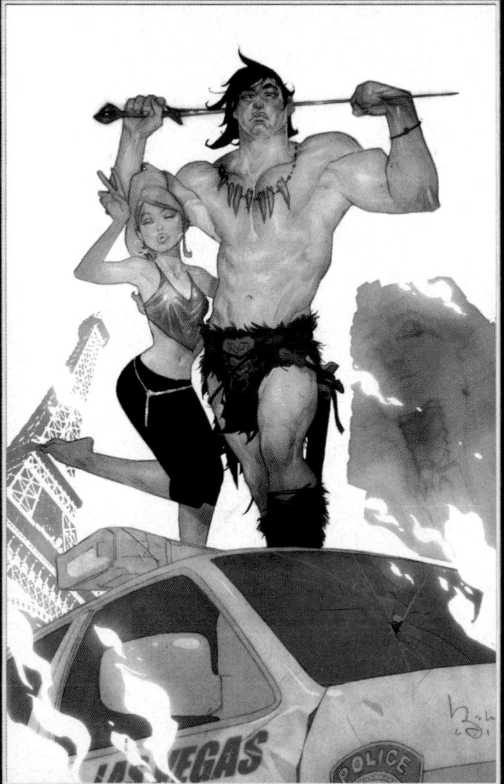
POLICE

#2 VARIANT BY BEN CALDWELL

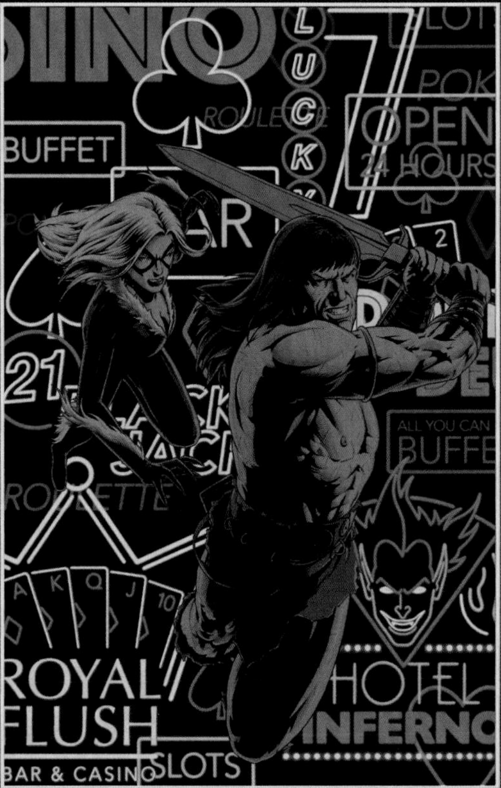
BUFFET
ROULETTE
LUCKY
OPEN
24 HOURS
ROYAL
FLUSH
BAR & CASINO
SLOTS
HOTEL
INFERNO

#2 VARIANT BY JOHN TYLER CHRISTOPHER

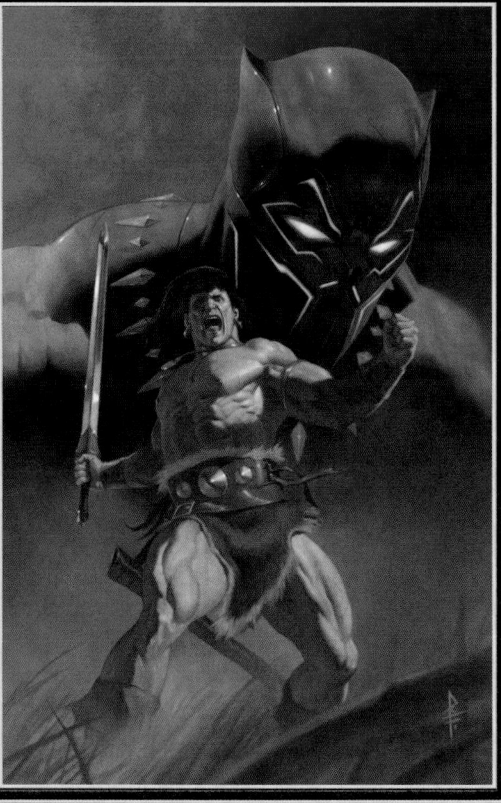

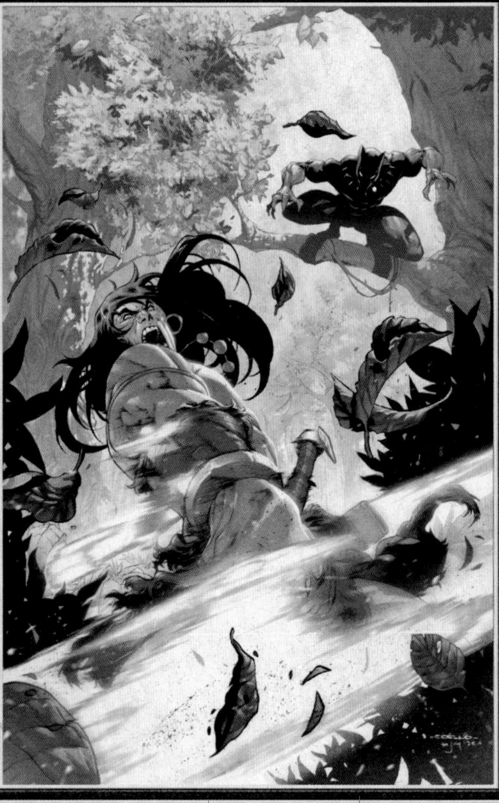

RICCARDO FEDERICI

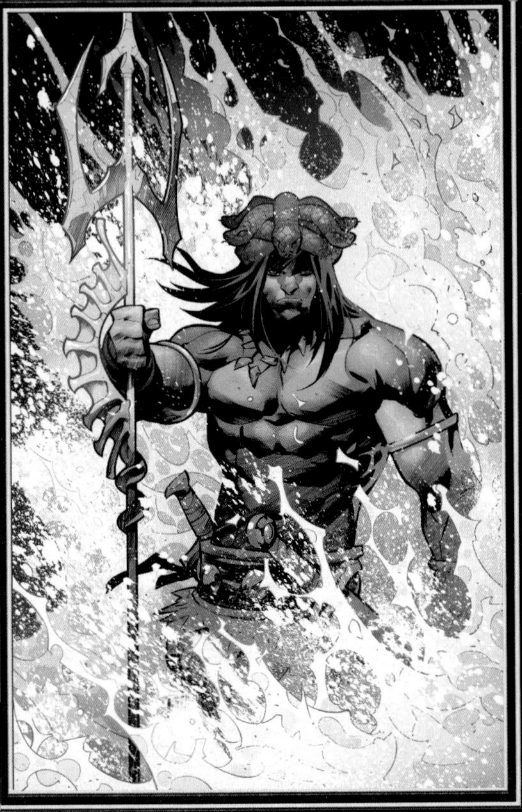

#4 VARIANT BY EDUARD PETROVICH

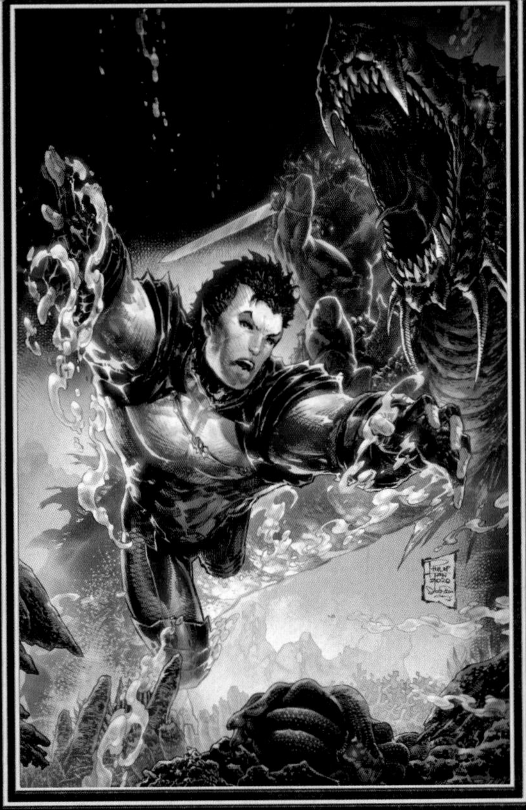

#4 VARIANT BY PHILIP TAN & SEBASTIAN CHENG

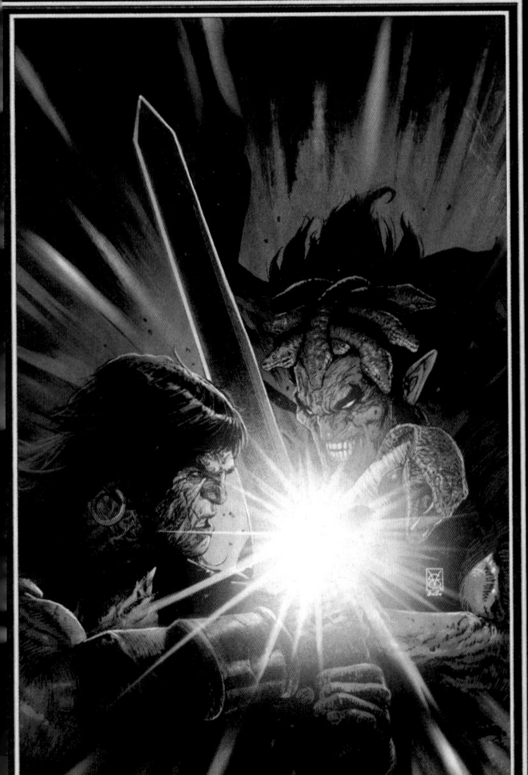

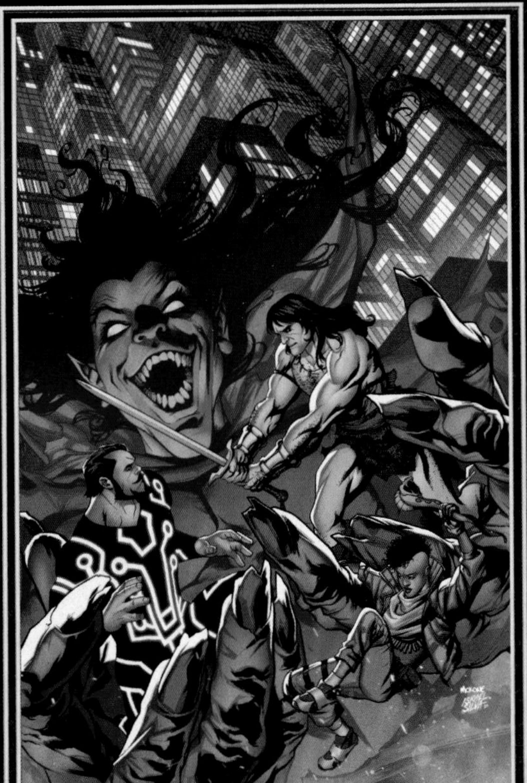